The Case for
Good Jobs

ZEYNEP TON

The
CASE
for

GOOD JOBS

How Great Companies
Bring Dignity, Pay & Meaning
to Everyone's Work

HARVARD BUSINESS REVIEW PRESS

BOSTON, MASSACHUSETTS

HBR Press Quantity Sales Discounts

Harvard Business Review Press titles are available at significant quantity discounts when purchased in bulk for client gifts, sales promotions, and premiums. Special editions, including books with corporate logos, customized covers, and letters from the company or CEO printed in the front matter, as well as excerpts of existing books, can also be created in large quantities for special needs.

For details and discount information for both print and ebook formats, contact booksales@harvardbusiness.org, tel. 800-988-0886, or www.hbr.org/bulksales.

The web addresses referenced in this book were live and correct at the time of the book's publication but may be subject to change.

Cataloging-in-Publication data is forthcoming.

ISBN: 978-1-64782-417-4
eISBN: 978-1-64782-418-1

The paper used in this publication meets the requirements of the American National Standard for Permanence of Paper for Publications and Documents in Libraries and Archives Z39.48-1992.

To my parents, Handan and Necmi Ton

CONTENTS

Everyone Wants Better

"Some jobs simply do not create enough value to justify higher wages," the CEO of a *Fortune* 100 company told me, yet he wasn't at all happy about this. Like many other CEOs and executives I have met, he was concerned that too many Americans have been left behind with low-paying jobs. For strong capitalism, he believed, there should be more good jobs with living wages. He just didn't see how it could be done.

In fact, in my earlier research, focused on retailers, I found two approaches to competing profitably based on low cost. The prevalent approach relies on seeing employees as a cost to be minimized, investing little in them, and—as a consequence—operating with high employee turnover. Companies using this approach operate in a vicious cycle in which their high turnover causes poor operational execution, poor customer service, and low productivity. All this erodes customer satisfaction and unit profits, but these companies can remain profitable by adding more units, by expanding their customer offering, or by ever more cost cutting. These measures, however, contribute to even higher turnover—there's the "cycle."

The other approach—much less known or understood—relies on seeing employees as a driver of profitability and growth, investing heavily in them, and—as a consequence—operating with low turnover. Companies using this approach pay their employees a lot more per hour, offer more stable schedules, and create more meaning and dignity in the work. They also create a system that makes their employees' work increasingly valuable—more than repaying the increased investment in them. These companies operate in a virtuous cycle of low turnover, excellent operational execution, and high customer service and productivity.

Companies in the vicious cycle generally believe that their cost-cutting approach to labor is the only way to win as a low-cost competitor. Even when they know about companies that take the other approach—such as Costco and Trader Joe's—they don't believe they can pull it off themselves. But that's just not true. It is specifically to highlight the fact that these two approaches are management *choices* that I refer to them as "strategies"—the bad jobs strategy and the good jobs strategy.

All of this was spelled out in my 2014 book, *The Good Jobs Strategy.* Since then, business leaders—from CEOs of large companies to managers of convenience stores—have gotten in touch with me to describe their own vicious cycle, express their desire to adopt the good jobs strategy, and ask for help. To meet this unexpected but very encouraging demand, Roger Martin—a leading management thinker—and my former MIT Sloan student Sarah Kalloch joined me in founding the nonprofit Good Jobs Institute. This has become the lab in which we have learned how to apply my academic research to real life—that is, much of what is in this book.

In that capacity, I have spent time with hundreds of executives (including dozens of CEOs) who run companies of all sizes and with hundreds of frontline employees and managers. No executive I met felt good about offering employees unlivable wages, poor working conditions, and a feeling of disrespect—yet that's what they did. No employee I met felt good about regularly disappointing customers—yet that's what they were set up to do. From bottom to top, they all wanted to do better.

Many, however, feel stuck in the system they're in and don't see the way out. Some executives can see the way out but can't see their CEOs or boards being willing to take it. Some leaders are ready to act but aren't sure how to get started. I wrote this book to help all such leaders get unstuck. I want to replace your justified worry about so much change with a justified confidence that this can be done, that you now know how to do it, and that you now know how to convince the skeptics around you that the good jobs strategy will give your company a powerful, enduring, and adaptable competitive advantage.

In *The Good Jobs Strategy*, the question for me was, How can a company offer its customers great service at low prices while simultaneously providing employees with good jobs and shareholders with superior returns? I could see that a few companies were making this work—but *how*? I found that the key to this approach was unusually high investment in people combined with a quartet of operational choices (spelled out in chapter 1), which produced operational excellence.

But knowing how a combustion engine works doesn't enable you to build a car and it doesn't even convince you that you need a car. For the past several years, the headwinds I've faced have focused on this disconnect between seeing a sound operational model and discovering the imperative and desire in an organization to adopt it. Overcoming that disconnect is the purpose of this book. The questions we'll address are:

- If you didn't found your company with the good jobs strategy, why should you adopt it now—especially if your company is profitable?

- How do you convince your board and your investors—and yourself?

- Once you're ready to start, what comes first?

- What works and what doesn't?

- How long does it take, and what kind of leadership does it take?

The answers to these questions come from my academic work and from our work at the Good Jobs Institute. We have worked with more than two dozen companies that explored adopting the good jobs strategy. We know more than ever about what does and does not work when you try to make these systemic changes to your organization. We have identified the most frequent barriers to change—but we have also identified how they can be managed. We have seen what order of changes works better and why. And we have seen with our own eyes how powerfully the operational choices that are key to the good jobs strategy—which I had originally observed in retail chains—and the thinking behind them apply to a much wider variety of industries, including financial services, restaurants, senior living, factories, hospitals, and hotels. All that hands-on knowledge is captured here.

After the next overview chapter, the book will progress in three parts. "Awareness" describes why a system based on high turnover is more expensive, less competitive, and less humane than most executives may think. "Courage" describes what holds some leaders back and what enables others to have the courage to pursue system change. "Implementation" describes how to prioritize this system change so that it really happens, what changes to make first, and how to stay the course.

We Need More Good Jobs—Now

The world is profoundly different today than it was nearly a decade ago when I first set out to convince companies of the value of good jobs. While good jobs alone won't solve all the following problems, it is hard to see how they can be solved *without* good jobs.

Workers are quitting their jobs at a record rate, especially in the low-wage sectors of the economy. Quit rates were already increasing since 2009 and the Covid-19 pandemic accelerated the trend, with record quit rates observed in 2021.[1] From health-care facilities to call centers, from fulfillment centers to factories, companies are having such trouble finding workers that some are adding signing bonuses as high as $3,000.[2]

America has lost its healthy middle class. Even before the pandemic, 53 million people—44 percent of the workforce—worked in jobs for which the median annual pay was just $17,950.[3] Black and Hispanic Americans are disproportionately represented in these low-wage jobs; economic and racial justice are, as Martin Luther King Jr. reminded us, inexorably linked. "Upskilling" workers to better jobs sounds good on paper but won't solve the problem, in part because most job growth is expected to come in low-wage sectors. Caregiving jobs are the fastest-growing occupation and are also notoriously bad jobs. But in fact, it isn't necessary that caregivers, waitresses, and so on upskill to become nurses and computer programmers. The jobs they have right now—in retail, restaurants, call centers, and senior living facilities—are important and *can* be good jobs with living wages, decent benefits, and opportunities for growth and success.

Indeed, many Americans are losing faith in market economies altogether, believing that capitalism inherently creates inequality and injustice. Even before the pandemic, 70 percent of Americans believed the economic system was rigged against them; 47 percent believed that capitalism does more harm than good.[4] Life expectancy in the United States has been declining since 2014. A major reason for the decline, according to economists Anne Case and Angus Deaton, is "deaths of despair"; that is, deaths from drug overdose, alcohol-related liver disease, and suicide.[5] Even among those who have succeeded most in this system, there are corporate leaders who believe that capitalism is broken.

Young and ambitious people are increasingly convinced that the only way to create a strong middle class and improve things for workers is to unionize for power.[6] The pandemic amplified the pent-up pressures—unlivable pay, unstable schedules, and lack of voice, respect, and dignity.[7] As I write these pages in October 2022, unionization—from Starbucks to Apple to Amazon—is on the rise.

On April 1, 2022, Chris Smalls made the news when he and his peers won one of the most historic labor victories in this generation: 2,654 workers at Amazon's Staten Island fulfillment center voted for the union and 2,131 voted against. Shortly after the victory, Smalls appeared on *The Daily Show with Trevor Noah.* Noah pointed out how dystopian the Amazon work environment seemed to those of us on the outside hearing about workers urinating in plastic bottles and about how, on Easter, Amazon posted a sign thanking workers for working on the holiday and told them that *if they meet their quota,* they may win a goody bag—water or soda plus a candy bar or a bag of chips—worth roughly two dollars. He asked Smalls if it was really that bad. The part of Smalls's response that really hit me was that "there was no human aspect" to the job. You don't have interactions with your managers, you don't move up, and if you get fired, it will be done by an app. Smalls brought up Amazon founder Jeff Bezos's trip to space in July 2021, in the middle of the pandemic, when Amazon workers were risking their health to work. After the eleven-minute thrill, Bezos said, "I want to thank every Amazon employee and every Amazon customer because you guys paid for this."

Presumably he meant well—sincerely grateful at that moment for his tremendous success—but imagine how those words came across to the workers, and imagine not having any idea how they would come across.

Then again, why would he, given the gulf between the haves and the have-nots? From 2020 to 2021, the ratio of CEO pay to median worker pay for three hundred low-wage employers—many of those whose employees were considered essential workers or heroes during the pandemic—rose from 604-to-1 to 670-to-1.[8]

That brings me to our trust problem.

If you are a customer, you resent being taken advantage of by companies pushing you to sign up for credit cards and loyalty programs and to buy warranties for products that ought to just work. You are tired of the hidden fees and the poor service—from waiting forever to get your call answered to having to use dirty bathrooms in understaffed restaurants to dealing with frontline workers who wish they could help you but aren't allowed or equipped to.

If you are one of the 53 million low-wage workers, you don't trust corporate leaders. They talk about purpose, inclusion, and equity but pay you unlivable wages and treat you with little respect and dignity. They have no idea what it is like to choose between paying rent and taking your child to the emergency room. Often, they seem incompetent, or at least unforgivably out of touch. There are real cases of company leaders thinking that the way to help people making less than $30,000 a year is to give them discounts on ski passes. There are leaders who send snow blowers to a store in Miami and then judge frontline employees' performance based on unsold inventory.

If you are an executive of a company with a large frontline workforce, maybe you're already protesting these accusations. You don't see much reason to trust those workers. They show up late, treat customers poorly, and can't even execute the simplest tasks well. They don't know how hard you work, or the performance pressures you feel every day.

Meanwhile, if you are a middle manager or a frontline manager in these companies, you feel stuck. Your boss wants you to be a long-term strategic thinker, but how is that possible when you are dealing with an unmanageable workload, you're running from one meeting to the next, and priorities change all the time? Employees cause problems. Customers yell at you because of high prices and long waits. No one has any idea that you are having anxiety attacks and are an inch away from quitting.

Even shareholders have a trust problem. If you are an institutional investor, you think executives don't have the same interests as their shareholders, who are in it for the long term. These investors resent being blamed for executives' tendency to focus on the short term.

Who Is This Book For?

With so much going haywire, what answers do I have and *whom* are those answers for? The primary audience for this book is business leaders at all levels who want their organization to be great—one that creates value for shareholders by winning with customers and providing jobs with respect and dignity. To put it another way, they want to work for an organization that both employees and customers can count on for good products, good services, and good jobs, and that shareholders can count on for good returns. The case studies in this book—from companies big and small, public and private, competing on low cost or on differentiation—will help you envision how you, too, can win through good jobs and the virtuous cycle that comes with them. You will see how to make the changes necessary for your particular company, how to reorient your company's decision-making processes, and—no less important—how to stay the course.

While I believe that business leaders can help solve this problem, they can't do it alone. Government, unions, customers, investors, boards, and business schools will all need to do their parts, and so this book is for them, too. If these influencers fully understand why companies are run the way they are—why jobs and service are as bad as they are—they can help by nudging those companies to change and by supporting the ones that do.

Still, it is CEOs and their management teams who will have to take the steps described in this book. These are the steps that are within *their* power—and no one else's—to take.

My goal is to show them that their status quo is worse than they think and that the way out of the vicious cycle doesn't involve jumping off a cliff into a raging river and hoping to come to the surface alive. Large investments in labor can be made in stages and with specific operational changes so that they begin to pay for themselves. Gambling on your workforce isn't really that much of a gamble. If you can prioritize this change, its implementation is less risky than you think. Companies in a variety of industries—not just retail—have already set out on adopting the good jobs strategy and have made impressive progress. You can join them.

Trends in labor markets—from rising minimum wages and other regulations such as fair scheduling laws to a tight labor market—make it even easier to make the case for change. Economists expect labor markets to be tight for a while for several reasons. The dependency ratio, which the Census Bureau defines as the number of people sixty-five and older for every 100 people of "working age"—between twenty and sixty-four—is projected to climb from 26 percent in 2022 to 36 percent in 2050. The Baby Boomers (those born between 1946 and 1964) are retiring, people are having fewer kids, and immigration is declining.[9] Employees and job seekers may have the cards in their favor for a while, a trend that will lead to rising wages.

Given that set of circumstances, if you stay with the status quo, labor costs will rise with the market, but employee turnover won't improve, and employees' output will remain the same—after all, the job is the same. But if you adopt the good jobs strategy, your higher-paid workforce will stay with you and generate more profit because their jobs are designed for higher productivity, contribution, and motivation. The pay increase is now an investment—a good one.

The case for good jobs is strong. Your company will be more competitive, more resilient, and more blessed with loyal customers and dedicated employees. So let's get down to business and see how best to carry out this transition to excellence.

Escaping Mediocrity

It was heartening how many executives reached out to me because they were interested in the idea of investing in frontline workers through higher pay or more stable schedules. But investing in workers alone was never my message and I soon realized that other aspects of the good jobs strategy—namely, that it is systemic, customer centric, and grounded in operational excellence—were not always understood as *essential*. (To emphasize the system aspect, I'll often use the term "good jobs system" to refer to the good jobs strategy.)

For example, the chief human resources officer (CHRO) of a large retail chain contacted me shortly after his company had raised hourly pay for store employees. Disappointingly, the retailer was still having trouble hiring people and keeping them. To his credit, he understood that going even further—namely, improving frontline work schedules—would help. Employees were working too few hours and their schedules varied week to week, which meant that their total pay was not only low but never the same—although the bills they had to pay didn't change. (This is a common problem in the service sector.) So his company wanted to "scientifically" study what would happen to store performance and workers' quality of life if workers were given more hours and steadier schedules. He figured that an expert on "workforce optimization"—namely, me—could help quantify the return on investment from better scheduling.

I was impressed that this thoughtful executive and his company wanted to take some real steps toward a strategy that would benefit not only the employees but also the customers and the bottom line. But there were two problems. First, he thought I was an expert on workforce optimization. People often see the title of my earlier book—*The Good Jobs Strategy*—and assume it's an HR book. But the secret sauce of the good jobs strategy is operations. The four operational choices—combined with unusually high investment in frontline workers—are the key to profitability, growth, competitiveness, and resilience.

The second problem was that he'd missed the point that the good jobs strategy is a *system*. You can't just implement one element—say, by raising pay or offering better schedules or empowering frontline employees to make decisions—and expect results. As an example, you can't improve scheduling without making quite a few other changes. Stable schedules require stable workload. If your deliveries are too unpredictable, if your visual merchandisers change their minds all the time about how to set up displays, if you offer too many sales promotions that create high variability in customer demand and throughout your supply chain, then you can't offer frontline workers consistent hours even if you sincerely want to.

So I want to make it clear to interested leaders that what I'm proposing is a *system* change grounded in operational excellence. I declined the offer to work with this CHRO's company just then but asked them to let me know if they ever wanted to consider a full system change. Several years later, they did. They were still having the same turnover problems but now their stock price had dropped more than 20 percent.

I made a presentation to the leadership team and was encouraged by the response—they really seemed to be getting how the good jobs system could help their company. But then the president said, quite matter-of-factly, "I didn't understand how important customer focus is to the good jobs strategy. That's really hard for a public company to do."

I was stunned. It's basically business canon that the best companies focus on creating value for the customer, and there is strong empirical evidence for that argument.[1] How could a company afford not to be customer focused? How could its leader openly say he is not customer focused in front of his team?

For that CHRO's company (as for many others), decision-making was primarily financial; that is, decisions were made to grow sales and profits. Okay, that's important, but don't you do it by making your customers happy?

Not always. In fact, there are many ways to grow sales and profits while ignoring customers. That's just what this company, like many others operating in a vicious cycle, was busy with. They bought other brands. They added e-commerce services to copy what startups were doing. (Those brands were later sold and some of the services discontinued.) They offered more products. To increase store traffic, they offered sales promotions. Of course, doing so complicated operations in the stores and in the supply chain. But promotions *did* increase store traffic, so they kept adding more and more—a new promotion every week. Customers stopped buying products at full price—why would they? Margins shrank. The company then added a rewards card. And then a credit card. Asking customers to enroll slowed down the checkout process, aggravating both customers and cashiers.

In a desperate attempt to show growth, they seemed to have prioritized everything except running their core business well—that is, giving their customers an experience that would bring them back for more. Their natural reaction to a quarter of poor financial performance—and this is true of many, many companies—was to add more and do more. But if what you are doing is not all that good, just doing more of it doesn't make it better. In fact, it weakens your core.[2]

And was all this financial decision-making at least helping the company's shareholders? Its stock price as I write is less than one-third what it was when I first talked to them in 2014. It may take years, but a commitment to financial decision-making over customer-centric decision-making will catch up to you sooner or later, as it did for General Electric, Toys "R" Us, Circuit City, and Sears.

Although the Good Jobs Institute did not end up working with that company, executives at different levels kept reaching out to us. One even said, "Deep in my heart, I know the good jobs strategy is what we need to do. But I can't see us doing it." He felt trapped, and he isn't alone. I hear similar statements from too many others working at large public companies. They see how broken their system is. They want to fix it. But fixing what's actually broken, which is many of the fundamentals—hiring the right people and helping them do a good job, designing their jobs to drive high performance, setting high expectations, facilitating end-to-end decision-making, having managers lead and improve performance versus firefighting all the time—seems an insurmountable task.

If you feel like this, you're not alone, either. You are trapped, and the trap you're in is worse than you think. At the same time, the way out is closer than you think. But before we start digging our escape tunnel, let's first understand where we're trying to get to.

What Is the Good Jobs System?

I originally studied four low-cost retailers (Mercadona, Spain's largest supermarket chain; Trader Joe's, an American supermarket chain; QuikTrip, an American convenience store chain; and Costco) operating in a virtuous cycle of high investment in employees and high performance. I saw that they all made four operational choices that made it possible to invest much more in their frontline people and deliver much more to their customers than their mediocre peers operating in a vicious cycle did—or than they themselves had been doing before taking the turn to good jobs.

Those four operational choices are:

- Focus and simplify[3]

- Standardize and empower

- Cross-train

- Operate with slack

FIGURE 1-1

The good jobs system

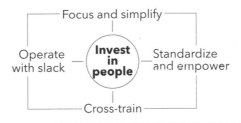

These operational choices make employees' work better. Still, even the best-designed work can't succeed without a stable, able, and motivated workforce. And even a well-paid, well-trained workforce will be defeated by the wrong operational choices. So these four operational choices must be *combined with* employee investment. I call this combination the good jobs system. It is a *system* that prioritizes customers and is *designed* to maximize employee productivity, motivation, and contribution. (See figure 1-1.)

Here is a brief overview of the elements of the good jobs system and how they differ from the system of companies that operate in a vicious cycle.

Invest in people

The mental model at companies that operate in a vicious cycle is primarily financial and therefore inevitably views employees as a cost to be minimized. Frontline wages are based on the going market rate in that area, as if labor were like any other input to production. High employee turnover is treated as something to live with, like equipment maintenance. Conversely, the mental model at companies with a good jobs system is customer centric and therefore recognizes that frontline employees—the ones face-to-face with the customers—are the ones driving differentiation, growth, and profitability. These employees aren't the picks and shovels—they're the gold. When you're customer centric, high employee turnover is a cost you can't tolerate. So those companies invest what it takes to attract the right people, train them, retain them, and keep expectations high. That investment includes higher wages, more stable schedules, promotion from within, and strong hiring, training, and performance management.

The following are the four operational choices.

Focus and simplify

The mental model at companies that operate in a vicious cycle is for head-quarters functions to make decisions to improve their own metrics and leave the frontline workers to figure out how to deal with the consequences of those decisions. Silos at headquarters constantly add products, services, projects, tools, and pilots. These activities—often uncoordinated—create an increased and uneven workload in the frontlines. Last-minute changes to deliveries, pilots, and corporate visits make the workload unpredictable. Meanwhile, at companies with a good jobs system, decisions always put customers ahead of short-term financial performance. But these companies also recognize that customer focus is not the same as being all things to all people. They maintain clarity about what value they offer their customers and what they give up. The mental model at these companies is that the most important work is done in the front lines where customers meet the company. Therefore, *everyone* should work on simplifying flow and work to ensure that the frontline workers can serve the customer well. Simplifying includes maintaining discipline in doing only what adds value for the customer, eliminating wasteful and low-value-added activities, and making the workload smoother and more predictable.

Standardize and empower

The mental model at companies that operate in a vicious cycle is command and control. Headquarters thinks and frontline workers do. There's a rule for everything. Information flows one way from the top to the bottom—there's no reason to build a structure for flowing information from the front lines to the headquarters. The mental model at companies with a good jobs system is to leverage frontline ability, knowledge, and time to serve the customer well and pursue bottom-up continuous improvement. These companies standardize routine processes—with frontline input—to increase efficiency and consistency and to reduce employees' mental overload, then empower employees to engage in improvement and to make decisions to increase customer satisfaction. These companies also create structures to hear employee ideas.

Cross-train

To cut costs, companies that operate in a vicious cycle either have their employees perform narrow tasks or ask them to cover more than they are trained or able to do. The mental model of companies with a good jobs system is to maximize the productivity of their employees and to foster ownership. To that end, they cross-train employees to do both customer-facing and non-customer-facing tasks so that they can adjust productively to changes in customer traffic. Cross-training is done in a way that ensures ownership and allows for specialization.

Operate with slack

When employees are seen as a cost to be minimized, the tendency is to staff the work environment with as few people as possible. Mistakes, burnout, and poor customer service are tolerated for the sake of keeping costs down. Companies with a good jobs system prioritize customers and see their employees as a driver of customer value and continuous improvement. They staff their businesses with more hours of labor than the expected workload so that employees can do their jobs without rushing and can respond to customer demand even during peak periods. Operating with slack also ensures that employees can take time off without letting their team down and managers have time to develop people and create a strong talent pipeline. Table 1-1 summarizes the differences between a good jobs system and a bad jobs system.

TABLE 1-1

Comparison of good jobs and bad jobs systems

Elements	The good jobs system	The bad jobs system
Invest in people	Invest what it takes to attract and retain the right people and set high expectations. Promote primarily from within.	Minimize labor costs by benchmarking the market. Hire "smart" managers from outside.
Focus and simplify	Maintain discipline in doing what adds value to customer. HQ decisions consider the impact on frontline employees and their ability to be productive and serve the customer.	Add to customer offering to reach new customers and grow sales at all costs. HQ functions optimize locally and ask frontline employees to make those decisions work.
Standardize and empower	Leverage frontline workers' knowledge, time, and ability. Standardize for consistency, productivity, and ease of empowerment. Invest in structures to hear the voice of frontline staff.	Command and control. Standardize to minimize mistakes and bad decisions. Few structures for HQ to hear frontline workers' input.
Cross-train	Design the work to balance specialization, flexibility, and motivation. Ensure ownership in an area that includes customer-facing and non-customer-facing tasks.	Design the work to minimize labor costs—either too much task specialization or requiring people to do too much.
Operate with slack	Ensure employees have time to serve customers, do their work without mistakes, develop a leadership bench, and have time for improvement. Minimize burnout.	To minimize labor costs, staff units with as few people as possible to get as much work out of them as possible.

A System with Interconnected Elements

Since the key to adopting the good jobs strategy is to understand that it's a system of interconnected elements, let's examine the workings of this system through one of the most successful examples I know: Mercadona, Spain's largest supermarket chain. Mercadona adopted the good jobs system, internally called the Total Quality Model, in the early 1990s to deal with tougher competition and declining profit margins.

Mercadona is my go-to case when I teach in executive education. During one session with executives of a large company, we started the discussion with Mercadona's investment in employees: higher wages and a yearly bonus that amounted to one or two months of salary depending on tenure; 5,000 euros spent on a four-week training course for new employees; operating with 85 percent full-time employees who received their schedules one month in advance and worked in consistent shifts; and 100 percent promotion from within. I asked the participants: "How can Mercadona invest so much more in its employees than its competitors do while also offering lower prices and making more money?"

One participant suggested low employee turnover. At 3.4 percent, Mercadona's turnover was less than one-fifteenth of what was typical in retail. That meant that Mercadona could spend fifteen times more per employee in training than a typical retailer. Low turnover also enabled high expectations—it's only when people mean to stay with a company that you can consistently demand and receive their best efforts. (Let me point out here that 3.4 percent turnover is astoundingly low. Don't be intimidated by it. You'll know with your own business when turnover is no longer a severe handicap, even if it is still a nuisance.)

Another participant said it was "because they empower their employees." Indeed, Mercadona's frontline employees make a lot of decisions that enable them to increase sales and reduce costs. They manage flow by opening cash registers or by changing their speed depending on customer traffic; they can accept a return without asking a supervisor for help; they can drop the price of tomatoes at the end of a Saturday if they believe too many kilos will go to waste otherwise (stores are closed on Sundays); and they are involved in improvement. Specialists in areas such as produce, bakery, and cosmetics are empowered to order products and talk to customers to understand their needs. When your employees contribute more—to customer service, sales, and costs—you can pay them more and still come out ahead. Empowerment also makes the job a better job, which lowers turnover.

But another participant was puzzled: "We've empowered our own employees and lost tens of millions of dollars." Why didn't that happen at Mercadona? Because, as noted earlier in the chapter, you can't apply just one element of the good jobs system and expect the results the system produces. Let's look further at Mercadona to see how the system's interconnected elements depend on and reinforce one another.

Mercadona can trust its employees to make good decisions because low turnover enables the company to hire the right people and train them well. Experienced employees know what they are doing, what their customers need, and how to help them. Because Mercadona offers fewer products in each category, employees can become knowledgeable about those products and suggest improvement ideas. Other forms of operational simplification (predictable deliveries, no sales promotions, and so on) mean that employees aren't spending their time and attention on tedious tasks. (The resulting higher productivity in turn enables higher pay, which in turn keeps turnover low.) Mercadona knows where to simplify operationally because there's clarity about what value it offers customers: the best quality-to-price ratio, the highest level of service, and the ability to complete purchases quickly.

Standardization of routine processes (such as unloading trucks, shelving, and cleaning) is done with employee input to make their jobs easier and safer. The combination of standardization and simplification reduces mental overload, which further helps employees make the right decisions. Operating with slack means that employees have time to make the right decisions, communicate improvement ideas, and understand customer needs. They aren't too busy to do a good job.

To see more of how interrelated the system is, let's examine how Mercadona can operate with 85 percent full-timers who have stable schedules even when customer traffic varies greatly throughout the day and week.

Remember, providing stable schedules is what the CHRO at the beginning of this chapter was after. And I noted that stable schedules require stable workloads. So, Mercadona looks for ways to smooth out the workload. It schedules activities such as deliveries, display changes, equipment maintenance, and product introductions on days and hours when traffic is likely to be low. These activities are performed with discipline—Mercadona minimizes last-minute changes. Operational simplification and the standardization of routine processes further reduce variability and make it possible to more accurately forecast workloads. During the day, as traffic varies, employees shift between customer-facing tasks (such as helping people find what they're looking for and manning the cash register) and non-customer-facing tasks (such as cleaning and restocking)— they have been cross-trained to do so. Stable schedules, in turn, keep turnover low and customers satisfied.

The Power of the Good Jobs System

When I studied Mercadona, it was offering its customers the lowest prices *and* good customer service. It had higher profitability and higher labor, inventory, and space productivity than its competitors.

You can feel the high performance and customer focus when you are in a Mercadona store. To me, being at Mercadona stores was like being at a Toyota factory—things were really humming. Stores were clean and orderly—even the back rooms and the small storage area for cleaning materials. Product locations were intuitive for the customer, with good signage. Price tags were at the center of each product's display where the customers could easily see them. The shelves were neatly stocked. The presentation of the produce and fish sections was impeccable. I saw many employees talking to customers. They didn't seem to be in a rush. All stores I visited had two checkout areas, each with multiple cash registers to reduce congestion.

Competitively, in addition to winning with customers, a system with capable and motivated employees and strong operations enables Mercadona to easily adopt new technologies, respond to changes in customer needs, and improve constantly. For example, Mercadona emerged from the 2008–2009 financial crisis with higher market share because it was able to cut prices by 10 percent—720 euros per family per year—while maintaining profitability.[4] That was a big deal for Spanish families during a period of high unemployment and shrinking gross domestic product. It wouldn't have been possible without Mercadona's productive and motivated employees, who came up with many ideas to reduce costs, and

What about the Toyota Production System?

If you are familiar with the Toyota Production System (TPS), it may have struck you by now that the good jobs system has a lot in common with TPS, which is synonymous with operational excellence and continuous improvement. Both investment in people and the quartet of operational choices are at work at Toyota. The values that guide the good jobs system and TPS are similar. The two systems are not, however, the same. Let me clarify here why the good jobs system might be an effective way to start if your company ultimately wants to adopt TPS.

During the last eight years, I had the honor of working closely with Jamie Bonini, the president of Toyota's nonprofit arm, Toyota Production System Support Center (TSSC), created to contribute to society by helping organizations outside the auto industry implement TPS. Since its founding in 1992, TSSC has helped over 480 organizations, from nonprofits to manufacturers to hospitals to city governments.

Bonini and his colleagues define TPS as "an organizational culture of highly engaged people innovating or solving problems to drive performance." The culture is supported by a philosophy promoting customer first, respect for people, shop-floor focus, and continuous improvement. But quickly identifying and solving problems when the evidence is fresh requires more than a philosophy; it requires technical tools to make problems visible and managerial tools to make sure there is a capable and motivated workforce that can safely identify problems and that knows about approaches to problem-solving. That means that developing people is at the heart of TPS—you can't just improve production or processes without improving the workers themselves.[a]

The way Toyota identifies and solves problems *one at a time* requires tremendous discipline and attention from top management. Some of the technical elements, like just-in-time, require deep operational competence. Referring to how demanding TPS is, one Toyota leader told me it is "almost against human nature."

Companies with a good jobs system do not have all the technical elements to conduct one-at-a-time problem-solving, but they all have built their own mechanisms to hear frontline ideas, surface problems, and improve. Four Seasons hotels, for example, have "glitch meetings" every day, where all the department managers get together to talk about problems their customers faced the day before and to find ways to delight them. At Mercadona, each process—including hiring and training—has a process owner whose assistants are at the stores all the time talking to frontline workers and hearing their ideas. At QuikTrip, there are employee resource groups to talk about common problems and then share ideas. At Costco, warehouse managers send a list of customer questions and issues to corporate at the end of each day.

You don't have to be the world's best at problem-solving to pursue operational excellence and continuous improvement. You just need a stable team with solid players—willing to learn and master the fundamentals—and you need to have the discipline to keep at it every day so that you constantly improve.

In short, although the good jobs system has much in common with TPS, it is not as demanding. Yet, it produces great results.

a. Like many others who have either worked at Toyota or studied TPS, Bonini is not happy about how frequently TPS is misunderstood and misapplied. It has been interpreted as a system whose objective is to drive efficiency—"lean and mean." That approach means cutting everything that looks like waste—including people. But TPS is in fact a good jobs system and cutting people is alien to its approach. It takes its inspiration from Dr. W. Edwards Deming, the founder of quality management. Both TPS and quality management have respect for people as a core value. With Bonini, I visited several companies TSSC had helped, including factories and service businesses, and saw firsthand how much TPS improved both performance and people's jobs—not just pay but also respect and dignity.

its strong system that enabled Mercadona to implement those ideas. And as the acid test of adaptability, thirteen years after I studied Mercadona, that retailer—like the other three I studied—still shines in the eyes of its customers, employees, and shareholders.

Lessons from Experience

For the last eight years, I have been observing and working with companies that are trying to adopt the good jobs system, whereas earlier, I had simply been observing companies, like Mercadona, that had long since mastered it. The Good Jobs Institute has worked with dozens of companies. My colleagues there and I have thus been able to identify certain approaches that matter most in making the transition from a vicious cycle of mediocrity to a virtuous cycle of excellence. These approaches will be reflected in the organization of the rest of the book (chapters 2–10).

Lesson 1: The importance of understanding how uncompetitive and inhumane a high-turnover system is

Few business leaders realize how damaging high turnover is to their business. And few realize how powerfully turnover and low employee ability are driven by low and inconsistent pay—due to low hourly wages and insufficient and inconsistent hours. So chapter 2 starts with the subject of pay, demonstrating that insufficient pay drives turnover and hurts employees, including their ability to maintain strong attendance and perform well, more than most businesspeople recognize.

Many executives I met didn't think the costs of turnover were high enough to justify higher pay. But they had never even quantified those costs. In chapter 3, we'll see that the direct turnover costs (hiring, onboarding, training, time to full productivity) are often higher than executives may suspect. The indirect costs from poor operational execution (lower customer satisfaction and loyalty, mistakes that reduce sales and increase costs, overtime costs, and low productivity) are even higher. In chapter 4, we'll see that the competitive and ethical costs of turnover are higher still—preventing companies from differentiating in the eyes of customers, adapting to changes, and offering basic dignity and respect to workers.

Lesson 2: The importance of changing from primarily financial decision-making to primarily customer-centric and ethical decision-making

In chapter 5, we'll see that a big obstacle to escaping mediocrity is that so many decisions that affect the frontline workers (and therefore the customers) are made looking at numbers alone—and often within silos—by managers who are held responsible for their own metrics, not for customer satisfaction or frontline performance. Many leaders of public companies have told me that they would *like* to be customer centric and values driven, but they are *obliged* to maximize sales and earnings before interest and taxes (EBIT).

In contrast, leaders who choose the good jobs system base their decisions *primarily* on competitiveness and ethics rather than *primarily* on financial outcomes. We'll meet these leaders in chapter 6. It is not that these leaders care less about creating value for their investors than those who focus on the financials. As we will see, their companies have done extraordinarily well for their shareholders. But they have a different mental model for how to create that value. They are interested in being the best, not necessarily the biggest. In their minds, if you can get everyone end to end to focus on creating value for the customer, maintain discipline in doing the fundamentals of your business well, and do the right thing, you will create great long-term value for the shareholder. An increasing body of evidence bears them out. In my first book, I had described the *what* of the good jobs system. This line of thinking is the *why* of the good jobs system. Once a company is customer centric, it must be frontline centric, designed to enable frontline employees to deliver great service, drive improvement, and be motivated and productive.

In chapter 7, we will meet leaders—mostly professional managers of public companies, which is to say, leaders under a lot of external pressure—

who had the courage to make system change. They didn't say, "What's the ROI on improving employee schedules or paying employees enough so that they can put food on the table? Get me the numbers!" Rather, they asked, "Can we be a great company—one that wins with our customers, adapts to changes, and conducts itself in line with its values—if we don't invest in our people?"

Let's go back once more to the CHRO who was interested in improving frontline scheduling. The question that guided his company's decision-making was financially driven and was asked in isolation: "All else being constant, does improving employee schedules pay off?" Here are two alternative approaches that would have led that company to the good jobs system.

Competitive case. First, what if the company had followed *this* line of thought: Our same-store sales growth is declining because we don't provide our customers with a compelling reason to shop with us. (They *were* aware of that.) Customers can't find the products on the shelves. They can't find an employee to help them or one who actually knows anything about the product they're looking for. They don't like the cluttered shelves and long lines. We can't create a good omni-channel experience if we can't depend on the stores to have accurate inventory or on store employees to find the products customers ordered online. Unfortunately, that's the best we can do with so many inexperienced and undedicated employees coming in and out. So we *have to reduce turnover*—whatever it takes. What it will take is to give our employees more hours and more consistent schedules so they can make a reasonable living. But to do that and not lose our shirts, we need much better logistics and smarter merchandising decisions so we're not wasting the time we're paying for and so our employees can serve customers.

Ethical case. Here's another line of thought that would bring the company much closer to solving its most serious problems: Our core values include respect for people. We say we care about diversity, equity, and inclusion. Yet our employees are not making enough money to live and have crazy-making schedules. Not to mention that those bad jobs are disproportionately held by women and people of color. If we're going to be an ethical company, we *have to turn those bad jobs into good jobs*—whatever it takes.

Both approaches would have enabled the company to be on its way to excellence. (And remember, all else doesn't have to be constant. Company leaders aren't lab scientists—they have both the permission and the power to *create* the right conditions for an experiment to succeed.)

Lesson 3: The importance of leadership conviction for adopting the good jobs system

Leaders who successfully adopted the good jobs system wanted their organization to be a great one. They were convinced that that wasn't possible without a capable and motivated workforce that can drive value for the customer. Their convictions gave them the courage to take on system change. In "Courage," I'll show what can undermine such conviction and how leaders have overcome those obstacles.

For example, many leaders deeply fear that investment in their frontline people, however well intended, will not pay off. They have been taught for decades that cutting labor cost is good business—they can't imagine operating any other way. Some are even told by their executive team, "We've raised wages before. It doesn't pay off." Some leaders are afraid to come off looking naive, paying their workers more than what others are paying and then getting nothing for it. To other leaders, the implementation risks seem high: How long will this system change take? Is it worth risking your own reputation—possibly even your job?

There are reasons that each of these fears is as common as it is. But, as we will see, there are also arguments and evidence that none of these objections is as definitive as it seems. Put another way, these are fears that you need not be afraid to face down.

Every single leader I know who committed to system change told me the same thing: "We had to take a leap of faith." But don't be fooled by this. It was faith in something that made perfect sense to them and that they knew was the right thing to do. Investment in people, one leader told me, was "a little bit like trying to quantify the net present value of buying a laptop. It's hard to do, but you know it's positive—having a personal computer versus not. So it's a little bit of a leap of faith, but intuitively you just know that some of these things will pay off." Another commented that the good jobs strategy was "blindingly obvious." No academic likes to think her work is obvious, but I'll take it. The four operational choices were considered to drive high performance and employee motivation long before I observed them at companies like Mercadona. Those choices made the high investment in people less risky—you are paying more for people but also improving their productivity at the same time. The new expense will more than pay for itself and you can see clearly from the start *why* it will.

It might seem scary that the good jobs system requires relying on the lowest-level people in your company to do a good job. Some of the corporate leaders who adopted the system were able to sidestep this fear because they had begun their careers on the front lines—pushing shopping carts in from the parking lot and similar entry-level jobs. They'd seen with their own eyes how good low-level employees could be if you put the whole company behind them. For this very reason, I advise my own MBA students at MIT Sloan to spend time working in frontline jobs before ensconcing themselves in higher management. Without this experience, you just don't know who it is you're managing, and you are very likely to underestimate one of your most valuable assets.

Lesson 4: The importance of prioritizing the transition to the good jobs system

In "Implementation," I'll show that once leaders prioritize system change, it proves to be less risky than it had seemed.

System change can sound daunting. If your company is in a vicious cycle and has created an entire system that assumes low employee ability, many interdependent changes will be needed. Which do you make first? As one executive aptly put it, "How do you eat the elephant?" Well, one bite at a time, but where you take the first bite makes a difference.

The most important ingredient for success is to get various corporate functions—finance, marketing, product design, supply chain, operations, HR—to recognize the need for system change and prioritize it. That is possible only if the good jobs system is necessary to survive and grow. As we will see in chapter 8, leaders who were successful in adopting a good jobs system did not think of that system—or present it to others—as something nice to have or as an investment (among any number of others) with a positive upside. The good jobs system solved a crucial business problem. They thought of it—and presented it to their teams and their boards—as the necessary response to an existential threat: "If we don't do this, we'll lose." To grow and survive, they had to become customer centric. The only way to become customer centric was to become frontline centric.

Once there's urgency to make system change, the tactical part of implementation is not as daunting as it might seem. The key is to make a set of changes to get out of the vicious cycle as quickly as possible without breaking the bank. Companies that were successful in doing that made two sets of changes simultaneously. They invested in people (pay, schedules, career paths, expectations) and subtracted from frontline employees' work (reducing and smoothing of workload) in a way that made their customer offering stronger. By reducing the workload, effective subtraction subsidized the pay investment and significantly reduced its perceived risk. These changes together reduced employee turnover, improved employee ability, and ensured there were enough people to take care of the customer. Now there was a solid foundation to develop managers, empower people, and create a system of continuous improvement.

From a $60 billion retailer to a fleet of call centers to a two-unit restaurant, there were similar high-leverage points for effective subtraction. But they required involving important headquarters functions so that their decisions considered the impact on frontline employees and the ability of those employees to deliver value to customers. In every company with which we worked—but most especially the large ones—the frontline workers and their immediate managers were buried with tasks and activities that came from headquarters. Too much had been added to the customer offering—more products, services, discounts, deals, hours, warranties, loyalty cards—just to increase sales incrementally. There was a steady stream of new pilots, reports, performance tools, processes, delivery schedules, and display layouts. Each of these demands had some value to the function that was making it, but few had any value to the customer, and the totality was seldom coordinated and sometimes incoherent.

In business, time itself is a risk, due to both opportunity cost and competition. So when assessing the risk of trying to break out of the vicious cycle, it's fair to ask: How long does it take to get results and how good are those results anyway? How long it takes to get on a virtuous cycle depends on the size of the company, how deep it is in the vicious cycle, how much mistrust there is between frontline employees and corporate, and how strong corporate's project management skills are. At a large company like Sam's Club, with around one hundred thousand employees and $60 billion in sales, results started showing within two years. At Quest Diagnostics call centers, a much smaller operation with less than one thousand employees in just two locations, results started showing within eighteen months. What were those results? Higher customer satisfaction and loyalty. Lower employee turnover. Improved attendance. More promotion from within. Better operational execution that resulted in higher productivity, quality, and same-unit sales and lower costs. (See chapter 7 for some numbers.) And—less measurable but even more important— increased competitiveness (differentiation and adaptation) and a more humane system in which people are treated with respect and dignity.

Looking back over these four lessons, the first one is that the trap you're in—largely due to low pay and high turnover—is worse than you think, but the final lesson is that escaping the trap is easier and less risky than you think.

And now, let's get moving. In chapters 2 through 4, we'll look more carefully at what's wrong with low pay and the resulting high turnover. That awareness (part 1) should set you on the road to courage (part 2) and then to implementation (part 3).

AWARENESS

Market Wages Aren't Enough

There's a lot more to low pay than not making enough money.

Obviously, even good pay doesn't guarantee a good job. You could be paid enough to make a living but have a soul-crushing job at which you are asked to work like a robot, your voice is not heard, your time and abilities are not respected. A company offering high pay could still have low productivity and poor quality if its operations are poorly designed.

But without sufficient pay, mediocrity is almost guaranteed. Nothing else you do will make up for low pay. And those of us who make more than enough to make ends meet often underappreciate the importance of pay for workers' well-being and ability to focus on the job—even for the simplest jobs.

Do You Know How Much Your Lowest-Paid Workers Make?

In 2017, a PayPal employee's house burned down. After helping that employee financially, senior leadership set up an emergency $5 million relief fund to help other employees experiencing financial hardship. The demand for that help—the volume of requests and the reasons for them—alarmed PayPal's leaders. Urgent requests were not necessarily due to calamities such as a fire, but more often to everyday events such as a steep medical bill, a car breaking down, or a student loan payment.

Another red flag came when a senior leader was doing community service at a soup kitchen in Chandler, Arizona, where PayPal had a large call center. As she was leaving, the director of the soup kitchen told her, "I just need you to know that many of the people that we have visiting our services are actually your employees." These were workers at a company whose mission was to democratize financial services, yet they were desperate enough to turn up at a soup kitchen.

To understand the financial health of its employees, PayPal examined paychecks of entry-level and hourly level employees and conducted a wellness survey of all its employees. The results showed that thousands of employees were financially stressed. Their net disposable income (NDI), defined as the percentage of pay left over at the end of the month after living costs and taxes, was so low that nearly two-thirds of the respondents to the surveys ran out—or nearly ran out—of money between paychecks and nearly one-third did not have enough to cover an unexpected yet reasonable expense. These findings surprised executives.[1] Dan Schulman, the CEO of PayPal, told me, "We pay at or above market rates. And you think that because the market is guiding you, that it therefore works for everybody." He continued: "The market forces are not working for them. . . . I had known that 185 million adults in the US struggle to make ends meet at the end of the month. But I felt like at a place like PayPal, where we are paying well compared to the market, that wouldn't be the same."

In 2019, Schulman led a global town hall to announce the "Financial Wellness Initiative," whose components included pay increases, reduction in health-care costs, stock equity grants, and financial education. PayPal wanted to increase NDI for its employees to 20 percent. In chapter 8 we will learn more about this initiative and what made it possible.

Mark Bertolini, the former CEO of Aetna, had a similar surprise in 2014. When he started asking workers about how they were doing and what was going on in their lives, he was surprised by how many of them mentioned pocketbook issues that created stress and real hardship. When he looked at data on his lowest-paid workers—about fifty-seven hundred employees, including white-collar workers such as claims processors and customer service reps, who were making $12.50–$13 an hour—he found that 81 percent were women. Many were single mothers. Their kids were on Medicaid because they couldn't afford Aetna's dependent coverage. Some were using food stamps.[2]

Bertolini told me, "If it was a machine, we'd take care of that machine every day. We'd make sure it's running properly, it's oiled properly, it's cleaned properly, it's shut down properly. We don't do that with our employees." He was also alarmed by the growing income inequality in the United States. For the holidays in 2014, he gave everyone on his executive team a copy of *Capital in the Twenty-First Century*, economist Thomas Piketty's bestselling book analyzing the growing wealth inequality in capitalist economies and its effects on social stability. Bertolini asked his team, "What are we going to do as a company to find a way to do something different?"

When Bertolini told Aetna's HR leaders that they had to raise pay, he faced resistance. They thought pay at Aetna was fine because, like Pay-Pal, they were already paying market rates. Anything higher would lower their ability to serve the shareholders. The HR team finally gave in and suggested a raise of 50 cents an hour. "Let's make it [starting pay] $16," Bertolini told them (a raise of $4 an hour). "Prove to me that $16 is wrong." They couldn't. The costs of low pay—yes, that's what I said, the *costs* of low pay—ended up being greater than all the benefits that could come from raising pay to a living wage.

Unlike Schulman and Bertolini, many company leaders are not yet alarmed by what they pay their workers, partly because they don't really know what they pay. They may know the number, but they don't know what that number means in real life—how inadequate it is. The CEO, COO, and CFO of a large specialty retailer were shocked when my students and I pointed out to them that 80 percent of their store employees, including managers, made less than $20,800 a year in 2016. Why did they make so little? Because hourly wages were low and they were assigned too few hours.

The company had relied on engagement surveys to assess job quality. According to those surveys, employees were doing just fine. When asked if their pay was fair, plenty of employees said it was. But meanwhile, turnover was 120 percent, meaning that the typical employee was staying for less than a year. Put another way, if you compared the rosters of employees at the beginning and end of the year, you might see all new names. Employees often left for a job that paid a dollar more an hour or offered more hours per week. All this time, actions had been speaking louder than the words on surveys—but no one had been listening. (This is why doctors don't just ask you if you have a fever. They take your temperature.)

When the Good Jobs Institute presents executives with data on what percentage of their full-time workers make below-subsistence wages, there's often silence in the room. Then someone says, "I had no idea we were paying that little." During a workshop with Lucky Eagle Casino & Hotel, owned and operated by the Chehalis tribe, when JaNessa Bumgarner, the CEO, saw the pay data, she told everyone it was sad. "I don't think when the elders wanted this casino, they imagined that we would be paying people too little to get by."

At several companies we worked with, more than half the full-time employees did not enroll in the company-provided health-care plans because it was too expensive for them. At one company, fewer than 10 percent of the hourly employees participated in the company's medical plan and fewer than 5 percent participated in 401(k) plans. Executives were often surprised that the uptake of their benefits was so low. Some thought, "Maybe they just don't value this benefit." They valued it. They just couldn't afford it.

Assuming Market Wages Work— Even When They Are below Subsistence

At both PayPal and Aetna, as at most companies, market wages were seen as the best practice for setting pay levels. PayScale's interviews with nearly five thousand companies showed that three-quarters had surveyed other companies about pay within the last year and 20 percent reported referencing market data for job titles daily or weekly.[3] Many large companies dedicate resources to (a) set wage rates according to competitor benchmarks and regional cost of living and (b) adjust wage bands annually according to complicated formulas. Some rely on HR consultants like Korn Ferry to provide market wages for specific jobs.

But what if you are operating in an industry where mediocrity is the norm—with below-subsistence wages, high disengagement, and high turnover? Would it make sense to benchmark against mediocre companies?

Of course not. Why, then, is this the predominant method? Why does market rate become so sufficient, so unarguable?

If your mental model is that people are just another input to production, it is easy to conclude that paying anything more than the market rate for them is unreasonable, like spending five dollars on something you can get for a buck at the Dollar Store. Even executives who publicly express concerns about inequality and worry that the version of capitalism that allowed them to succeed is not sustainable for our society are hesitant to raise frontline pay above market rates. Over the last two years, the pandemic and then the protests after the brutal killing of George Floyd raised awareness of racial injustices. Many company leaders have spoken out about what they are doing to address those injustices. Almost every large company has an initiative to promote diversity, equity, and inclusion. Yet those companies are still unwilling to pay their lowest-paid employees—who tend to be disproportionately people of color—enough so that they can live with dignity and have the opportunity to succeed.

Paying market wages is faithful to the basic economic principle that the price or value of something is determined by its demand and supply. So, wages should be where demand for labor equals supply of labor. But labor markets don't really work like other commodity markets. Wages are sticky. When demand for labor decreases, for example, we should expect the price to decrease. But wage cuts are a lot rarer than a supply-and-demand model would lead you to expect; wages certainly don't bounce up and down like the price of gas or airline tickets. For that very reason, executives think twice before raising wages during periods of lower

What Do CEOs Think?

Shortly before I was to moderate a panel at a conference, the Business Roundtable had changed its statement of purpose from one that solely pursues profit maximization to one that includes a commitment to invest in workers. This change provoked a lot of press coverage and commentary—both jubilant and indignant. So, at the conference, I asked the panelists whether this new purpose statement would encourage CEOs, especially those operating with a large low-wage workforce, to improve job quality for their workers.

One of the panelists said that CEOs were already doing everything they could for their workers. He mentioned Howard Schultz at Starbucks as an example. It intrigues me how often Starbucks is identified as a company that does well by workers. They do offer health benefits to part-timers (after working at least 240 hours in a three-month period), and that's a big deal. When you talk to their leaders, they seem to care about their employees, whom they call partners.

But they haven't necessarily paid more than others in their sector or in retail, and frontline work schedules have been as unstable at Starbucks as anywhere else. According to surveys conducted by the Shift Project at Harvard's Kennedy School, 63 percent of Starbucks employees made less than $15 an hour in 2021. That percentage was 68 at Dunkin' Donuts and 53 at Walmart.[a]

Instead of making these points, I just suggested that more CEOs could do more. I pointed out how many Americans make too little to live and then pointed out how much more certain companies—those with a good jobs system—pay their workers. "Clearly," I said, "most CEOs are *not* doing everything they can." This produced a palpable chill in the room, and I realized I had better move on to what these CEOs wanted to talk about: the skills gap! The skills-gap argument, of course, is that we can't pay people more until they *become*—sometime in the future—worth more. There's some basis for this argument, but it ignores the fact that wages not only reflect but also affect ability.

After the panel, a friend from a worker organization said to me, "I'm glad you pushed them, but I'm also glad you didn't push more, because we want business leaders to continue coming to these events." But I was frustrated. Why weren't they acknowledging the problem?

As I reflect on that panel and on my many other interactions with executives, I have come to believe that CEOs like the one who said most were doing all they can are not in some self-serving state of denial so much as genuinely unaware. They've never spent much time analyzing and thinking about frontline take-home pay. And because most C-level executives have not been exposed to a world in which take-home pay (versus a "salary") means counting every penny, they really do have no idea how much it matters. My MBA students aren't too different. In class, when we discuss the research that shows how much a small increase in pay can improve worker behavior and health—the documented effects include fewer unmet medical needs, better nutrition, less smoking, less child neglect, fewer low-birthweight babies, and fewer teen births—at some point someone almost always starts a sentence with "I had no idea that . . ." The sentence may end with: "the conditions of low-wage workers could be that bad" or "a small change in income can have such a big effect on someone's life" or "low wages hurt children this much" or "how important pay can be for someone's dignity and sense of worth."[b]

a. Company wage tracker by Shift Project and Economic Policy Institute can be found at https://www.epi.org/company-wage-tracker/ (accessed December 2022).

b. Kelly P. McCarrier, Frederick J. Zimmerman, James D. Ralston, and Diane P. Martin, "Associations between Minimum Wage Policy and Access to Health Care: Evidence from the Behavioral Risk Factor Surveillance System, 1996–2007," *American Journal of Public Health*, February 2011; J. Paul Leigh, Wesley A. Leigh, and Juan Du, "Minimum Wages and Public Health: A Literature Review," *Preventive Medicine* 118 (January 2019): 122–134; "Raising the Minimum Wage Would Reduce Child Neglect Cases," News at IU, Indiana University, August 16, 2017, https://news.iu.edu/live/news/24033-raising-the-minimum-wage-would-reduce-child; Kelli A. Komro, Melvin D. Livingston, Sara Markowitz, and Alexander C. Wagenaar, "The Effect of an Increased Minimum Wage on Infant Mortality and Birth Weight," *American Journal of Public Health*, August 2016; Lindsey Rose Bullinger, "The Effect of Minimum Wages on Adolescent Fertility: A Nationwide Analysis," *American Journal of Public Health*, March 2017.

supply; they don't want to be stuck with those higher wages when the supply goes back up. As I write this book, after two years of Covid-19, not enough people are willing to work at restaurants, cafés, and grocery stores for the wages and working conditions offered to them. Yet, wages are rising a lot more slowly than you'd expect from the market. Some believe raising wages will result in losing market share to competitors that don't raise wages.

Labor is also different from other inputs of production. Each unit of labor is not the same. Some people are more productive than others. Some work harder than others. That's why economists argue that paying above market—that is, paying efficiency wages—can indeed be good for companies. But the causation can go both ways; wages aren't just a *reflection* of worker quality; they are also a *determinant*. Low pay affects the quality of labor by harming health, cognitive functioning, and ability on the job—even for the simplest jobs.

In business schools, when we teach about pay and when we conduct research on pay, we typically focus on how the amount and composition of pay (for example, what percentage of pay should be fixed versus variable, how to design performance-based pay, and what benefits to offer) make it easier or harder to attract, motivate, and retain the right people. We do not focus on the effect of low pay on the people receiving it: how it affects their health and the quality of their work and thus their productivity. In effect, we're busy studying the benefits of a healthy diet and not too interested in the effects of malnutrition.

The Problem of Low Pay

Low pay is a two-pronged problem: One, low hourly wages. Two, insufficient and inconsistent hours.

Support for a $15 minimum wage has grown over the years. A 2019 Pew Research Center survey found that two-thirds of Americans are in favor of increasing the federal minimum wage to $15 an hour.[4] A growing list of employers have announced their commitment to a $15-an-hour wage floor.[5] You may think that $15 an hour is a decent wage—or at least livable—but let's see if that's true. If you live in Cleveland, Ohio, a representative US city in terms of cost of living, and if you are part of a household with one child and with both parents working, $15 an hour is below the *living wage* of $17.60, according to MIT's living wage calculator (as of June 2022).[6] If you are a single parent with one child, then $15 an hour is way below the living wage of $29.66. (This is a big chunk of the population. In 2019, almost a quarter of the children in the United States lived with a single parent.[7])

If you are a single parent living in Cleveland and working a steady forty hours a week, you would make $2,580 a month—$1,589 less than your likely rent, childcare, transportation, food, medical expenses, and personal care. That's not even counting taxes, cable/phone bills, going to a movie once in a while, and unexpected expenses such as a broken cell phone—and certainly not any savings. (And the MIT living wage calculator has a built-in assumption of $420 per month for food, which is basically a diet of rice and beans or ramen noodles. So actually your child is more likely to be sick due to a poor diet, which brings on *more* medical expenses that you *don't* have the money for.)

In short, a full-time worker cannot make ends meet with $15 an hour. Even a working married couple with one child can't do it. That's why so many Americans have more than one job. That's why millions of *working* Americans must rely on government assistance. In 2019, 25 million working people and families received $61 billion in earned-income tax credits (EITC). Other social safety net programs, such as the Supplemental Nutrition Assistance Program (SNAP), Supplemental Security Income (SSI), Medicaid, and the Children's Health Insurance Program (CHIP), also cost taxpayers over $40 billion a year.[8]

It gets worse. In the calculations above, we assumed a forty-hour work week, but many workers don't get that, even when they are full-time. This is part of the reason why the Brookings Institution found that 53 million Americans—44 percent of all workers aged eighteen to sixty-five—worked in jobs with median annual earnings of just $17,950. "There are so many of us, but each with few hours," is a common complaint I hear from workers.

At a restaurant chain we examined, nearly 98 percent of the kitchen staff and almost the entire front-of-the-house staff worked fewer than thirty hours a week. Forty-eight percent of the kitchen staff and 78 percent of the front-of-the-house staff worked fewer than twenty hours a week. The most extreme case of inadequate hours I've seen is a specialty retailer with over one thousand stores; the median hours per week there was thirteen. A typical worker there made $8,320 a year. In a chain with more than fifty thousand employees, barely any were making a living there. With so few hours, it's no shock that people didn't care about their jobs. Is it any surprise, then, that average annual employee turnover there was 120 percent? With such high turnover, managers can't even know their workers, never mind develop them.

Additionally, the variability in hours—different numbers of hours from week to week—makes an already-low income also unpredictable. Jonathan Morduch and Rachel Schneider found a 30 percent rise in US year-to-year income volatility from 1971 to 2008.[9] This is especially the case in retail and fast food. In 2014, the *New York Times* published a story about a Starbucks employee—Ms. Navarro, a single parent—who made $9 an hour. She rarely learned about her schedule more than three days in advance, and her hours and income changed all the time. She described how she worked until 11 p.m. and then had to start another shift at 4 a.m. Many readers, at the time, were surprised that even Starbucks, with its reputation for progressive political stands, offered such low wages and unstable schedules.

I've met hundreds of Ms. Navarros at different companies. "You don't know from week to week how many hours you're going to have," one worker told me, "but your bills are still the same amount. . . . You can't even make enough money to pay your internet fee." Using data from 27,792 hourly workers at large US food service and retail companies, Daniel Schneider and his colleagues found that two-thirds received their work schedules with less than two weeks' notice and about one-third received them with less than one week's notice.[10] In the month before they were surveyed, these workers had experienced 32 percent variation, on average, between the hours worked in the week with the most hours and that with the fewest. Twenty-six percent reported being on call and 14 percent reported having had their shift canceled at the last minute.

This is frustrating and unhealthy for the worker. You can't schedule— or keep—doctors' appointments. You can't get to the grocery store in a regular way. You can't go to school and be sure you'll make it to all your classes. You can't get your homework done between shifts that end at 11 p.m. and start at 4 a.m. Arranging childcare becomes a nightmare. You can't even sleep properly. "My life is always in a turmoil because you can't sleep," one retail worker told me. "You can't just go to sleep on cue."

Having multiple jobs makes life stressful. A department manager at a senior living organization told us that their caregivers, who were paid close to minimum wage, often worked 7 a.m. to 3 p.m. there and then until 11 p.m. somewhere else. Most of them were women who were also taking care of their own families. Not surprisingly, six out of ten caregivers left every year.

Life for low-paid workers is tumultuous for other reasons, too. There's no margin for error: a sick child, a broken cell phone, a flat tire. A 2021 survey found that 32 percent of Americans couldn't absorb an unexpected $400 expense.[11] And while social safety net programs exist, you have to apply to each program separately, each application involving a pile of tedious paperwork that takes time that's hard to find.

Working multiple jobs and not being able to meet obligations increases stress, which undermines mental and physical health. Low pay is associated with heart disease, stroke, diabetes, opioid use, and even suicide. Inconsistent and unpredictable schedules are associated with psychological distress, poor sleep quality, and unhappiness.[12] One of my students, a medical doctor, told me he came to business school because he concluded that he can make more of a difference for people's health by improving their paychecks.

Low pay and financial stress directly affect workers' children and that naturally affects the workers themselves. One study found that students from low-income families entered high school with average literacy skills five years behind those of high-income students.[13] Standardized tests administered by the US Department of Education found that students classified as low-income trailed their higher-income peers by two to three grade levels in reading and math across all age categories.[14] In 2016, high school dropout rates for students whose families were in the lowest quartile of income were 3.7 times as high as those whose families were in the highest quartile.[15] Children who grew up in families below the poverty line during early childhood (up to their fifth birthday) had income as adults that was less than half that of children whose families had incomes over twice the poverty line and were more than twice as likely to report poor overall health.[16]

Low Pay Hurts Performance on the Job

When workers don't make enough money or have inconsistent hours, they are constantly juggling expenses and making trade-offs. What to pay late, what critical expenses to cut, how to manage childcare. All the stress associated with poverty lowers cognitive functioning. According to a study published in *Science*, "Preoccupations with pressing budgetary concerns leave fewer cognitive resources available to guide choice and action. Just as an air traffic controller focusing on a potential collision course is prone to neglect other planes in the air, the poor, when attending to monetary concerns, lose their capacity to give other problems their full consideration," creating a "bandwidth tax" equal to a loss of thirteen IQ points.[17] Employees with financial insecurity find it difficult to be fully present at work and focus on the job.

Naturally, this kind of financial stress undermines the performance of individual workers, their teams, and their company. A study of certified nursing aides (CNAs) found that those with greater financial insecurity were less likely to notice threats to the safety of their patients—even though it was obvious that they cared very much about them. A study of truck drivers showed that those with financial insecurity had higher accident rates. A field experiment with workers in India randomized the timing of when workers were paid and found that on days when workers had more cash on hand, they were more productive and made fewer errors.[18]

Using data from the large retailer mentioned earlier, where the median hours worked per week was thirteen, my colleagues Mahdi Hashemian, Hazhir Rahmandad, and I found that the combination of too few hours and low take-home pay is associated with lower worker productivity. Having a typical employee work twenty-four hours a week instead of thirteen—and without changing overall staffing levels—could increase the company's productivity by 10 to 29 percent.[19]

When workers' lives are in turmoil, their attendance is less reliable—a frequent cause of involuntary turnover (that is, getting fired). At PayPal, reasons for absenteeism included not being able to afford the gas to go to work or not having bus money that day. In my work with companies, I've met a lot of *full-timers* who worked multiple jobs, creating even more unpredictable schedules and, of course, attendance problems.

Pay doesn't just *reflect* workers' ability and value, although that's the theory. As all this evidence and more shows, it *affects* their ability and value.

The Vicious Cycle

What we see here is a vicious cycle for workers (see figure 2-1). Workers who make mistakes, can't focus on the job, or have attendance problems likely won't be promoted and will continue getting low wages. (Not to mention that low-wage employers typically provide little or nothing in the way of a clear path to advancement; that's another investment in people they don't see any good reason to make.)

Indeed, this vicious cycle shows up in aggregate data. One study that measured the ability to increase one's income (as measured by earnings deciles) during two periods—1981 to 1996 and 1993 to 2008—found that workers with low incomes in their first jobs were likely to make low incomes decades later, while those who began with higher incomes tended to maintain them.[20] By 2018, households in the top 20 percent of earners

FIGURE 2-1

Workers' vicious cycle

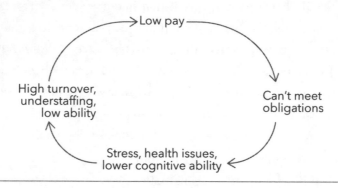

made 52 percent of all US income, up from 43 percent in 1968.[21] According to one study, in 2018, the average annual income of Americans in the top 1 percent was 39 times more than that of the bottom 90 percent, while the average annual income of Americans in the top 0.1 percent was 196 times more than that of the bottom 90 percent.[22]

Low Pay Means High Turnover

In company after company after company, we at the Good Jobs Institute have seen that low pay is a top driver of turnover. Without sufficient pay, other perks and benefits did little to reduce turnover or attendance problems. A McKinsey study in 2022 found inadequate pay to be the number two reason why employees quit their jobs (after career development and advancement), across all jobs.[23] In particular, low pay has been a big reason that K–12 teachers quit their jobs—even before the pandemic.[24]

Yet, a lot of low-wage employers we've worked with did not look at actual pay data when assessing whether they were offering good jobs or why they had turnover problems. Many companies assessed job quality based on engagement surveys. It's always surprising to hear "We just got our engagement scores and they look great" at companies where employee turnover is way north of 50 percent. "Ninety percent of our employees are proud to work here. We must be doing something right." Yes, your employees may tell you in a survey that they are proud to work at your company. They may even say they think pay is fair. But when you have high turnover, your sample will be skewed to represent new employees who have not had much experience on the job yet. And if many of them are leaving shortly after they start working for you or you have attendance problems or you can't hold on to frontline managers, you are not offering good jobs, no matter what the survey says.

Because a lot of executives are out of touch with how hard it is to live paycheck to paycheck, many think that employee appreciation or cool but insufficient benefits or a rousing company purpose can make employees stay. "I just don't understand," the CEO of a health-care company told our Good Jobs Institute team before the pandemic. "I care so much about our employees and we do so much to show our appreciation, but they still keep leaving." He was proud that his company celebrated major employment milestones for all workers and offered certain discount programs. Yet many of the caregivers had to work two jobs to make ends meet and every day they faced problems on the job, including understaffing, that got in the way of their professional care—and heartfelt concern—for their patients. Some executives suggested offering discounts on ski lift tickets as a perk, not realizing that a frontline worker making minimum wage can't possibly afford to go skiing even with a free ticket.

In some companies, leaders thought that encouraging employees to be themselves—to display tattoos, wear whatever they want—was the way to offer good jobs and retain employees. The ability to express individuality may indeed be important to employees. But it won't pay the bills.

None of this is surprising. In Maslow's hierarchy of needs, pay would be at the bottom level—representing physiological needs—followed by the other four levels: safety, belonging and love, esteem, and self-actualization. Frederick Herzberg, whose two-factor theory is one of the most influential theories of motivation, identifies pay as a "hygiene factor"; that is, its absence causes dissatisfaction, but its presence does not guarantee job satisfaction. Figure 2-2 illustrates employee needs.

FIGURE 2-2

Employee needs

Higher needs

Meaningfulness Work itself and significance to customer	**Personal growth** Learning, creativity, problem-solving	
Belonging Team, pride for working at the company, mutual respect	**Achievement** Have autonomy, tools, time, and resources to do great work	**Recognition** High expectations, feedback from others and job

Basic needs

Pay and benefits Fair for the work and compared to others, meets needs	**Schedules** Consistent and predictable schedules, adequate hours	**Career path** Clear and fair advancement to higher pay	**Security and safety** Keep job if perform well, safe conditions

Low pay also undermines motivation and engagement. As organizational psychologists have shown us, what really engages and motivates employees is a sense of belonging, achievement, recognition, meaningfulness, and personal growth. When companies pay little and operate with high turnover, they end up making many interrelated decisions that hurt their ability to meet those needs. Management, seeing itself as saddled with a low-ability, easy-come-easy-go workforce, uses more and more top-down control to make up for employees' individual skill, judgment, and dedication. That, of course, doesn't develop belonging and achievement—it erodes them. Managers who are constantly fighting fires have no time or resources to provide feedback. That doesn't develop career opportunities. As a worker, when you constantly worry about making ends meet, can't focus on your job, fail in front of the customer every day, or feel that your time or abilities are not respected, it is hard to find meaning in your work—regardless of what the company's purpose is or the social good it may actually do. I once met with leaders of a company that spent a lot of time and consulting resources to develop their mission. They wanted to feed the human spirit. During one of our calls when they kept talking about this mission, I asked how much their frontline employees were making. It was about $9 an hour.

Are People Worth Higher Wages and Good Jobs?

If you are thinking, "But some people may not be worth $15 an hour" or "Some jobs may not create enough value to justify higher wages," you are not alone. I've heard these counterarguments from many corporate leaders and MBA students. The first reflects how deeply ingrained the idea is that a worker's work depends solely on his or her inherent ability and motivation, which is deemed to be relatively fixed for each person.

But as we've seen in this chapter, a worker's worth is not fixed. Ability itself is affected by low pay. It can be reduced or increased by external conditions (as well as by the worker's own decisions and actions). If you operate in a setting with low pay, you may develop a distorted view of people. You see employees not showing up, not focusing on the job, falling asleep because they just came from another full shift, making mistakes, or behaving poorly—and you conclude that they are lazy or that they can't do any better. Organizational psychologists call this *fundamental attribution error*: the tendency to overemphasize personality-based explanations for another person's behavior and to underemphasize situational explanations.

As for the second objection, if you assume that some jobs are "unskilled" by definition, it's easier to devalue that work and justify low pay. But this category is rather overpopulated. Since 1917, when the census began categorizing work into skill levels, "unskilled" jobs have been the most populous category—from farm and factory workers in the twentieth century to retail and restaurant workers and health aides in the twenty-first century.[25] People of color, immigrants, and women have historically been disproportionately represented in these jobs. Calling these jobs and the workers who hold them "unskilled" also makes it easy to find fault in the workers rather than in their jobs. That's why so many leaders are eager to talk about upskilling workers rather than about improving jobs.

Some people are more productive than others. But you can give the same worker the same job in two different settings and his or her output would be different—possibly *very* different—depending on how the work is designed. (See the NUMMI story below.) The important question is not whether a particular worker is worth $15 an hour or whether a particular job is worth $15 an hour, but rather whether that person's work—the job—has been *designed to contribute* $15 an hour.

And that, fundamentally, is what companies with a good jobs system have done: design their frontline jobs to be worth relatively high pay through smart operational choices, then find workers who can do those well-designed jobs well and keep them for a long time (not necessarily in the same job) so that they get even better and their value to the company grows.

We will see different examples of the same workers creating more value when their companies started adopting the good jobs system—in call centers and retail stores. My favorite historical example comes from a General Motors plant in Fremont, California, which was known to have the "worst workforce" in the auto industry. The reputation seemed well deserved—high absenteeism, drinking on the job, low productivity, poor quality, and strikes. In 1982, that plant closed. But at that time, Toyota was interested in coming to the United States and GM was interested in learning how to make small cars. So, in 1984, the two companies created a joint venture, New United Motors Manufacturing Incorporated (NUMMI), that would produce a small car in that plant of evil reputation. Within two years of Toyota's taking over operations, absenteeism dropped from above 20 percent to below 4 percent. Labor productivity improved; total labor hours per unit produced went from forty-three to twenty-one. Product quality improved significantly. All this was done with 85 percent of the same hourly workforce and with the same union that had performed so poorly before.

A team leader at NUMMI, Rick Madrid, described the difference: "When I was with GM, I hated management and everything about the plant. Work was just an eight-hour interruption in my day. I couldn't have cared less if somebody had driven a forklift right through a wall just to break the monotony. And sometimes we did. . . . At NUMMI, I am constantly learning new things. Right now, I'm part of the 1989 Nova model project team. All the homework and extra work is rough, but it's exciting to be constantly tackling new problems. At GM, they left me in the truck-tire-mounting department for eight years of mind-numbing repetition. It was degrading!"

Not every GM employee rose to the higher expectations at NUMMI, but over 95 percent did (more than eighty employees out of about twenty-two hundred were let go during the first two years because of absenteeism problems). Bill Borton, Stamping Department Manager, said, "Our assumption at NUMMI is that people come to work to do a fair day's work. There are exceptions and you would be foolish to ignore them. But 90 percent of people, if you give them a chance to work smarter and improve their jobs, and if they find that by doing that they have created free time for themselves, will spontaneously look for new things to do. I've got hundreds of examples of that."[26]

If you design a system around the minority who are not able and motivated enough to do a good job, then you get 100 percent of your people behaving and performing that way. And a big part of any design like that is low pay—even if it is market rate.

Turnover Is Ruinous

In October 2016, I got an invitation from Quest Diagnostics, a leading company in the clinical laboratory industry. The note said that my book had been read by hundreds of leaders and managers there. I was curious, because *The Good Jobs Strategy* had focused on retail. A diagnostics company found it useful? A few weeks later, I learned that Quest was integrating the good jobs strategy in their call centers to get them out of the vicious cycle in which they were operating.

Here's how the vicious cycle had unfolded there. In 2013, the company had consolidated its twenty regional call centers into two in Lenexa, Kansas, and Tampa, Florida, low cost-of-living places where the call center industry was already established. The consolidation was supposed to cut costs.

But by 2015, the two call centers were way over budget and delivering poor customer service. They suffered from high turnover, poor attendance, and understaffing. Three of every five reps—the customer service representatives—left in their first year. Overall turnover was 34 percent, costing Quest up to $10.5 million a year in hiring, training, and lost productivity. Unplanned absenteeism was 12.4 percent. The cost of poor service, though it hadn't been measured, was significant.

Not surprisingly, the call centers frequently had too few people to handle the call volume, which was bad for callers, reps, and management.

Capacity management is foundational to operations management. If you can't manage capacity well, many things fall apart. Callers suffered frustration and possibly genuine worry if they couldn't get test results. Reps endured overwork, frustration at being rushed and having to rush the callers, and the embarrassment of—and possibly punishment for—making mistakes from being in a rush. Management in turn expressed frustration at continued customer complaints and, eventually, loss of business.

By now, you won't be surprised to know that one of the top reasons for all this turnover and absenteeism was low pay. Starting pay, at $13 an hour in 2015, was slightly above market rate, but the market consisted of other companies that also operated with high turnover (undoubtedly for the same reason). Furthermore, the job at Quest was harder than similar jobs at other call centers. Beyond the natural complexity of a typical call center—answering over 100 calls per shift, multitasking with different screens and systems to find and communicate information—Quest reps had to have a basic understanding of the testing procedures—there were over three thousand—and medical terminology. There was also an emotional component: some callers had serious health issues and needed to be treated with empathy.

Beyond low pay and a taxing job, the reps did not see a clear career path and had little sense of belonging. Before consolidation, the call centers had been colocated with labs, and reps had felt like part of the lab's work culture. Some had worked in the lab, so they already had the technical background. Turnover then was in the low teens and, over the years, many reps built relationships with their clients—physicians' offices and hospitals. With the consolidation, those relationships were mostly lost.

Supervisors were also unhappy. They spent most of their day on the phone, handling calls that reps had forwarded to them because the reps themselves could not answer the client's question or couldn't even understand it. One supervisor said, "We were caught in a negative feedback loop. We were so focused on productivity and getting the next call answered instead of thinking about how I can better assist this caller so it decreases the amount of [future] calls. There wasn't time to think about if there was a better way."[1] Another said, "There would be many days when I wouldn't sit down. I would literally go from desk to desk because I had sixteen brand-new people."

Quest's low investment in its reps fueled the vicious cycle. High turnover and understaffing often meant either that a call wasn't answered on time or that the customer's question couldn't be answered and had to be transferred to a supervisor. Only half of calls were being answered within two minutes. Twelve percent had to be transferred to a supervisor. All of these issues made the whole operation more expensive and less effective. Poor service led to lost accounts. Jim Davis, executive vice president of General Diagnostics, told me, "When patients have a bad experience, they complain to their doctors and then the doctors, if they hear five patients who had a bad experience at Quest, they're going to flip their labs to the other guy." Davis kept getting emails and calls from Quest's commercial team saying, "Hey, your call center screwed up this relationship and I just lost a million dollars of business." All this made it harder to invest in reps and when reps could not do their jobs well, they became unhappy. Some quit. Sometimes they just didn't show up.

Another Vicious Cycle

I could now see why Quest leaders were interested in the good jobs system. They recognized the retailers' vicious cycle described in my book as their own. And they wanted out.

In 1998, when I began my research on retail supply chains, my colleagues and I found that retail stores were full of operational problems such as misplaced products, inaccurate inventory data, and obsolete products still occupying the shelves. One specialty retailer I studied had an 18 percent stockout rate and a 1.6 percent shrink rate. As for inventory accuracy, for 30 percent of the SKUs, there were reported sales while at the same time the inventory system said they were out of that item. (Talk about ghosts in the system! I wish we had the data to show how many nonexistent items were returned.)

But that mess wasn't even exceptional. Poor operational execution was common and expensive. At two retailers, we estimated that lost sales from misplaced products and data inaccuracy amounted to more than 10 percent of profits.[2] But that's just lost sales *now*. These problems hurt future sales and profits by undermining supply chain performance. If you make supply chain decisions based on inaccurate data (e.g., you think an item is not selling because there is no demand, but in fact it's not selling because it's still in the back room), those decisions will be bad. In addition to lost sales, these problems undermined customer service and labor productivity. Employees wasted their time and customers' time trying to find items that were shown as in-stock. At retailers that were trying to integrate their online channel with the brick-and-mortar channel, online customers might be told that a product was at a store, then go to the store and find that it wasn't. Of course, all this confusion hurt customer satisfaction, sales, and profits.

Poor operational execution manifested in many other ways, such as pricing errors, long checkout lines, and messy shelves, and was pervasive—much more so than top management usually realized—in large part due to low investment in people. Stores that had more employee turnover and too few people on deck to get all the work done had more operational problems. Those problems then reduced sales and profits—for example, when a sale was lost because the store had what the customer wanted but no one could find it. Finding sales and profits down, the typical response was to cut the labor budget, causing more underinvestment in people. More underinvestment meant more operational problems—another vicious cycle.

Figure 2-1 showed the vicious cycle from the workers' perspective; figure 3-1 shows that cycle from the operations perspective.

But why did retailers invest so little in their people? Because retail is a low-margin business, many retailers do everything they can to reduce their costs. When you see people as just another cost, you try to pay as little as possible for them (which, as we saw in chapter 2, ends up being market rate) and try to staff your units with as few of them as possible.

When there is financial pressure, reducing headcount and/or cutting hours tends to be a first resort rather than a last because it's relatively

FIGURE 3-1

Operational vicious cycle for companies

easy. One company that fell into this trap is Home Depot. When Bob Nardelli became CEO in December 2000, having come from GE, Home Depot was known for its outstanding customer service and entrepreneurial culture. During his six-year tenure, Nardelli created a culture of cost cutting and "making the numbers." One way to cut costs was to reduce the percentage of full-timers. Another way was to reduce staffing; the average number of employees per store dropped from 200 in 2000 to 170 in 2006. The savings were immediate. Home Depot's profitability improved. The losses come later. Referring to the costs of lower people investment, Arthur Blank, the cofounder of Home Depot, said, "It reduced sales, so they reduced labor some more, then it reduced sales. . . . Before you know it, you're doing a fraction of the business you were doing before."[3] But Nardelli managed to increase overall sales anyway—by buying other businesses and expanding internationally. When he left, Home Depot's customer service scores were among the worst in retail on the American Customer Satisfaction Index. Home Depot's same-store sales growth had dropped to negative 2.6 percent in 2006 and it performed significantly below its largest competitor, Lowe's, throughout Nardelli's tenure.[4]

At several retail chains, I've seen store managers cutting labor hours during the week just to meet their short-term targets for payroll as a percentage of sales. They knew cutting hours would ultimately hurt their performance. But those short-term targets mattered. Many retailers used automation solely to cut labor—even when that same automation might impair customer service. My colleague Daron Acemoglu calls this type of automation "so-so" because it doesn't improve productivity or service.

An executive at a large retailer told us: "Every time we make an innovation, we remove labor. I know we have to because of margin pressure. But in our case, our innovation is directly tied to taking hours out." Another said, "When we set our budget for 2020, we literally had to find [so many million] dollars."

New technologies to cut labor costs do not always produce the intended savings and sometimes lead to further understaffing, as the replaced worker could do more different things than the technology can. One frustrated frontline manager said, "I think [headquarters] thinks the self-checkout kiosks can stock shelves, which I'm still waiting for them to do." One reason technologies don't work is that companies often are unable to involve the frontline employees in developing, adopting, and scaling them. (We'll see why in chapter 4. In chapter 9, we'll see how investment in people enabled Sam's Club to effectively develop, adopt, and scale new technologies.)

It's not just retail. A call center at a financial services company implemented a virtual assistant to save labor costs. While on a call, the virtual assistant would encourage customers to ask questions on a screen and then answer them. The company calculated how much time the virtual assistant would save and reduced staffing accordingly—*before* rolling the program out. But once in action, the virtual assistants' answers often weren't quite right, which meant the reps had to spend more time explaining the answers the bot gave. Ultimately, the company ditched the virtual assistant.

My colleagues at the Good Jobs Institute and I have seen this vicious cycle up close in dozens of companies. Consistent with my earlier research, units of restaurants, call centers, and health-care organizations that had understaffing and high turnover also had worse operational execution, which then reduced sales and profits, which then caused more understaffing and turnover. And we've seen how this vicious cycle *interlocks* with the workers' vicious cycle from the previous chapter:

FIGURE 3-2

Interlocking vicious cycles

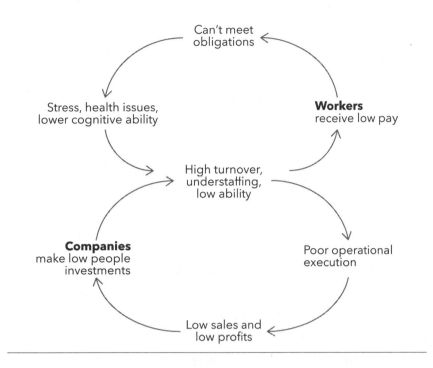

From our work with companies, I've also learned that, in one respect, I was wrong about the operational vicious cycle when I first wrote about it. It's *more expensive* than I calculated back then—both because of the direct costs of turnover and because of the system such turnover inevitably creates.

Direct Costs of Turnover

In addition to the costs of poor operational execution, the direct costs of turnover—hiring, onboarding, training, and time to full productivity—can be high.

At Aetna, the direct annual cost of voluntary employee turnover was $27 million—more than twice what it would cost the company to raise its minimum wage from $12 to $16 an hour. One call center of a financial services company had nearly 40 percent turnover for its phone reps, meaning that a caller was almost as likely as not to be dealing with an inexperienced rep. How could the supervisors and the more experienced peers have time to help the novices, who nearly outnumbered them? As at Quest, the technical knowledge required to staff this call center meant a long training period. The company estimated the direct costs of turnover to be around 45 percent of total payroll costs. Imagine a ship whose crew spends 45 percent of its time just bailing water. It is exhausting for the crew, and they have no time to look up to see danger on the horizon. Even the captain is belowdecks and not thinking about how to get safely to the shore. But a ship has the luxury of being repaired in dry dock; a company has to repair itself on the high seas. (Yet it can be done, or I wouldn't be writing this book.)

At a chain of senior living facilities, average caregiver turnover was nearly 60 percent. Frontline manager turnover was over 35 percent. Caregiver turnover alone cost the company about 10 percent of total payroll. At a restaurant chain with more than 120 percent turnover for hourly workers and nearly 40 percent for managers, the total direct cost of turnover was 25 percent of payroll. In retail—including grocery, specialty, and convenience stores—the Good Jobs Institute has observed 60 percent to 120 percent turnover for hourly workers, which costs those companies millions of dollars. At one convenience store chain, direct costs of turnover were about 2 percent of total sales and more than 20 percent of total labor costs.

And it isn't just the service sector. The technician turnover at Nissan's Smyrna assembly plant between 2019 and 2020 was as high as 38 percent in some departments. The direct cost of turnover alone was $15,000 each time an assembly line operator left.[5]

These are significant costs, yet most companies we worked with had not even calculated or paid much attention to them. Neither did their investors. When we showed one private equity investor the direct costs of turnover and its association with low productivity, low customer satisfaction, low sales, and high material costs, he told us, "We've never looked at turnover before."

Some don't even think of turnover as a bad thing. One executive at a large public company told me they are "numb" to high turnover numbers. Other executives and some of my colleagues have asked me, "Can't high turnover be good for companies?" This may seem like a reasonable question. If a thriving company like Amazon reportedly operates with roughly 150-percent turnover in its fulfillment centers, how bad a problem can high turnover be?[6] Some argue that not depending on a capable and motivated workforce in the fulfillment centers is what enabled Amazon to grow so quickly.

It's an old industrial line of thinking, the kind Henry Ford must have used in 1913 at his plant in Highland Park, Michigan. "Why is it," he famously asked, "that I have to hire the whole person, when all I need is a pair of hands?" Forced, as he saw it, to manage all these unwanted aspects of a human being, he made the tasks at his plant so simple that he could hire "anyone" to do them and didn't have to spend much on onboarding or training. A line worker's task would be to put two nuts onto two bolts or to attach one wheel to a car—just that, over and over. He would never be involved in ordering parts, procuring tools, repairing equipment, or inspecting for quality. He wouldn't necessarily have any idea what the worker next to him was doing.[7] More than fifty languages were spoken at Highland Park and most workers could not speak English, so there was little or no communication with supervisors or even with coworkers. Amazon, the modern-day equivalent of Highland Park, operates in a similar way. We will see the full costs of this mistaken strategy in chapter 4.

Toyota taught the world that making your workers' ability and motivation irrelevant to the success of your system is not the best way to make cars; investing in assembly line operators and empowering them to identify problems and engage in solving them drives continuous improvement in quality and costs. Ford, General Motors, and Chrysler could not survive against Toyota without making significant changes, including significant changes to their work design and people practices.

Indirect Costs of Turnover Are Even Higher Than Direct Costs

Recall from the last chapter that Mark Bertolini at Aetna challenged his HR team to prove that raising starting wages from $12 to $16 to reduce the turnover that drove a vicious cycle would not work. He asked them to list all the benefits that could come from higher pay (though pay was not the only change Bertolini implemented). When they presented the $27 million per year of direct voluntary turnover costs, Bertolini asked them to calculate all the indirect costs—absenteeism, rework, overtime, mistakes, and customer service (measured at Aetna as Net Promoter Score, a measure of customer loyalty).[8] With the indirect costs, total turnover cost $120 million per year. With all the costs in front of them, Bertolini and his team considered how much improvement was realistic if people were paid enough to be able to focus on their jobs, and they estimated the possible savings from those improvements. Bertolini himself did not believe that spreadsheets would give them the truth, but running the exercise was helpful. He told me, "The spreadsheet gives us a ladder of risks that we, as a team, have to stand back and say, 'As a team, do we believe we can confront these risks and manage them effectively to make this work?'" When compared to the $120 million total costs, the $10.5 million wage investment by upping base pay to $16 per hour didn't seem risky at all.

How Much Does Low People Investment Cost Your Company?

Although spreadsheets may not reveal everything, it's helpful to quantify financial costs of low people investment. When corporate leaders are presented the costs of direct employee turnover and poor operational execution, a common response is that "intuitively, I knew low people investment was expensive; I just didn't know how expensive." We've already covered the direct turnover costs above. When we work with companies, we encourage them to quantify the costs of poor operational execution in

FIGURE 3-3

The costs of low people investment

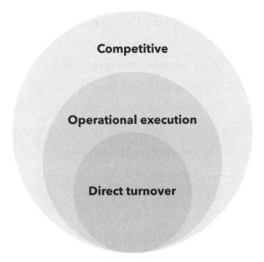

three ways: lost sales, higher costs, and lower productivity. As we will see in chapter 4, the competitive costs of low people investment are even higher than the poor operational execution costs. (See figure 3-3.)

Lost sales

In many settings, the biggest cost of low investment in people is lost sales from operational problems and poor customer satisfaction. In retail, research shows that reducing the occurrence of misplaced products by one standard deviation across the company could increase sales by 1.2 percent—and in retail, that's a big sales increase.[9] Not surprisingly, retailers with the good jobs system have much higher sales per square foot and higher same-store sales growth than their bad jobs competitors.[10] In fast-food restaurants, the biggest benefit from better execution often comes from serving customers more quickly, which means handling more customers during busy lunch or dinner periods. And in all services, there are missed sales when employees do not have enough expertise to help the customer or to offer substitutes when an item is not in stock. During Covid-19, we all experienced the most categorical of all causes of lost sales: *Closed* signs. How many times did each of us walk up to a store or restaurant that should have been open—that would have been open at that time on that day a year or two earlier—only to discover that it was closed because it simply didn't have enough people to operate? From mom-and-pops to national chains, Covid-19 taught American businesses a new and painful lesson: when labor markets get tight, low turnover can be the difference between staying in business and failing.

Higher costs

High turnover and sporadic attendance lead to more overtime, which can be expensive. And then there's the cost of mistakes or execution problems from turnover, low ability, and understaffing. In 2009, a typical convenience store spent 1.6 percent of sales on shrink—damaged or stolen merchandise. But at QuikTrip, a company that has a good jobs system, that figure was only 0.6 percent. A study of the convenience store industry found that the store's relative wages—after controlling for employee characteristics, the store's socioeconomic environment, and other factors—were negatively associated with employee theft.[11] Lower wages meant more theft. In nursing homes, falls and injuries—especially in memory care—can be the provider's largest cost outside real estate, labor, and food. As you would expect and as repeated studies have found, such mistakes are more frequent the more inexperienced and/or overworked the staff.[12] At restaurants, wrong orders can amount to a significant loss; one restaurant chain we analyzed spent about 1 percent of sales correcting wrong orders.

Lower productivity

High turnover and low ability mean productivity losses. If you've ever been in a store looking for something and an employee told you it was in stock but then you both wasted ten minutes searching for it but never found it, you know what I'm talking about. Or perhaps you've wasted time with a call center rep who wasn't able to answer your question or solve your problem. Those are just the productivity losses that are visible to customers. There are more behind the scenes. Companies that operate with high turnover tend to rely largely on computerized training. You might spend ten hours and go through all the modules without paying any attention and be paid for learning almost nothing. One of my students spent a few weeks working part-time at a large retailer that was about to open a new store in New York. She carefully tracked 4,965 minutes (82.75 hours) on the job, of which 725 minutes—15 percent of her time—was idle because she finished her tasks earlier than planned or because the manager who would assign a new task was nowhere to be found. Eight percent of her time was wasted on useless tasks—for example, when the manager purposefully knocked over towels for her and her colleagues to refold or when she had to redo work that had been done poorly or incorrectly. Anita Tucker shadowed 26 nurses in 9 hospitals for a total of 239 hours of observation. She found that nurses were interrupted once every hour due to operational problems or errors. Dealing with these issues took valuable time away from patient care—an average of thirty-three minutes per nurse per 7.5-hour shift.[13]

You *Can* Escape the Vicious Cycle

The good news is that it is possible for companies to transition from a vicious cycle of low employee investment, high turnover, and low individual and corporate performance to a virtuous cycle of high employee investment, low turnover, and high performance. Quest's call centers did it. Aetna did it. Mercadona did it. We will see more examples in chapters 7 through 10.

The bad news is that you can't get there just by raising pay. As we saw before, pay is a hygiene factor—necessary for good jobs but not sufficient. Its absence causes dissatisfaction, but its presence doesn't guarantee engagement and motivation. When Henry Ford raised pay to $5 a day in

1914, turnover reportedly dropped significantly. Higher pay was a big deal for workers and their ability to support their families. But higher pay alone didn't do much for motivation or ability to contribute more. The jobs were still mind-numbing. How productive can you be—how much value can you create—if all you do is turn screws?

Remember that a virtuous cycle of low turnover and high performance requires not this or that policy, but a *system* that prioritizes customers and is *designed* to maximize employee productivity, motivation, and contribution. And here let me repeat that the good jobs strategy—the escape from mediocrity—is at least as much an operations initiative as it is a people initiative. A doctor can afford not to care much about how stethoscopes are manufactured, but an executive who wants to bring his or her company or unit out of the vicious cycle has to learn, know, *and care* about operations.

Quest didn't just raise pay. Here's a brief summary of how the four operational choices played out:

- **Focus and simplify:** At Quest, this manifested as avoiding unnecessary calls and creating a well-designed self-service option for customers. Simplification also included other changes to reduce workload and cutting the number of skill codes by more than half.

- **Standardize and empower:** Quest started standardizing by initially working with two "pods," each with a group of reps and a supervisor. Reps in the pods learned about basic quality principles, and each day they held a nine-minute huddle. Quest also implemented an idea system to collect, evaluate, and implement ideas from reps.

- **Cross-train:** Quest cross-trained reps to handle more than one region to react to changes in customer demand.

- **Operate with slack:** Quest created new support roles to ease the burden on reps and supervisors. These new roles included subject-matter experts and dedicated trainers.

These four operational choices helped increase reps' individual productivity and their collective contribution to profits. In this way, the reps themselves made Quest's increased investment in them affordable. (That's the good jobs strategy in a nutshell.) Those investments included raising starting wages from $13 to $14 an hour; adding further increases at three months, six months, and one year; implementing an annual incentive program that could amount to 6 percent of pay to recognize good work; and creating a clear career path that showed reps how and when they could advance to higher pay. In chapters 9 and 10, we'll learn more about implementing these changes, including which ones to make first.

The strategy worked. In under two years, Quest's turnover dropped more than 50 percent—down to 16 percent. Absenteeism declined 12.4 percent to 4.2 percent. Calls transferred from a rep up to a supervisor dropped from 12 percent to 9.5 percent. Calls answered within sixty seconds went from 50 to 70 percent.

Quest was no longer losing accounts because of a mediocre call center. And despite all that investment in people—which cost plenty—Quest's overall annual costs were reduced by $2 million.

The Problem Is . . . Mediocrity Is Profitable

When I introduce the concept of the vicious cycle to company leaders in workshops or to participants in executive education, I often ask, "Does this look familiar?" Many hands go up. "It's like you are describing us," they say. "We are in that cycle." One executive of a large company said, "Everything is about cost and, at some point, you cut the muscle. That's where we are right now."

They acknowledge all the costs to their business. None of them is proud when they see how little their full-time employees make. Those who are aware of the high turnover aren't proud of it. They know they are working for a mediocre company. When I share the case studies from Quest or other companies that made system changes, they get excited about how much better things could be for their own customers, employees, and investors.

But even then, many don't think the costs are high enough to convince their leaders to change, because they haven't quantified those costs and because mediocrity *is* profitable. Fred Reichheld, inventor of the Net Promoter Score (NPS), shows that McDonald's, a nearly seventy-year-old company, has one of the lowest NPS scores and the lowest same-store sales growth in the fast-food industry. Yet, McDonald's is still profitable and growing. And that's one of the biggest reasons companies stay mediocre. The way decisions are made at these companies—with heavy reliance on examining past data and analytics—makes it hard to escape mediocrity.

In fact, my colleague, Hazhir Rahmandad, and I have shown that mediocrity can even be profit maximizing.[14] We found that companies competing on the basis of low cost can maximize profits in two opposite ways, either by paying employees as little as possible, operating with high turnover, and designing the work on the assumption of low employee ability and contribution (cost minimizing) or else by paying higher wages, operating with low turnover, and designing the work on the assumption of high employee productivity and contribution (contribution maximizing). In our model, however, we needed to make some simplifying assumptions, one of which was that mediocre companies that operate with high turnover will execute just as well as companies that have a stable and motivated workforce. Obviously, that's not the case. So mediocrity is actually costlier than our theoretical model predicts.

Nevertheless, our theoretical model provides an important insight as to why the cost-minimizing model is more prevalent: it requires less managerial competence. The playbook is simple—pay as little as you can, make the job as easy as you can, and hire anyone who is willing to work under those circumstances. The contribution-maximizing model, on the other hand, is context dependent. Competent managers need to find the pay levels and job design levers (e.g., empowerment, cross-training, operating with slack) that best fit their situation. This insight should be a motivation for competent managers to pursue something that will confer significant competitive advantage and that competitors can't easily imitate.

Your Company
Is Vulnerable

"Profit can hide many sins," said Greg Foran, CEO of Walmart US from 2014 to 2019. "It's what your customers and [frontline employees] say about your business that indicates whether it's vibrant and healthy."

By 2014, Walmart had become the poster child of the vicious cycle of low pay, unstable schedules, high turnover, and low customer satisfaction. The company was still profitable—and even growing. But alarm bells (finally) started sounding when the company had nine consecutive quarters of declining same-store sales growth.

When Foran became CEO, he discovered that "the stores weren't where we needed them to be in terms of basic things like cleanliness and items in stock. The engagement of [frontline employees] wasn't where it needed to be. The supply chain wasn't working as well as it should have been. Each rock I turned over indicated that our business was past its prime and starting to struggle." And that's the thing about companies in a vicious cycle. Problems are everywhere because the entire system is weak. "It's the basic stuff we can't execute on," a manager at a health-care company told our Good Jobs Institute team.

Here's why her company and many others I've observed or worked with could not execute the basic stuff.

When companies operate with high employee turnover and understaffing (as we saw with Quest call centers, turnover and understaffing almost always go hand in hand), they end up making many interrelated decisions that make their system incapable of supporting best practices related to operations and people. Here, specifically, is what they cannot do:

- Hire the right people and train them well.

- Trust frontline employees to solve problems for customers or to engage in improvement.

- Match labor supply with workload—that is, manage capacity well.

- Develop or retain strong unit managers.

- Hold employees to high expectations.

That's a lot of "cannots"—or, you might say, a lot of corporate disabilities. I wouldn't argue if you wanted to call it management malpractice. I'm going to go over each of those disabilities in detail because there's a lot to understand about how they come about and how disabling they really are. But don't despair, because in chapters 9 and 10, we'll discuss how to address each of them.

Corporate Disability 1: You Can't Hire the Right People or Train Them Well—the Firefighting Loop

Companies operating in a virtuous cycle of low employee turnover, strong operational execution, and high performance can implement best practices in hiring. Mercadona has clarified what attributes matter most to succeed in their environment and uses a variety of methods—from structured interviews to role-playing scenarios to technical tests—to hire such people. They then invest in training to make sure that new hires are ready to perform the job well from day one. Companies operating in a vicious cycle, on the other hand, often can't hire the right people or train them well—even if they have decent hiring practices on paper.

In 2016, my Good Jobs Institute colleague Sarah Kalloch spent nine weeks working at a large retailer. This wasn't an undercover operation; the CEO of the company knew that Sarah was working there. She applied with her real résumé, yet the hiring manager never bothered—or perhaps never had time—to ask why someone who had just completed her MBA at MIT Sloan would be applying for a job stocking shelves. No one called her references, either. She was hired after a brief interview, a quick background check, and a drug test—that was it.

Sarah approached her job there as a real job—she wanted to deliver.[1] She worked forty-one training hours, but twenty-three of those hours were wasted, largely due to technology glitches, not having enough computers for all six trainees, unproductive shadowing outside her department, and just standing around waiting to be told what to do next. Once she got to work, she rarely had the equipment she needed. Part of her job was to open boxes, for example, but she was not given a box cutter and had to spend time finding one or open the boxes with her house key. During her nine weeks of employment, having worked 178.5 hours, she received zero feedback about her performance.

Sarah's experience is not unique. From the point of view of a mediocre company in the vicious cycle, it makes sense. Why bother with rigorous hiring or training when you know most people aren't going to last long? Even if you have great hiring and training practices on paper, managers operating in mediocrity often have little time to cultivate new employees because they are constantly fighting fires.

Since frontline pay is low, there aren't many people attracted to the jobs. This has always been a problem for mediocre companies, and a tight labor market has made it worse. Among those who do apply, some are not a fit or are unreliable. Managers often know they're hiring a potentially unreliable person, but with turnover so high, they'll take almost anyone they can get.

Meanwhile, those who really are capable and motivated aren't set up for success. The design of training is often poor. Orientation often consists of paperwork and a few videos; no one explains the company's

Managers Are Often Unaware of How Mediocre Their System Is

In a fantastic *Harvard Business Review* article—"Why Do We Undervalue Competent Management?"—Raffaella Sadun, Nicholas Bloom, and John Van Reenen show that leaders often don't realize just how mediocre their companies are.[a] Interviews at twelve thousand companies in thirty-four countries showed that in most companies, operations are not excellent or even good. By the authors' measure, only 6 percent of companies scored 4 or 5 (out of 5) in implementing best practices related to operations and people management, 11 percent scored 1 or 2. That left 83 percent of companies scoring 3.

So, nine out of ten companies were mediocre or worse. One in ten were excellent or good. What's more, real-world results were aligned with these survey scores: companies with lower scores really did have less productivity, innovation, and growth.

Still, when the surveyed managers were asked simply to rate their own companies' management and operations, the ratings were typically higher than what was merited by their answers to questions about best practices. This was true in all thirty-four countries.

Can this misplaced confidence be overcome? Justin Kruger and David Dunning found a correlation between incompetence and overconfidence, but

history, its values, and how it creates value for the customer. Often there is heavy reliance on computer training, which tends to be glitchy, easily gamed, and hard to administer. On-the-job training—assuming there is any—can be ad hoc, assigned to whoever might be around. For Sarah, it was a cashier who only spoke Spanish. Sarah doesn't speak Spanish, and her job didn't involve working at the cash register.

I don't think we need to write the problem off as unsolvable.[b] The fact that those survey participants didn't see the self-contradiction doesn't mean that at least some of them couldn't acknowledge it if it were pointed out to them and backed up with numbers. That's why, at the Good Jobs Institute, we make such an effort to use data to help companies face their own mediocrity. What percentage of full-time employees make below subsistence wages? What's your employee turnover? Here are your direct and indirect costs of employee turnover.

Many business leaders have some idea of what's wrong but have no sanctioned opportunity to acknowledge and discuss it and every reason to ignore it, to "see no evil." At least some of those executives would like to do better and, in my experience, they eagerly jump at what they view as the first plausible chance they've ever had to address the problem. And people who work for them are delighted when they see the possibility of moving from mediocrity to excellence. A Quest senior manager who had been there for fifteen years told me, "When the company said, 'We are going to do this,' I was like 'Okay, my gosh, after all these years! This is what we've been waiting for.'"

a. Raffaella Sadun, Nicholas Bloom, and John Van Reenen, "Why Do We Undervalue Competent Management?" *Harvard Business Review*, September–October 2017, https://hbr.org/2017/09/why-do-we-undervalue-competent-management.

b. Justin Kruger and David Dunning, "Unskilled and Unaware of It: How Difficulties in Recognizing One's Own Incompetence Lead to Inflated Self-Assessments," *Journal of Personality and Social Psychology* 77, no. 6 (1999): 1121–1134.

All this mediocrity in hiring and training—along with the low pay—naturally results in a significant percentage of employees who aren't good at their jobs and who make mistakes. This, in turn, causes operational problems we saw in chapter 3, which beget even more mistakes. Meanwhile, one level up, managers spend their time covering for employees who didn't show up, jiggering the ever-changing schedules, and fighting fires.

The manager of a supermarket with over $20 million in annual sales told me he spent most of his days working at the cash register or solving equipment and customer problems. Of course, he had less time to make sure he was hiring the right people and then coaching and mentoring them. That, in turn, made it harder to delegate responsibilities—he didn't have many supervisees he could trust with more than simple tasks—which left him even more overwhelmed. He told me he had all kinds of ideas for improving store performance but almost never had time to carry them out.

What we see here is another vicious cycle or reinforcing loop that, over time, makes the business less and less competitive.

Corporate Disability 2: You Can't Empower Employees—the Trust Loop

One of the four operational choices of the good jobs system is "standardize and empower." Empowerment of employees is enormously valuable—when combined with a stable workforce who have expertise in what the company makes or sells, who have time to help the customer, and whose job is designed in a way that reduces mental overload. Empowerment is a key ingredient of motivation and engagement. As we saw with Mercadona in chapter 1, empowerment also contributes directly and profitably to customer service, process and product improvement, and innovation and adaptation.

But remember the executive in chapter 1 who said, "We've empowered our own employees and lost tens of millions of dollars"? Empowerment relies on trust. And while companies with a good jobs system can trust their employees, the ones operating in mediocrity can't. Let's start from where we left off in the previous section. You haven't hired the right people or provided sufficient training. Of course, you're going to see employees making mistakes at work or skipping work altogether. How can you trust them to make on-the-spot decisions that are in both the customer's and the company's best interests?

Top management's solution is backward; that is, to put in *more* controls and remove *more* decision-making from the frontline staff. An executive at a workshop said, "We are building systems assuming people can't do anything right." A cashier at a large retail chain told me she was not authorized to:

- process returns

- terminate a transaction (e.g., when the customer didn't have enough money to pay)

- correct a mistake (e.g., if the customer scanned something twice)

- take a coupon

Does the customer have a coupon? Call a manager. Did you type the wrong product code? Call a manager. Basic cashiering tasks were not trusted to cashiers. Can you ever be customer focused if you are wasting your customers' time like that?

Frontline controls often include tracking every minute of work time.[2] A restaurant worker told us how his supervisor watched staff on the security camera and counted how many times each one went to the bathroom. Lacking basic autonomy, this worker started having panic attacks. When Amazon workers first tried to unionize, one of their big complaints was lack of autonomy; tracking systems and cameras monitored their every move. I'll never forget the retail worker who told me, "We are a dime a dozen, just human robots, really." People don't like being treated like robots, or, as Henry Ford would have it, just a pair of hands. We like to have some control over our work, make decisions, and solve problems.

Companies that adopt the good jobs system don't try to turn their people into machines. "We never ask a person to do what a machine can do," a leader at Mercadona told me. If you're going to design the work so there's no decision-making, use real robots, not human robots.

Bad as this kind of top-down, "just do what we say" job design is for factories and warehouses, it's even worse for service operations.[3] With all the variability that comes from interacting with customers—when they arrive, what they want, how they react to other people—it's impossible to specify every interaction in advance. The more management tries to add standards, policies, rules for unpredictable situations, the more often their specifications and scripts are going to be useless, counterproductive, or infuriating in practice.

This disconnect between command and control of the frontline workers and good outcomes for customers and the business sometimes becomes comically obvious. Our Good Jobs Institute team once walked into a discount retailer in Ipswich, Massachusetts, that was stocked—just as corporate had ordered—with New York Yankees gear. For heaven's sake, I grew up in Turkey and have never been a baseball fan, but even I know that selling Yankees gear in Red Sox Nation is not going to work. The store where my colleague Sarah worked received a big shipment of beach chairs—in New England in September. They didn't sell. Our Good Jobs Institute team visited a store that was part of a large national chain. This store was in a low-income neighborhood. Pointing out hair-care products that were in the $20–$40 range, the store manager said, "They do not sell in this store. It's shrink." By shrink, she was referring to theft or damage. Likewise, the store's selection of yoga pants and weighted blankets "just sit and collect dust, when something else could be sitting here and sell." Our team asked if she let the district leader or someone from merchandising know about this. The store manager laughed. There was no way her voice would be heard, she said.

When employees see enough bad decisions like those, they lose trust in HQ's ability and decide they don't really need to do what HQ tells them to do. Sometimes a requirement from HQ makes more sense than frontline workers realize, but since the reasoning is often not explained to them, they are left to their own judgment. Supervisors may feel that there's no point in taking time to explain everything HQ does when there are so many fires to fight and the employees are changing all the time anyway.

Employees who decide to disregard what strike them as foolish rules may feel they are doing the company a favor and improving performance. In some cases, they would be right. But they may also be taking some revenge for the disrespect they feel. At the notorious General Motors plant discussed in chapter 2—where there was no empowerment and no explanation for many of the rules and regulations—one final inspection found loose steering arms on two hundred cars; a worker had done it intentionally.

You might suspect such an event would wake management up to a bad reality. Often it has the opposite effect. It just makes it more clear to HQ that employees have low ability and low motivation. They need *more* controls and *less* empowerment—yes, another vicious cycle.

Most leaders know at some level that it's not possible to deliver great service if frontliners who interact with customers every day are not empowered to make decisions for customers or solve their problems. Most leaders acknowledge it's a missed opportunity not to involve frontline employees in improving their own work. After all, the frontline staff know their own jobs better than anyone at HQ. Most leaders intuitively know that it's harder to roll out new technologies successfully without employee input.

But companies operating in mediocrity *cannot* leverage their employees for customer service or continuous improvement or adopting new technologies. The trust isn't there and frontline managers lack the time, capability, and necessary systems for helping employees make decisions and involving them in continuous improvement. You can't just "set people free" and call them "empowered." Instead, you must create the conditions for people to be empowered by investing in them and designing their jobs so that they can use their freedom constructively and keep getting better.

Corporate Disability 3: You Can't Match Labor Supply with Demand—the Understaffing and Loss-of-Focus Loop

As companies operating in a vicious cycle find their productivity, customer service, and sales deteriorating, there is performance pressure, especially at companies with aggressive financial targets. Even when there isn't any performance decline, there's often reaction to noise; one week of slow sales might cause panic for managers under pressure to meet targets. As we saw in chapter 3, they may resort to cutting costs by cutting back on head-count or on workers' hours. They also may try to increase sales by add-ing more products or services or offering discounts.

Adding more just to meet financial targets is possibly even more dangerous than cutting labor costs. In addition to increasing costs, increas-ing operational complexity, and undermining customer service, it can undermine companies' value proposition to customers. An executive at a large public company lamented that "financial pressures lead us to be all things to all people. And that's not a strategy." I have witnessed this in many companies, even when HQ itself knew perfectly well that their coupons, promotions, new products, price changes, and so on would worsen the customers' and the employees' experience and weaken their core.

One insurance firm, for example, realized that a quick way to entice new customers would be to offer discounts. But that meant that a call with a potential customer that should take five minutes took twenty-five min-utes because the rep had to figure out the discount in each case and explain it. And later, when those discounts expired, frustrated customers would call back asking why their premium had suddenly gone up—another lengthy and probably unsatisfying call that wouldn't have happened if the premium had been left alone. That company's business model was to com-pete on low cost, but any short-term gains in sign-ups from the promo-tion were lost to higher costs down the line from the problems the promotion caused. Now they found themselves having to choose between high prices or lower margins.

To grow sales, one retailer pushed unnecessary warranties to custom-ers. Our Good Jobs Institute team saw a mother buying swimming gog-gles for her two daughters. The cashier, who had targets for how many warranties she needed to sell per shift, told the mother she should get the warranty. When the mother declined, she told her, "You can spend $5 now and save $20 when they break next year."

The most heartbreaking example I ever witnessed of offering more and having it backfire was in a senior living facility. It was supposed to accept only relatively healthy residents. Faced with financial pressures, it started accepting "high-acuity" residents—that is, residents with significantly more serious medical problems. These high-acuity residents had different needs than lower-acuity residents—not just more needs, but different ones—and they required more time, but the caretakers' hours were not adjusted accordingly. The same workforce was trying to do significantly more work. They had to provide new kinds of care for which they may or may not have been trained and in which they may or may not have had much experience. Of course, all this change led to more mistakes, more falls, and more injuries—for both patients and staff. Meanwhile, the healthier residents were frustrated; they were getting less care than they had signed up for (and were still paying for).

Top management went so far as to ask the facility director to hide the high-acuity residents when potential residents and their families visited to check the place out. Of course, the staff hated being forced to take part in a dirty trick like that, not only deceiving potential customers but also showing such disrespect for the most vulnerable residents. All this contributed to higher turnover and worse care. With higher turnover, residents were less likely to have caregivers who had gotten to know them—how they liked their hair combed, what they liked to eat, what activities they liked, which way they were likely to lose their balance, who would be coming to see them. Residents and their families became as unhappy as the staff.

Beyond the cost of falls or other accidents and the cost of turnover, it may be hard for the management of a senior living company to see how much harm mediocrity does. After all, vulnerable people—especially those with dementia—may not complain much to their families. And you don't have repeat purchases—or the lack of them—as feedback. But there's an ethical cost to all this mediocrity.

One company that understands the problems created by adding more but keeps doing it anyway is Starbucks. As one manager there told me, "Store complexity is a huge indicator of [employee] satisfaction, which directly impacts customer satisfaction and a store's financial performance. We're constantly throwing new products at our stores, which require training. They need to know the recipes and technology changes—things like new tablets, point-of-sale updates, and inventory tracking systems. But we're not giving them the proper time and resources required to train and adapt to these new technologies."

What makes things even more difficult at Starbucks are the frequent promotions—some lasting just two to four days—that disrupt the stores and make it harder for employees to serve customers. One example: the Unicorn Frappuccino introduced in April 2017.

It was heavily hyped, alluringly described by Starbucks as a "color-changing spectacle of purple and pink, finished with whipped cream and sprinkled with pink and blue fairy powders." The promotion lasted only a few days, but it was a nightmarish few days to many employees. A barista in Colorado published a video rant on social media describing how difficult it was to make this complicated drink. "Please don't get it," he said in the video. "I have unicorn crap all in my hair and on my nose. I've never been so stressed out in my entire life."[4] On Reddit and Twitter, there were many more complaints. It struck baristas as a waste of their time to learn to make this complicated drink that wouldn't even be on the menu a few days later. They also hated the way it slowed up their service, not only because it was complicated to make, but because many stores had only two blenders and, with a run on Unicorns, two weren't enough to fill all the orders that used a blender. Managers didn't see fit to increase staff (or the supply of blenders) just to manage this one promotion, so the employees on duty had to absorb the surge. Some stores were told it would be a one-day promotion, but then it lasted three. They ran out of supplies and found themselves dealing with frustrated and sometimes angry customers who had come to get this special treat.[5]

So here we see yet another loop. Poor performance leads to efforts to increase sales by adding more. Increased workloads while running lean leads to turnover and understaffing, which drive more mistakes and customer service problems, which drive even poorer performance.

Companies with a good jobs system, on the other hand, pursue a disciplined focus on the customer. They change all the time, with improved products, services, and technologies. But they do so without making life difficult for their employees or hurting their value proposition. At Mercadona, one of the principles is: "Anything that doesn't provide value for the customer is not done." By value, they don't mean anything customers may happen to love or mention in social media, but what Mercadona wants to be the best at—namely, "the best quality-to-price ratio, the highest level of service, and the ability to complete purchases quickly." At Toyota, anything that doesn't add value is considered waste. That's why Toyota does not overproduce and simplifies its operations by using common parts and specifications.

Corporate Disability 4: You Can't Have Strong Managers

Unit managers—those who run a single factory, store, hospital, call center, or hotel—are arguably a multiunit organization's most critical employees. At every company I've observed, units with more-experienced managers perform better than those with less-experienced managers. At one restaurant chain, units with general managers who had been there for more than two years had 25 percent higher EBITDA and 45 percent higher sales per square foot than those with general managers who had less than a year's experience.

Mediocre companies can't consistently retain and develop strong managers. Many burned-out and frustrated managers leave. We have worked with organizations with unit manager turnover higher than 30 percent and department manager turnover higher than 50 percent. Here is what several had to say: "I'm on call 24/7. . . . I'll leave at 7 p.m. and get back in at 7 a.m. and I'll already have thirty emails." "This job is a burden on my family. I never see my partner and kids." "By the time I finally go to bed at midnight, after spending six hours on the phone answering questions about work or figuring out a schedule, it's time to work in five hours. You burn out."

Things have gotten even worse during the pandemic. Companies that couldn't attract and retain employees before the pandemic had major understaffing problems during it, making life even harder for frontline managers. We saw managers asking to be demoted because the workload was becoming a health issue—physical and mental—for them.

Good Managers in Bad Systems

By now, you've likely found in your memory some exception to some of the vicious cycles and loops I've described. You know a manager thriving in a bad situation, or a hire that worked out brilliantly. I don't doubt it. Bright spots exist in every mediocre company I've ever studied or worked with. There are always some managers who are just awesome. Their units beat others on many metrics. But some executives draw the wrong conclusion from the bright spots. "Look at those units that are performing much better," they will say. "All we need is some more great managers like those." This line of thinking convinces some executives that they don't need a system change.

But those great unit managers are performing well *despite* a bad system and that's never going to be the norm. (One vice president at a convenience store chain told us—clearly frustrated—that corporate expects every manager to be like Michael Jordan. People make that comparison for a reason: there aren't many Michael Jordans. What's more, when you're Michael Jordan, you're sought after. Few Jordans would choose to work at mediocre companies.)

At a workshop for a large retailer, one participant mentioned hiring a great manager away from Costco, known for the quality of its managers. What a catch! Yet this manager proved to be a disappointment in his new environment. What went wrong? Costco's investment in people and in strong operations means that things run smoothly. Managers, who are almost all promoted from within, can therefore spend most of their time leading people and improving performance. But in his new job, the ex-Costco manager was dealing with high turnover, understaffing, and continual customer service problems; he hardly had time to be the good manager he had been at Costco.

When managers leave mediocre companies, it takes a while to replace them because the pipeline is weak. We worked with several companies that had numerous units without general, assistant, or department managers because they couldn't hire as quickly as people were quitting. Newly hired managers are often ineffective at first. The desperate need for them means sometimes their training gets cut short, just like the training for frontline employees. If they're hired from outside, they don't yet know their coworkers or the ins and outs of the organization.

The talent pipeline is weak because the hiring and training of new employees is weak and once they are on the job, their managers have no time to develop them into viable candidates. At the Smyrna Nissan factory, for example, zone supervisors reported spending 47 percent of their time filling in for no-show operators, addressing quality concerns, and managing attendance. Only 16 percent claimed to accomplish all their tasks each day.

Corporate Disability 5: You Can't Have High Expectations

When operations are designed to allow frontline employees to be productive, empowered, and customer focused, companies and frontline workers can expect a lot from one another. Low turnover allows QuikTrip to hire the right people and train them well. On the job, employees are held to high standards. For example, they must initial each completed task. Peer pressure also helps—part of everyone's pay is tied to the store's customer service score. Full-timers enjoy profit sharing.

But it's not a one-way street. QuikTrip employees expect to be rewarded for their productivity and contributions. In 2017, news broke in Oklahoma that a teacher with a bachelor's degree could teach for seventeen years before reaching QuikTrip's starting salary for a full-time employee with a high school diploma.[6] All managers are promoted from within. QuikTrip employees also expect the company to respect their time and knowledge. If a coffee machine breaks down, employees expect facilities management to fix it immediately, so they don't have to disappoint customers.

Expectations are dismally low at companies operating in mediocrity. You haven't hired the right people, you haven't trained them well, deviation from standards is often the norm, and you can't even manage capacity. With staffing so unstable, it's hard to know who did or should have done what. In such a world, low performers are often tolerated. At one company, a manager told us why he didn't fire an employee who had attendance problems: "I had to work all day, go home, work overnight—I worked five out of seven shifts. This is what happens when you let someone go."

Meanwhile, even employees eager to do a good job have a hard time finding out what that means. My colleague Sarah was told at the company she joined that she had to do two things: "Be on time, and do not steal." Other than that, she had no idea what *good* looked like to her boss or to the company or how they thought she was doing. Another of my students spent some time as a frontline employee at a large retailer and found herself in a similar fog: "I asked during our training period what metrics managers care about. Some of the answers included sales, compliance, processing order pickups and deliveries on time, minimal missing/stolen items, accurate price matches." But she could never find out what any of these numbers were supposed to be or what they currently were. There was also no information on individual performance. "The manager would say, 'Show up on time, work hard, and you'll get noticed.' But how about positive interactions with customers or increasing sales? What does 'working hard' mean?"

Unsurprisingly, there's no ownership culture at these companies. Instead, there is what psychologists call learned helplessness. When employees feel that they have no control over their situation because of decisions from headquarters that waste their time and prevent them from serving customers well, they give up. People at headquarters give up, too. Things go wrong all the time so they are buried with issues from frontline workers and have no time to address them all. To create more of an ownership culture, some companies have tried monetary incentives—linking compensation to performance. Some have tried employee stock ownership. Neither incentive is effective when the rest of the system is what we describe above. You can't hang lead weights on people and then offer them a bonus for the high jump.

The Entire System Is Less Competitive and Less Humane

These five corporate disabilities make a company less competitive. If you are operating in a vicious cycle of high turnover and low performance, you probably have most if not all of them, because they work together to reinforce one another.

There are two competitive costs of this system: you can't differentiate in the eyes of your customers and employees, and you can't easily adapt to changes.

Inability to differentiate

If you can't deliver a good product or service to customers, it can be fatal. Almost every mediocre company we've worked with had "customer first" or "customer focus" as a core value. But almost everyone there knew it was just talk. These companies were designed to deliver poor service. Poorly paid, poorly trained, overworked employees who aren't empowered can't offer good service—though it's a testament to human nature how hard some of them try anyway.

One employee at a specialty retailer told me, "Every day, I think more and more that my company—they don't even deserve to exist. . . . They trick the customer with pricing. . . . Sometimes, there would be rats in the basement. And we still had to sell those shirts full of rat hair. And they wouldn't care." Many executives have told me their own customers wouldn't be able to tell the difference between them and their competitors. "Our design principle," one told me, "is to disappoint customers." There are *many* online fan clubs for Trader Joe's, Costco, H-E-B, and other companies that treat their frontline employees with respect. You don't see that for companies operating in mediocrity.

Customers buy from mediocre and bad jobs companies because they don't yet have a better choice. But once a stronger player enters the market, this becomes a problem. It certainly was for the "Big Three"— Chrysler, GM, and Ford. Today, Amazon is making online shopping so easy that brick-and-mortar retailers that do not offer a compelling reason to shop in their stores are closing down. Sears was founded in 1893 and was the largest retailer in the United States between 1950 and 1980, but it went into bankruptcy in October 2018. Circuit City, Borders, and Toys "R" Us have gone under, and they probably aren't the last of this wave. The United States is still "overstored," with 24.5 square feet of retail space per person versus 16.4 square feet in Canada and 4.5 square feet in Europe.[7] The mediocre stores that don't make their customers want to keep coming back will find it hard to survive.

Inability to adapt

Companies operating in mediocrity also find it hard to adapt to changes in regulations, technologies, customer needs, and labor markets because, with weak managers, weak employees, and weak processes, they just don't have the execution capability.

The pandemic and a tight labor market accelerated technology investments. But technologies don't implement themselves. A robot won't walk in the door, shake hands with its new coworkers, and get to work. Adopting new technologies requires involvement from the frontline staff, who are often the users of the technologies. Home Depot under Nardelli invested $1 billion on automating merchandising and store processes, but many of the systems either failed or fell short of their promised impact, largely because they were designed and rolled out without frontline involvement. They were forced on the associates and store managers, and there was a lack of fit to in-store needs.[8]

Right now, higher minimum wages and a tight labor market are making it tough for many low-wage employers to attract and retain people. It's not just the lowest-paid frontline employees who don't want to work at mediocre companies anymore. Higher-level managers and even executives want work that is less aggravating and more meaningful. Candidates for higher and better-paid positions are increasingly rethinking whether they want to work for a company where they know those below them have lousy pay, lousy hours, lousy training, and lousy prospects. For one thing—as we've seen—it's draining and dispiriting to try to manage such a workforce. For another thing, some find it embarrassing or even immoral. Millennials and Gen Z have gained a reputation for wanting to work for companies that are purpose driven. I certainly see that in my classroom with Gen Z students. Just last semester, I was surprised when a student turned down what seemed like a great job offer. It was a company, however, that had been in the news for some unethical practices. As he explained it, "I couldn't tell my mom I was going to work there."

Investors may also start putting pressure on bad jobs companies. Not only are investors increasingly concerned with social issues, they're also starting to connect the dots on mediocrity—the low productivity, high costs, poor customer satisfaction and sales, lack of continuous improvement, inability to differentiate, and inability to adapt—that's spawned by a lack of people investment. They may come to see mediocrity as not only an ethical mistake but also a business mistake and therefore feel justified in pushing companies toward a better system.

At the least, investors may start pushing for transparency of employee-related data such as take-home pay, turnover, and internal promotion—metrics which over time affect the company's bottom line and investor returns. There are already efforts to make employee-related data transparent for all to see. The Shift Project at Harvard's Kennedy School, led by Daniel Schneider, uses Facebook to survey employees of large companies about their pay and schedules and publishes the data. Gary Gensler, who became the Chair of the US Securities and Exchange Commission in February 2021, is looking for ways to make companies disclose their human capital data. Companies including Intel already disclose annual take-home pay buckets by race and gender.

Executives be warned! A weak, mediocre system that has survived so far may not survive the full light of day.

Companies with a good jobs system, on the other hand, can differentiate and adapt. I started studying Costco, Mercadona, Trader Joe's, and QuikTrip more than a decade ago. Since then, a lot has changed in retailing. Yet, these companies have been able to stay ahead in the eyes of their customers and their employees.

Ethical costs

What caps it off, though, is how needlessly inhumane this system of mediocrity is. The pandemic revealed the poor working conditions at meat plants, fulfillment centers, nursing homes, and retail stores. We've learned that people who are essential to the functioning of our economy are treated with little respect and dignity. They earn too little to make ends meet.

Leaders at these companies know, deep inside, that they are not doing the right thing for their customers and employees. One health-care CEO who contacted me to explore the good jobs system in his company wrote, "I have grown increasingly troubled by the 'livability' of typical caregiver compensation, instability in the caregiver workforce and the impact it has for our customer, and the unpredictability that caregiver instability creates in our business outcomes. I'm prepared to do something about that in our company."

In "Courage" we will see what challenges that executive will face if he really means to "do something"—and what it will take for him to prevail.

COURAGE

Fears, Doubts, and Lack of Imagination

We are not a company that tends to make
bets on its people.

—Senior vice president of a retailer

At the end of the fall semester in 2021, I received a note from a student who'd taken my class after watching a panel discussion I had with Craig Boyan, president of H-E-B, a Texas-based supermarket chain. H-E-B is one of the most loved and trusted supermarket chains in the country. Not surprisingly, it is also one of the best employers in retail. H-E-B begins every year by committing to increase pay for employees—whom it calls partners—and to lower prices for customers. It challenges those partners to earn their higher pay and make it possible for H-E-B to offer lower prices in part by contributing their innovative ideas. Every year, the partners come through.

During the panel, Boyan talked about how grocers typically see labor as their largest cost. The leaders of H-E-B see labor as their greatest investment and expect different results. Boyan asked the students, "Can you imagine more productivity? Can you imagine greater hospitality? Can you imagine real spirit? Can you imagine more teamwork? Can you imagine higher sales per square foot?"

Well, it turns out that a lot of people can't, including my student who sent me the note. He wrote that he thought our panel conversation had exposed him to a set of operational principles that he "didn't think could be more than a pleasant bedtime fairytale. The story seemed too good to be true." He signed up for my service operations course anyway because, "Deep down, I wanted to believe that there was another way of doing management practice, one that was both more empathetic and could still be profitable for all stakeholders involved."

He's not the only one who starts my course with doubts. Once, right before we started discussing the Mercadona case, a student asked whether Mercadona was a real company or a fictitious business school case. Could a retail company really have such low turnover and manage its business that well? Several students told me that the transformation at Quest call centers seemed too good to be true, until they met the leaders and heard about it from them. Over the years, many students have told me that they just couldn't believe that investing in people could go hand in hand with high performance in frontline service jobs until we discussed the Quik-Trip case and they heard from QuikTrip's CEO, Chet Cadieux.

It's not just my students who find what I'm telling them too good to be true. Generations of business leaders can't imagine it either. When there is so much written about how pursuing operational excellence and offering good jobs is not only a humane business strategy, but also a strong one, and when you have as much evidence for that as we do at the Good Jobs Institute, you can get a bit frustrated by the resistance to the idea. The truth is, most leaders meet the message with a lot of yeah buts: "Yeah but . . . X, yeah but . . . Y."

Instead of getting frustrated about this, I've tried to understand what is driving resistance to a strategy that will make companies more competitive, more resilient, more humane. I think it comes down to three things: fear, doubt, and lack of imagination. And these three things have their origins in how leaders are taught and in the accepted orthodoxy of data über alles. Let's explore this issue.

Leaders Who Can't Imagine That Investment in People Could Be Good for Business

Deep down, many executives have doubts about investing in frontline employees despite the academic studies, case evidence, and logic. This doubt is often rooted in what they've experienced and how they were taught. They've been taught that labor is just a cost to be minimized. Lean and mean is what drives efficiency. In their mind, bad jobs—with low wages, scant benefits, unstable schedules, and few opportunities for success and growth—and the resulting operational mediocrity are simply what one must accept in their industries. They have been convinced that if they pay market wage or slightly more—even if that wage is not actually a *living* wage—this is all they can and should do. If their employees have inconsistent schedules and too few hours—well, that's what it takes to operate in a service industry.

During a conversation with a board member of a large hospitality business—a business in which quality of service obviously makes a big difference for customer satisfaction—I asked if they had ever investigated if market pay, which is what they said they were paying the frontline workers, was actually enough for their employees to be able to live on or to stay with the company. The response was, "We are not running a charity. We are running a public company." I outlined the benefits of investing in people and making operational choices to leverage that investment, but the board member's response stayed the same: paying their frontline staff any more than the competitors did would put them at a disadvantage. I pointed out there were companies in retail that had been doing just that for years or even decades and had never found it to put them at a disadvantage. Maybe so, she acknowledged, but she couldn't imagine that it would work in hospitality. (It does. You'll see in chapter 6.)

In the summer of 2020, I reached out to the chairman of a large public company after hearing him speak about racial and economic injustice. When I mentioned that one way he could help reduce the problem was to improve jobs at his own company, he got defensive. "You have to understand the economic proposition," he told me. "Markets don't have a conscience. My investors tell me if I go with BlackRock and the ESG [environmental, social, and governance] stuff, I'm out." I replied that one doesn't need to do this to support ESG but rather to win with customers; there were companies—including one of his own competitors—that paid their employees about 50 percent more than his company did and created as much if not more value for their shareholders. He said those were exceptions.

I then mentioned the changes at Walmart and Sam's Club. Walmart could have become a Sears or JCPenney, but since 2014 it has become a stronger company partly because of its investment in people. His response was that Walmart's EBITDA had not improved all that much. Besides, the only reason Walmart could invest in people was because the Walton family owned a big share. It didn't make business sense.

When I wrote *The Good Jobs Strategy*, I described a set of excuses people use for not investing in people, including "Big companies can't do this because there aren't enough good people." At the time, Walmart was the poster child for low people investment. I wrote then that if Walmart were to start offering good jobs, someone might offer the opposite excuse: "Walmart is so big they can do anything they want to do." Unfortunately, that prediction was perfectly accurate.

When the CEO of a large manufacturing company described his company's stated mission to care for its people, I asked if they paid workers enough to make a living. That would seem to be a rather minimal requirement of caring for one's employees, but he had a strong negative reaction. First, he talked about how pay didn't matter for engagement, but the care employees felt did. (He's right that pay doesn't necessarily drive engagement, but, as we've seen, in the absence of sufficient pay, things start falling apart both for workers and for operations.) He then talked about how paying more than the market—that is, more than the going rate— would make companies less competitive.

As long as American consumers want low prices, he explained, manufacturers will do everything they can to locate their factories where labor costs are low. He had seen that happen multiple times. First, companies closed their unionized factories and opened new ones in right-to-work states where pay was lower. Competition then forced them to close those factories to open new ones in Mexico, where pay was even lower. And then they closed those factories too when they couldn't compete with Asia, where the pay was even lower than in Mexico.

I mention the manufacturing example, even though most low-wage employees work in the service sector, because America's manufacturing decline seems to have shaped many people's beliefs about investment in people and about competitiveness in general. For example, when I was sharing how companies like Costco and QuikTrip promote almost all their frontline managers from within, the CEO of a *Fortune* 100 company immediately connected promoting from within to complacency, which (he believed) had caused America's manufacturing decline, and he then connected complacency to unions—and his company had no interest running a union shop.

Show Me the Money!

When we run workshops with companies or investors, after the first or second day even the skeptical people end up believing that investment in people combined with operational choices can drive outsize value for *other* companies. But that still doesn't mean they can see it working in their own company. They need more proof. To get there, they often look at historical data.

Here's what happened at a large public company whose leaders wanted to explore whether the good jobs strategy would work for them. During a workshop, the participants—mostly senior vice presidents—recognized their own vicious cycle and corporate disabilities. Many in the room agreed that if they didn't change, they would be heading for trouble. Financial pressures had caused them to add so many new products and services that they had lost customer focus. Customers came to them because they had a lot of convenient locations, but it was only a matter of time before a stronger competitor would eat their lunch. They were losing managers who could no longer deal with constant firefighting, lack of autonomy, and understaffing.

These leaders were not happy about the quality of service they delivered to their customers or the quality of jobs they offered to their employees. Operating in mediocrity is exhausting. It's also demoralizing. Now, they could see what they had to do to get out of the vicious cycle. They could see how much better things could be. But that required convincing the CEO and other executive leaders. To do that, they knew they needed bulletproof analysis showing that investment in people—including higher wages—would pay off.

Naturally, they turned to their analytics team for help. How much would they need to spend to bring everyone to a minimum of $15 an hour (this was before the pandemic)? What would be the performance benefit of higher pay? Calculating the cost of the investment was straightforward. Calculating the upside was trickier. To estimate the benefit, the analytics team looked at what had happened a couple years earlier when they had increased hourly pay. Had it reduced turnover? And if so, had that improved customer service and sales?

The analytics team found that the link was there. The last time they raised pay, turnover dropped, which then improved service, which then increased sales. Yay! But the effects were tiny. Based on this analysis, the team estimated that increasing pay to the proposed minimum of $15 an hour would lead to a single-digit decrease in employee turnover, which would then lead to a small increase in customer service and sales. Although more analysis was needed to get a fuller picture, it was already looking clear to them that higher pay would not pay off. Yikes!

"The CEO wants to invest in people, but the data shows that it won't be worth it," one of the senior VPs told me. "Everyone is afraid because they don't want to be wrong. It's a bet. And we are not a company that tends to make bets on its people." He sounded defeated.

The analysis came to be seen as "proof" that investment in people would not pay off. But what did the analysis prove, really? It didn't show what would happen if they didn't change the status quo. Could they offer a compelling reason for their customers to buy from them if they didn't fix turnover and all the corporate disabilities that came with it? Could they ever fix turnover without raising pay? Could higher pay combined with other interventions make a more significant change in turnover and engagement than the pay raise alone had done before? They didn't ask these questions.

Nor did the analysis consider how higher pay could improve other factors such as fewer mistakes, higher labor productivity, lower manager turnover, lower overtime costs, and higher sales from better execution. Even for the effect it did consider—reduction in employee turnover—how accurate was the prediction? Was it true that all they could do was to reduce turnover by less than 10 percent? The analytics team acknowledged that their estimates were on the conservative side. Wouldn't you want to be on the conservative side if you were working at a company that has always emphasized minimizing labor costs? Wouldn't you be scared to make a different recommendation? As we saw in chapter 3, Quest Diagnostics was able to reduce turnover by more than 50 percent. We will see other examples of companies that were able to reduce turnover between 25 and 70 percent. Why should the prospects for this company be so much less?

In *The Design of Business*, Roger Martin highlights that a key reason why leaders struggle to change or innovate is that they insist on justifying every decision analytically, often using historical data. While using historical data can help them optimize the status quo and capture greater profits that can be reinvested in the business, it's an impediment to innovation because no innovation's effects can be proven in advance. The same logic holds when companies are making a system change. If your company has been operating in a vicious cycle, then historical data will only point you to optimizing that current state. It won't help you estimate the expected value of system change—or, as Craig Boyan from H-E-B reminded my students, it won't help you *imagine*.

Looking at Effects in Isolation

Another reason that the analytics team's estimate of the effect of a pay raise on turnover was so low was that the small pay raise was *all* they did that time. There was no system change, only a tweak of one component of their mediocre system, leaving most of the corporate disabilities in place. I've seen the same results with other changes. "We've increased staffing levels and lost money" or "We've empowered people and lost money."

Why would they choose to look at such a limited analysis? It is tempting to look at one factor in isolation because doing so is considered a hallmark of scientific thinking. It allows "rigorous" analysis of cause and effect. We academics love this type of analysis, in which we isolate the effect of an independent variable (pay) on a dependent variable (turnover). Read any empirical paper and you'll likely find a sentence like this: "All else being equal, increasing independent variable β by X would lead to Y amount of decrease/increase in the dependent variable α." Randomized controlled experiments are the gold standard for establishing such causality. In large, siloed organizations, looking at such data—how a specific decision affects an outcome—helps different groups make a point.

Of course, there is a place for scientific thinking and data analysis in business. When you are forecasting demand for your existing products or services, managing inventory levels, or determining how many people you need to hire, data analysis can be extremely useful. QuikTrip's algorithm for site selection enables it to determine—with great accuracy—the revenue and EBITDA of a potential store at a particular latitude and longitude. Mercadona is one of the best examples of using scientific thinking in retail. Every time the company makes a process change, such as changing the displays or the order in which a new employee is taught things, it examines the impact of that change—as much as possible, in isolation— before rolling it out.

Still, it's a mistake to equate data analysis with rigor. As Roger Martin eloquently explains, the outcomes of many business decisions are not determined by inescapable laws of science, but rather by determined leaders who have agency to make choices that can radically change situations. Investor Charlie Munger of Berkshire Hathaway talks about "physics envy," referring to how cause-and-effect analysis doesn't work in complex systems—we just *wish* it would. Martin reminds us that even Aristotle, considered the father of the scientific method, warned about when science applies and when it doesn't. "Most of the things about which we make decisions, and into which we therefore inquire," he wrote, "present us with alternative possibilities. . . . All our actions have a contingent character; hardly any of them are determined by necessity."[1]

Aristotle was right. In the world of complex organizations, "all else" is *never* going to be "equal." There's no law of labor, like the law of gravitation, that tells you that when you increase pay this much, turnover will decrease that much. It matters how you increase pay and what else you do along with it. It matters whether it's 1990 or 2020. Heck, it matters whether it's 2020 or 2022. If all you think you can do is reduce turnover by less than 10 percent, it is unlikely that this investment will pay off. But why that low? Quest Diagnostics and others were able to reduce turnover significantly because they didn't just increase pay. They made other changes, including focusing on the customer, simplifying operations, creating career paths, giving employees time to do their jobs well, and empowering them. They didn't just change a tire—they rebuilt the engine.

Cutting Competitive and Ethical Corners

Financial and siloed decision-making, without considering competitive and ethical costs, which aren't as readily calculable, is dangerous. Charlie Munger calls it "man-with-a-spreadsheet syndrome." If you are going to reduce a complex system, like a large organization, to only the elements that can be calculated, then you will undoubtedly ignore important variables.

Business schools have contributed to this problem. We teach our students data-driven, "rigorous" decision-making, often with the objective of maximizing profitability. Many business schools, including MIT Sloan, offer a degree in analytics. Many MBA students would be uncomfortable making a case for increasing pay if they couldn't show—with the numbers all lined up on a spreadsheet—that higher pay would pay off financially.

The effect of this kind of training can be seen and felt in the real world: using data from all publicly traded firms in the United States from 1992 to 2014, researchers found that when a CEO with a business degree takes over from a non-MBA, there is an average 6 percent decline in wages at the firm during the next five years, but no improvement in productivity.[2] Researchers estimate that an increase in the fraction of workers employed by business managers accounts for 15 percent of the slowdown of wage growth since 1980.[3]

Numbers may not lie, but they can mislead because they only tell you about the things you thought to count or that you find easy or cost-effective to count. Numbers might tell you, for example, that it's more profitable to go cheap on cleaning and maintenance. Perhaps that's what happened to Family Dollar. In February 2022 the US Food and Drug Administration alerted the public to unsafe products sold by Family Dollar.[4] FDA's inspection of a distribution center in Arkansas had found unsanitary conditions, including rodent infestation. There were live rodents nesting and dead ones in various states of decay, rodent feces and urine, plus bird droppings and dead birds. A fumigation of the facility revealed more than eleven hundred dead rodents, and company records showed that the problem had been going on for at least eleven months. On February 19, 2022, Family Dollar announced that it would temporarily close 404 stores served by that distribution center. These were stores that sell food and other essential products.[5]

If saving money was the goal, even without specific data it's not hard to imagine that the unmeasured costs of product recalls, store closings (404!), and reputational damage likely outweighed whatever the company should have spent on pest control and cleaning.

Data, for example, might tell you that it's more profitable to understaff your units even at the risk of putting people's lives in danger. Large pharmacy chains, hospitals, and senior living organizations have all been reported to have too few people to do all the required work without making mistakes.[6] Not surprisingly, errors that harm patients and residents are not rare in these health-care settings, leaving managers and caregivers feeling frustrated and defeated. Marlena Pellegrino, a nurse of thirty-five years, recalled an experience at an understaffed hospital: "I [was so over-worked that I] could not get to [my patient's] room for over two hours.

When I did get into the room, she had tears in her eyes, she was crying and holding onto me. And when I looked into her bed she was soiled in urine. I felt like I did a bad job. I felt less than the nurse that I know I am." She explained, "There's not a shortage of nurses, there's just a shortage of nurses willing to work under those conditions."[7]

It's the same with any number of organizational decisions. Financial and siloed decision-making rarely points you to increasing investments or accepting short-term losses for longer-term gains, especially when those gains are less measurable than revenues and profits. If sales are falling short, data will show how more products and promotions will increase them—but it doesn't show the hit to customer service, employee satisfaction, or even turnover, which may come later than the surge in cashflow. It doesn't show the hit to your value proposition and hence your differentiation. If labor costs have gone up, data can show how cutting those costs by offshoring manufacturing can immediately goose earnings. It's more difficult to see the supply chain complexity creating quality control problems and longer lead times causing more stockouts and more excess inventory—with all that reducing customer satisfaction.

Financial decision-making can push companies toward cutting competitive and ethical corners, yet it has become the accepted approach to business. With the exception of some big events that make the news—GM having to recall several million cars, Boeing's faulty flight control system causing its planes to crash, pharmacy chains giving people the wrong meds, food poisoning outbreaks at Chipotle restaurants—cutting corners generally doesn't seem like a big deal.[8] Boards certainly aren't firing CEOs for it.

They Don't Prioritize the Work Frontline Employees Do

There are cultural reasons that leaders fear and doubt the good jobs idea, too. Many don't see frontline work as a critical enough driver of performance. They simply don't view the work as all that important to what they're trying to accomplish.

My MIT colleague Suzanne Berger argues that one reason for the decline in US manufacturing is that many people—including policy makers—
think that manufacturing is not important work.[9] Investors and some
leaders also insist that it isn't that important to make your own product—
only to design and sell it. The ethos is that anything that's not a "core com-
petency" should not be done. Gary Pisano and Willy Shih from Harvard
Business School argue that this approach has hurt not just businesses but
the entire US economy. The United States is losing—or has already lost—
the knowledge, skilled people, and supplier infrastructure required to
manufacture many of the cutting-edge products invented in the United
States. This includes such key industries as electronics, pharmaceuticals,
and semiconductors. And because manufacturing has deep connections
to product design and innovation, the United States is losing its ability to
design new products in some of those industries.

But this view that frontline work doesn't matter much extends well
beyond manufacturing. Even in many service industries, the number of
transactions trumps their (lack of) quality. An operating partner at a
private equity firm told me that his firm didn't sweat over how well the
work was done at a restaurant chain they owned. Quality of service at the
restaurants—even basic things like serving the burgers at the right temperature or the accuracy of orders—didn't matter much. Good enough
was all they needed. What mattered to company leaders was growing
the stores and making money. One executive, referring to her company's
call center reps, said to our team: "I'm going to be quite honest with you.
In our world, a lot of times, when you think about value-added jobs, not
many people are going to jump to the fact that a frontline customer rep
is one of the most important jobs you have in your company. They will
default to your more strategic products. Maybe marketing. Just anything
other than your core back-office operations team."

Her own company had focused on creating scale by acquiring other
companies. They spent extravagantly on advertising their services.
Running the core business well and improving the quality of service to
customers was not a priority. Meanwhile, at the other end of the value-
creating chain, a frontline manager at a senior living organization told

our team: "HQ, please come and see the work we do. . . . You can look at numbers all day long, but you have to see it to understand it." The leaders never took the time to visit the frontlines. They had the numbers.

In the service world, when the work is not a priority, it follows that serving customers well is not a priority.

As a teacher, I can see how this cycle of undervaluing certain types of work continues. During the last decade, many young entrepreneurs have internalized the unfair view of frontline work and incorporated it into their pitches for new companies that rely on gig workers—for housecleaning, building security, in-store jobs, and even babysitting. Their business plans assume that you can just mix and match people depending on moment-by-moment demand and thus keep costs low. How—and how *well*—that work gets done doesn't matter. A sense of belonging to a team of people doing something useful for other people doesn't matter. The skills of teamwork and coordination don't matter.

I try to point them to companies that approach business this way and learned hard lessons. A distribution center we analyzed tried to solve its labor shortage problem by introducing temp workers. After all, they're just picking and packing, right? No. Each new worker was around 30 percent as productive as a fully trained and experienced employee. Productivity went down. More-efficient workers grew frustrated with wasting their time training the revolving door of temps; their own productivity dropped. They began to see headquarters as unimpressively out of touch with the job they did and how complex it was to deliver the results they had been delivering. Resentment grew, as did turnover. It's the same vicious cycle over and over again.

Theory X Managers

This cultural dismissal of the value of certain work and workers is rooted in the fact that many leaders just don't trust frontline employees. Based on their experiences, they have concluded that frontline employees are unskilled and lack motivation. If these were truly hardworking and competent people, they reason, wouldn't they have better jobs?

In *The Human Side of Enterprise*, Douglas McGregor, one of the most influential management professors of the twentieth century, wrote about how much leaders' assumptions about employees shape their policies and practices. He described two types of managers. Theory X managers generally assume that employees are unreliable, lazy, unambitious, irresponsible, and unintelligent—they work only for money. Theory Y managers, on the other hand, assume that employees work hard, want to take responsibility, and—under the right circumstances—find meaning and satisfaction in their work.

McGregor had been a student of Abraham Maslow and argued that human nature was more consistent with Theory Y assumptions. But, he acknowledged, "[Theory X] assumptions would not have persisted if there were not a considerable body of evidence to support them." If you have ever spent time at a company with low pay and high turnover, you must have seen employees making mistakes, not showing up, and not focusing on the job. If you've been a student of the decline of US manufacturing since the 1970s, you may think some of that decline was due to workers who had good wages, benefits, and job security but slacked off and behaved badly. The auto industry, in particular, is full of stories of bad worker behavior, including gambling, drugs, and sabotage.

But wait. Remember the fundamental attribution error (cited in chapter 2)—attributing a person's behavior entirely to his or her inherent nature rather than at least partly to his or her circumstances. One of McGregor's most powerful lessons exposes this bias in leaders who take a Theory X approach. McGregor argued that whatever managers assume about people will be proven right because they'll end up creating a system that promotes the behavior they expected. Put in our terms, bad jobs aren't the natural habitat of bad workers; bad jobs go a long way to creating bad workers. Good jobs—with the four operational choices supporting them—make it possible for a majority to be quite valuable workers.

McGregor encouraged leaders to ask themselves certain questions: Do you believe people are trustworthy? Do you believe people seek responsibility, accountability, and meaning in their work? Do you believe people naturally want to learn? Do you believe people prefer working to being idle? Below are a few indicators of Theory X thinking. If you find yourself agreeing with these assessments, consider that you are falling prey to the attribution error that ultimately puts your company in a vicious cycle.

1. Your first instinct is to fix people

Imagine a fast-food chain with operational problems. The lines are too long, the fries are soggy, and there are mistakes with online orders. This chain might have turnover problems, it might be seriously understaffed, the menu might be too complicated, there might be something wrong with the equipment or the ordering system. But a Theory X mindset will lead you to first think about improving either the workers' skills (e.g., improve training) or their motivation (e.g., change incentives) when those may be effects of the problem, not causes.

(I love a story that's told of Peter Drucker, the legendary management theorist. He asked a group of senior executives to raise their hands if there was a lot of dead wood in their companies. Many in the audience raised their hands. Then he asked, "Were people dead wood when you interviewed them and decided to hire them, or did they become dead wood?" In either case, he's cleverly pointing out, it's management's fault. Either you hired poorly or lost them.)

W. Edwards Deming, considered the founder of Total Quality Management (TQM), teaches us to look at the system in which the workers operate—not the workers themselves—to understand the root cause of problems. Companies that pursue operational excellence follow Deming's advice. When Mercadona implemented its own Total Quality Management in the early 1990s, one of the first changes was to declare a set of principles, starting with "Everyone is reliable." That means you can rely on people to do their work. And if you can't, you need to look at what impedes them—that is, the system or the job design—and what *you* can do as a manager or executive to overcome those obstacles.

This instinct—to fix the people, not the system—rises to public policy levels. I've spoken with leaders of many foundations, nonprofits, and impact investment firms who recognize the need for improving job quality in the United States to buoy the economy. Yet, when it comes to fixing this problem, almost all of them start with policies for fixing the workers rather than fixing the jobs. They support workforce training. They focus on K–12 education. They seem to believe that these workers are not yet worthy of higher pay—but with hard work and good intentions, we can get them there.

2. You hire "smart" managers

Another sign of a Theory X manager is that he or she doesn't promote frontliners to be supervisors or managers, but rather looks for outsiders, often ones with college degrees. Amazon, according to its former HR vice president, intentionally limited upward mobility. A 2014 proposal to create more leadership opportunities for hourly employees was rejected because Amazon's leaders believed in hiring "wicked smart" frontline managers with college degrees.[10] Amazon leaders are hardly the only ones with that belief.

Companies like Costco, Mercadona, the In-N-Out burger chain, and Toyota—companies that have long been operating in excellence—don't just give opportunities to frontliners, they promote almost exclusively from within. Referring to companies that hired managers from outside, Chester Cadieux, the cofounder of QuikTrip, said, "It seemed un-American to deprive hardworking employees the chance to advance. Their logic completely escaped me—why not hire capable people and reward them for the skills and knowledge they acquire?"

3. You believe the best decisions come from headquarters

This is the most obvious tell of a Theory X manager. HQ is strategy, frontlines are execution to be told what to do. Decades of research shows the costs of command and control. Some executives are aware of the costs of too much centralization, which, as we saw in chapter 4, include decisions that don't work, causing the frontliners to lose trust in headquarters; a complex operation of workarounds to help customers because headquarters doesn't respond to challenges it doesn't know are out there; and missed opportunities for improvement because frontline workers aren't heard or don't offer suggestions, knowing they won't get anywhere. Yet, for a Theory X manager, the cost of trusting workers appears even higher. When you assume that frontline workers aren't good enough to drive sales and lower costs through better execution, you resort to other ways to grow sales and profits.

Do any of those attributes or behaviors resonate with you? Still not convinced? Fear, lack of trust, lack of imagination—these are powerful forces. For all the evidence we provide, many leaders still can't get past their Theory X biases. I've learned from working with companies that changing beliefs is a challenge; in some ways, it's *the* challenge.

Changing Beliefs

I started this chapter by saying that many of my MBA students begin my class on service operations with doubts. With them, I have months to build conviction that investing in people is good business—if it's done with smart operational choices. I have time to show them the power of people investment in retail stores, restaurants, airlines, manufacturing, hospitals, insurance, even in pest control. They see it in the context of public and private companies, small and large companies.

They meet Theory Y leaders. Michael Fisher, the CEO of Cincinnati Children's Hospital Medical Center, explained to my class why he raised the minimum wage from $11 an hour to $15 for about three thousand people who worked in areas such as janitorial services, food services, and sterile processing units—functions that may not seem that important. "I can tell you," he said to them, "if you are a parent or a grandparent and if your child is in one of our intensive care units, you want that person to know what they are doing, to be skilled and compassionate, every bit as much as the doctor." Leaders like Fisher who lead with good jobs and operational excellence have a completely different orientation toward work. They believe that the work frontline employees do drives a competitive advantage for them. Those workers aren't a drag on the bottom line—they're where the bottom line comes from. Prioritizing the work frontline employees do and doing the fundamentals of business better than anyone else helps those companies provide their customers with low prices and excellent service. That, in turn, makes it unacceptable to operate with high employee turnover. To them, cheap, easy-come-easy-go labor is not a cost saving, it's a foolish expense they can't afford.

My students also meet a few frontline workers. Some students take my advice to work in the front lines as a part-time employee, and they tell me it's life changing.

MaryAnn Camacho, who led the transformation at Quest Diagnostics, tells them about how much call center reps and supervisors wanted to do better. Early on in the journey, Camacho asked for call center teams willing to identify problems, design solutions, and implement change—all while keeping up with their own daily work—in order to help *all* the call centers improve. Team supervisors had to give a presentation explaining why their own team should be selected for this considerable volunteer effort. Camacho said that "each one of the supervisors was so hungry to have investment and training and receive from us the belief that they could do the job, they blew us away. . . . Members of my staff were in tears and said things like, 'I didn't know they had it in them. I can't believe what I just saw.' And I said, 'You know, you invite people to the table, and they'll rise to the occasion.'"

With you, reader, I don't have an entire semester. But I hope the first four chapters have already convinced you that the status quo—bad jobs and corporate mediocrity—is expensive financially, competitively, and ethically. I hope this chapter has persuaded you that the well-established views and fears that can make a commitment to excellence seem too much of an uphill battle are not at all as well founded as they seem. They reflect the widespread experience of being trapped in a vicious cycle, but not the factors that let you escape the trap.

In the following chapters, I'll introduce you to leaders whose beliefs about people and the importance of their work gave them the courage to start companies with excellence or to transform existing companies toward excellence. What they have been able to accomplish for their customers, employees, and investors, I hope, will give you the courage to change.

Convictions and Values

Seventy cents of every dollar we spend to
run our company goes to people.

—Jim Sinegal, cofounder of Costco

At a talk at the Aspen Institute in 2014, someone asked me what role leadership played in the good jobs strategy. I answered that the strategy was all about operations. How I wish I could go back and fix that answer! Yes, the "what" of the good jobs strategy is all about combining investment in people with specific operational choices: focus and simplify, standardize and empower, cross-train, operate with slack. But the "why" of the good jobs strategy has everything to do with leadership.

We've just laid out the doubts and fears that, for many business leaders, make good jobs and the escape from mediocrity that good jobs promise seem either unattainable or delusional. Now, we will meet leaders who have overcome the mediocre status quo.

Something that struck me forcibly once I started spending time with leaders who either had already adopted a good jobs system or were determined to do so is that they "think different." Like all business leaders, they want their companies—and themselves—to succeed. But they have a different mental model of what drives success than the leaders we met in the last chapter. They see their primary fiduciary duty as being to customers. And once they placed winning with their customers ahead of short-term financials, then operating with high turnover and not prioritizing frontline work became unacceptable. How can you improve the quality of products and services to customers if you can't trust employees to make decisions, and if you don't give them enough time to do their work well? These leaders aren't operating on faith that maybe this will work. They're sure. They can't even imagine running a successful business with untrusted, unempowered workers.

They wouldn't invest in workers—with higher pay, more benefits, and cross-training—if they thought workers were lazy or incompetent. They wouldn't operate with slack if they thought their organization was already full of slackers. They wouldn't empower employees if they didn't trust them to make good decisions or have good ideas for improvement.

When making decisions, these leaders always consider competitiveness and ethics, regardless of what spreadsheets say. It is unacceptable to add products or services inconsistent with the value they want to offer customers, to trick customers with deals that don't provide value, to compromise the quality of service by understaffing, or to go cheap on wages or benefits, regardless of how much such tactics might improve short-term profits.

Such beliefs and values aren't just expressed in words. They are put into action daily by the choices and investments these leaders make—including what they could do but don't. Let's meet some of those leaders who have developed the convictions and values to escape mediocrity. In their stories you will find courage and inspiration. We start with Jim Sinegal, cofounder of Costco and CEO from 1983 to 2012.

Jim Sinegal

Sinegal is worth studying as a prototype leader pursuing excellence. He was practicing what I'm proffering here well before I started studying it.

He's considered an icon in retail and beyond, celebrated by people ranging from investors Charlie Munger of Berkshire Hathaway and Tony
James of Blackstone to presidents Barack Obama and Joe Biden. Munger,
a Costco board member since 1997, described Sinegal as "a moral leader
as well as a practical leader." Shortly before Sinegal retired as Costco's
CEO, Jena McGregor of the *Washington Post* wrote, "It's hard to imagine anyone with less pretense, more discipline or more integrity leading a
major corporation today."[1]

If you ask Sinegal to speak, he'll spend most of the time talking about
Kirkland products (Costco's house brand) or Costco employees—not
about himself or his leadership principles. While running Costco, Sinegal
had a tiny office, answered his own phone, and made much less money
than his CEO peers were making because, to him, it was wrong to have
an individual make two or three hundred times more than someone working on the floor.

Sinegal is as down-to-earth as you can imagine—a humble leader. The
word humble comes from Latin *humilis*, which literally means "on the
ground." When he was running Costco, Sinegal used to spend two hundred days per year on the ground—that is, visiting the front lines. That,
he always says, is where the most important work gets done. That's where
Costco makes its money.

Which it does well. From 1985 to 2022, Costco's revenues grew at
a 12 percent compounded rate, profits at a 13 percent compounded
rate, and stock price at a 17 percent compounded rate. The S&P 500's
growth during that same period was 9.3 percent. In 2022, Costco was
the world's third-largest retailer—behind only Walmart and Amazon—
with $223 billion in sales, 304,000 employees, 838 warehouses worldwide,
119 million cardholders, and a membership renewal rate of 93 percent
in the United States and Canada.[2]

Since 2014, Sinegal has been coming to my class every year. After class,
we take a group of students on a tour of the Costco warehouse in Waltham,
a suburb of Boston. In the following pages, I'll share what we have learned
from him.

Investing in People Is Obvious!

Costco has been offering the highest pay and the best benefits in retail from its beginning. In 2021, the median hourly wage for Costco's hourly employees was over $25, more than 80 percent higher than the median hourly wage for retail salespeople, which was $13.79. In 2020, 89 percent of Costco's employees were eligible for health benefits and 97 percent of those eligible were enrolled.[3] (Unlike the unfortunate employees mentioned in chapter 2, Costco frontliners can afford their own company's health plan.) Costco offers a consistent forty hours for full-time employees and more than twenty-five hours for most part-timers. Department, warehouse, and field management positions are filled almost 100 percent from within. "We have put a priority on loyalty to the people we have working in our company," Sinegal told my students. "We are creating careers for people. Not just jobs. They are opportunities for success." Promotion from within applies to the home office, too. Corporate employees and many pharmacists also come from the front lines—they put themselves through college while working at the warehouses.

Costco's average employee tenure in 2021 was nine years. Sixty percent of employees had been there for five or more years, 33 percent for more than ten years.[4] Turnover of employees who have been with Costco for at least a year is about 6 percent.

Costco's investment in people is extraordinary in retail, but that's not how Sinegal sees it. He thinks it's the obvious strategy. (That is what I mean by "thinking different.") "It's not altruism," he always tells my students, "It's good business." When I asked him how he had gained his original and rather unintuitive conviction that paying such high wages while competing on low cost would be profitable, he said:

> Seventy cents of every dollar we spend to run our company goes to people.[5] So if you think about it, all the other costs of running your business—rent and utilities and supplies and fixtures and

everything else—are only 30 cents. Well, that tells you pretty significantly how important people are. It is a people business. If you don't do that well, you are going to screw up your company pretty badly. And we think that we've proven that we're getting better productivity that works when you're paying higher wages.

He added: "I guess it's easy to look and say the job is not worth more than $10 an hour. I suppose that's an easy conclusion to come to. But it's a fool's errand to think that you can hire somebody for $10 an hour and that they are going to stay with you for any length of time. If you have your managers running out there and hiring the first warm body that walks in the building . . . they are not managing their business anymore."

To the leaders of the retailers I studied for my first book, investment in people is so obvious that they are puzzled as to why anyone would choose *not* to operate that way. "Paying people more than they expect has been one of QuikTrip's secrets to success, even though it's never been a secret at all," wrote cofounder Chester Cadieux. "QuikTrip attracted better people and kept them longer. Reduced turnover saved time and money. It was such a simple idea I was (and am still) shocked that our competitors never copied it."[6] (In 2019, the average tenure of a part-time employee at Quik-Trip was two years. For a night assistant, a full-time entry job, average tenure was four years. Store manager tenure was sixteen years and assistant manager tenure was nine years. In 2021, if you started as a full-timer at QuikTrip in Tulsa, Oklahoma, you could have made more than $44,000 in your first year. One hundred percent of frontline managers are promoted from within.)

Joe Coulombe, founder of Trader Joe's, wrote, "Time and time again, I am asked why no one successfully replicated Trader Joe's. The answer is that no one has been willing to pay the wages and benefits and thereby attract—and keep—the quality of people who work at Trader Joe's. . . . Grocers seem to spend more effort squeezing payroll than squeezing cost of goods sold, though there is at least five times more opportunity to save money in the latter."[7]

Todd Miner at Costco

One Saturday, when I was visiting Costco in Waltham, Massachusetts, I could see Todd Miner's frustration from far away. Todd is the meat manager, and the meat area is behind a glass window, so customers can see what's going on inside. "You see this rib eye?" he asked me. It looked all right to me, but not to him. "The fat trim is supposed to be a quarter-inch thick," he explained. "When there's more fat, it's not good for members. When there's less, we can lose eight pounds of meat per day, which means over $2,000 a month of hidden shrink, just for the rib eye. These are not a quarter-inch thick!" It was amazing to me that Todd could immediately tie the fat on the rib eye to performance for Costco. Not meeting the standard was not acceptable to Todd. What it meant to him was that *he* had to do a better job teaching his staff.

When Todd comes to my class at MIT Sloan, he talks about his expectations, from the fat trim on the rib eye to the right type of overhead light to make sure the presentation is right. "You always find ways to raise your standards," he says. You can feel his pride when he talks about how he has the lowest shrink in the region and among the highest sales. "I paid for my payroll with the sales from endcaps," he told me one day, signaling how well he and his team had presented their merchandise.

Investment in People Is Obvious
If You Want to Win with Customers

Sinegal's retail career began in 1954 working for Sol Price, the founder of Fed-Mart, a chain of discount stores. At eighteen, his first job was to unload mattresses. He ended up working twenty-four years for Price. He often says that his business success came from what he learned from Price, especially Price's business philosophy and values.

How could meat managers at mediocre retailers even have time to worry about the trim on the rib eye? They are worried about filling in for someone who didn't show up that day, dealing with a constant influx of new employees because turnover is so high, and other problems caused by a system of mediocrity. Todd, on the other hand, can focus on meeting the highest standards because Costco—the system in which his own work is embedded—runs well. He knows about each product because Costco carries fewer products. Todd has a stable team who show up at work on time. He really knows his team—their individual and collective strengths and weaknesses, what they care about. He takes satisfaction in the people who are promoted. He points with pride to Angela, the deli manager, and Pedro, a meat manager: "They are my protégés." He knows that no one has been promoted just because somebody had to fill the slot. He knows that anyone on his team who is promoted has earned it and that he helped them earn it.

I've known Todd for a long time now. He's very talented and quite passionate about what he does—he even has a butcher's knife tattoo on his arm. He may be the best meat manager at Costco. So even if you put Todd in a vicious-cycle company, he could still shine. But Costco, like other good jobs companies, tries to make every manager shine—even those who do not have their work tattooed on their arm!

Price's philosophy was simple. The first fiduciary duty of a company was to the customers: provide customers the best value possible—excellent products at the lowest prices. In a memo to staff in 1967, he wrote, "Margin must never be done at the expense of our philosophy. Margin must be obtained by better buying, emphasis on selling the kind of goods we want to sell, operating efficiencies, lower markdowns, greater [inventory] turnover, etc. Increasing the retail prices and justifying it on the basis that we are still 'competitive' could lead to a rude awakening as it has with so many."[8]

You can see the prioritization of customers at Costco. Since 1983, Costco's operational mission has been to bring members quality goods and services at the lowest possible price. Strong operational execution is critical for achieving that mission. Poor handling of fresh produce or frozen products could increase costs significantly. If employees forget or don't have time to replenish empty shelves, sales will be lost. High volume is key for keeping costs low and paying employees well; Costco can't achieve high volume if customers aren't processed quickly at checkout, if empty boxes aren't immediately removed from the shelves, or if shopping carts are not brought back in from the parking lot. Reducing costs requires continuous improvement. The company can't improve if managers never have time to observe operations calmly and carefully and don't hear ideas from the people doing the work.

When Sinegal takes my students on a tour of a Costco warehouse, they see how he can look at the store through the eyes of the customer, attentive to the details of each product and to how it is priced and presented. He'll point out a jar of Kirkland brand cashews and talk about their size, consistency, and freshness. He'll point out some Kirkland shirts and invite the students to touch them and feel the quality and compare the price to others. I once saw him write a note to himself to look into why strawberries in the Waltham warehouse were cheaper than those in a California warehouse he had just visited. But that amount of attention to detail is not just Sinegal; it's pervasive throughout Costco. And the point here is that it matters because, in Jim Sinegal's eyes, *the frontline work matters*. It's not just stocking shelves and sweeping floors. It's what gives members great service at low prices, which is what makes Costco valuable for investors.

Leaders outside Low-Cost Retail

Leaders of other companies in which serving customers well is a priority have also concluded that being customer centric requires you to be frontline centric.

Isadore Sharp, the founder and chairman of the Four Seasons luxury hotel chain, told me that since the founding of Four Seasons in 1960, luxury there has been defined by service. The hotel's guests count on time-saving, problem-solving, fast, personal, unobtrusive, and error-free service. A chipped plate that's unnoticed by a dishwasher, an under-staffed pressing department that makes a customer wait in his under-wear for his suit to show up, or a rude waitress could ruin the service experience and damage Four Seasons' reputation. Their goal is 100 percent satisfaction. Even an error that the guest doesn't notice is considered unacceptable. "The outcome in our industry," Sharp explains, "nor-mally depends on the frontline employees—doormen, bellmen, waiters, maids. . . . These frontline staff represent our product to our custom-ers. In the most realistic sense, they are the product."[9] That's why, whenever Sharp visits a new hotel, he gathers all the staff in a ballroom to let them know where the company is going and their role in making that happen.

If frontline employees are the product, it's unacceptable—not to men-tion, irrational—to forgo investment in their ability and motivation. Sharp used a similar logic for why Four Seasons chooses to operate with lower turnover: "The books may show that employees represent the largest share of expense. They don't show that they also earn the largest share of rev-enue."[10] (Another example of how misleading perfectly accurate numbers can be.) How could Four Seasons not invest in people when a disappoint-ing customer contact could turn a potential lifetime patron into an ex-patron griping on Tripadvisor?

Frontline employees are also where the good ideas come from. Sharp told me that not getting ideas from frontline staff to improve the busi-ness is not acceptable because "every employee knows more about some part of our work than we managers do." He then talked about the power of compounding—those small improvements add up to create a huge gap between Four Seasons and its competitors. Leveraging the knowledge of frontline workers to continuously improve value for the customer is at the heart of the Toyota Production System and Total Quality Management, too.

Sharp has been leading Four Seasons for more than sixty years. He has opened hotels all over the world, from Istanbul, Turkey, to Papagayo, Costa Rica. When I asked him how he can trust thousands of people all over the world to make important decisions for customers and the company every day, he responded with a question: "Do you know anyone who doesn't want to succeed?" Experience has shown him that people can be trusted to do their jobs: "People everywhere just want an opportunity to succeed." That's the assumption on which Sharp built his business.

In the insurance world, an exemplar of reliance on and investment in frontline work is Progressive Insurance. Its innovations for customers and its ability to do the most important things in its industry—assessing risk, servicing customers, and managing claims—better than its competitors enabled Progressive to grow its insurance revenues at an annual compounded rate of 13 percent from 1991 to 2021 and become one of the three biggest insurance companies in the United States.[11] Many insurance companies lose money on the operational side and make their money on investing.[12] Progressive has always made money on the operational side. My students asked CEO Tricia Griffith how Progressive could maintain a competitive advantage with services developed decades ago. Why hadn't the competitors copied them? Griffith replied, "Operational excellence is a mindset"—and therefore not easily copied. She went on to describe the importance of the work frontline employees do. "Claims are our product," Griffith says. Her first job at Progressive—as a claims representative trainee, crawling under cars and doing estimates in body shops—showed her how important customer service is. It matters that the claims reps have long tenure. It matters that their work is designed to enable them to shine in front of the customer. It's not surprising, then, that Progressive invests in its employees, including the frontline claims reps.

In the fast-food world, an exemplar of a good jobs system is In-N-Out Burger. Harry Snyder, the founder of In-N-Out Burger, believed that if the burgers weren't done properly, customers wouldn't come back. Attention to detail was extremely important, so he would use only four to five slices of the thick middle part of onions and beefsteak tomatoes, the crisp inner leaves of a head of lettuce, and the freshest, higher-grade meat, pota-toes, and produce. Snyder didn't believe in cutting corners. Lynsi Snyder, current CEO of In-N-Out, told *Forbes*, "We didn't ever look to the left and the right to see what everyone else is doing, cut corners, or change things drastically or compromise."[13] Because quality was so important, so was paying higher wages and keeping turnover low. When In-N-Out first started in California, the minimum wage in the state was 65 cents an hour. Snyder paid a dollar an hour, plus one free hamburger per shift. From the beginning, he also emphasized internal promotion—creating careers, not just jobs.[14]

For these leaders, creating trust with customers and employees isn't an extra burden on top of running a business. It is not in opposition to running a business. It *is* running the business. It's a big part of what enables their companies to win competitively and deliver strong returns to their shareholders. And from this customer-centric conception of what the business is, the various frontline-centric elements of the good jobs strategy flow naturally. There's just no other way to win what these lead-ers are trying to win.

But, as we will see in the next section, it requires tremendous discipline.

Discipline in Focusing on the Customer and Keeping the Core Strong

Steve Jobs famously said, "I'm as proud of what we don't do as I am of what we do." Companies that focus on the customer have tremendous discipline in keeping that focus. Costco won't carry a product if they can't save customers money on it, even if spreadsheets tell them carrying that product would improve sales and profitability. (Trader Joe's has the same policy.) For a long time, Costco didn't carry disposable diapers, a big seller in supermarkets, because they couldn't sell them any more cheaply than they were already being sold elsewhere. Data analysis would have said it was a great idea. Shoppers already in the store would be glad to pick up some diapers for no more than they'd cost anywhere else. But such a data analysis doesn't have a sense of purpose. Numbers can't remind you: we're not here to do everything—we're not the only store in the world—we're here to do what we do as well as it can possibly be done.[15]

Loss leaders are common in retail, but Sinegal believes that selling things below cost is dishonest. To ensure Costco could still make money and keep the price of its famous hot dog and drink combination at $1.50, the company started manufacturing the hot dogs in-house. (Joe Coulombe, founder of Trader Joe's, also didn't believe in tricking customers with discounts: "I have always believed that supermarket pricing is a shell game and I wanted no part of it.")

Costco has a rule for not marking up any branded item more than 14 percent and any Kirkland item more than 15 percent. Even if their costs go down and they could pocket the difference, they lower the price to stick to the markup ceiling—customers' willingness to pay is irrelevant. Sinegal tells the story of selling Calvin Klein jeans for $29.99 that others were pricing at $50 or more. When Costco buyers were able to get a shipment at a much lower price, they cut the price to $22.99. "I didn't have to go to the buyer to lower the price," Sinegal proudly explained to my students. "They did it automatically because that's what we do. . . . Do you know how tempting that is, if you got five hundred thousand pairs of jeans and you know you can make seven bucks a pair on them? Well, once you do, that's like taking heroin. You can't stop. It becomes addictive and then you've changed your business plan totally."

Costco offers only thirty-seven hundred SKUs, meaning a limited product variety within each category. Spreadsheets may show that more variety would increase sales, but Costco doesn't do it. They even have a term for this: intelligent loss of sales. Sinegal tells my students how the company almost killed off its Kirkland shirts when they added slim-fit shirts. The increased variety made it harder to predict demand and manage inventory. It reduced labor productivity at the warehouse. If standard shirts are acceptable to most members, losing the customer who doesn't buy the standard fit would be an intelligent loss of sales. Once Sinegal saw that the warehouse carried two similar air fresheners, one for $3.59 and another for $4.29. Why not just offer the better product? Selling the better product was more efficient from a labor perspective and it meant fewer returns. Losing the customer who would only buy the cheaper product was another intelligent loss of sales.

Discipline is important not just for low-cost businesses. Sharp told me, "We didn't join with frequent flier giveaways. No one is coming to Four Seasons because we have the best price." Four Seasons doesn't do loyalty programs, even though they might boost revenue and attract new customers. The company's way of boosting sales and attracting new customers is to offer consistent service and rely on word of mouth. Other Four Seasons executives have suggested to Sharp that the chain add different types of hotels to its portfolio, just as many of their competitors have done, to accelerate growth. Sharp resisted. Four Seasons would stick to operating its high-touch service, medium-size hotels.

In restaurants, Texas Roadhouse, which according to Fred Reichheld has one of the highest NPS scores in the restaurant industry, has shown remarkable discipline by continuing to open only for dinner. And if they add an item to the menu, they are required to take something else off.

Discipline in Growth—the Best, Not the Biggest

One of the biggest enemies of excellence is growing more quickly than you should just because you need to justify a high earnings multiple. High valuation can, in fact, be a curse because of the pressure it puts on unsustainable growth—to do the easy things mediocre companies do to create bad growth.

"We never set out to be the biggest retailer," Sinegal said:

> We set out to be the best retailer. . . . We're going to have the best refund policy of any retailer in the country. You're guaranteed satisfaction on everything you buy. Your membership is guaranteed 100 percent as well. We would not carry seconds or irregulars. We wouldn't use a lot of superlatives to try to push goods on people. . . . There'll be limits on how much money we would allow ourselves to make on any given product. . . . And nobody's going

to be able to say that we're making money off the backs of our employees. We're going to pay the highest wages and offer the best benefits that are available in the retail business.

Early on, the growth rate at Costco was determined by the availability of experienced managers, not the availability of capital:

> Over the years, we've had people—and, most particularly, Wall Street people—suggest to us, "These things are so successful. Why won't you open 100 [stores] a year?" Well, we wouldn't have been able to manage 100 a year. I said, "No way." . . . Anytime we look at a new market, the first question we ask ourselves is, "Who do we have to manage these places? How many managers are going to be able to come up?" . . . You would probably be surprised at how much time we spend on succession planning. . . . If we're going to promote from within our own company, we better have a pretty good succession plan in place.

Leaders bent on excellence don't decide on the growth rate by what's optimal financially. They consider what's sustainable organizationally. Can they maintain the quality of their customer offering? Can they maintain the quality of their talent? To them, growing too quickly at all costs is just another example of cutting corners. That is, it's a way to look like you're successful without running the business all that well.

Indeed, Sharp told me how he stopped growth at Four Seasons for a period when he realized that the general managers running the hotels were not strong enough. They hadn't established trust with their employees. They acted more like inspectors looking for mistakes than teachers and coaches who developed people. Some on his team complained about slowing growth, especially because the hotels were doing well financially. Some ended up leaving the company. But Sharp kept his discipline.

Progressive Insurance's objective is to grow as quickly as it can at or below a 96 combined ratio (a measure of profitability in the insurance industry), which means they have to make at least 4 percent profit on the operational side. My students were shocked when CEO Tricia Griffith said, "We won't grow if we aren't able to handle our customers in the way they deserve. There have been times where we said, we have to stop growing. And we'll pull down advertising and do some things to make sure we can take care of our customers."

These strategies stand in stark opposition to recent history, especially in the startup world, where the obsession with fast growth at all costs has driven much of the economic activity. Moving fast and breaking things, tolerating poor management and processes, ignoring profitability for a long time, and constantly changing the management team are seen as tolerable, even necessary, for the explosive growth desired.

Much of this obsession with fast growth has been due to a belief in winner-takes-all dynamics—that is, that the best performers will capture a very large share of the available rewards. That belief drove high capital investment, which then could only be justified by high growth. The winner-takes-all dynamic might be relevant when it comes to businesses built on bits and bytes with strong network effects; the success and near-monopolies of companies like Microsoft, Google, and Facebook make a somewhat persuasive case. But for businesses with real human beings delivering a product or a service, winner-takes-all doesn't seem to work—even when there are network effects. In the US ride-sharing industry, for example, researchers find that capital doesn't translate to winner-takes-all; large companies don't gain market share over time and they pay more for labor than smaller companies in the gig economy.[16] Eighty percent of gig workers do similar work for competing companies.

It's not just the startup world that has gone growth crazy. After a CEO told me about how bad things had become for his large company—operational problems, high turnover, poor customer service, poor productivity for all assets—I asked how things had gotten that bad. He said a big reason was earnings growth pressure. Their core business wasn't doing well. Productivity wasn't improving. They weren't keeping their customers and getting a bigger share of their customers' wallets. Instead, they kept opening more units, more than they could handle. They picked suboptimal locations. They gave keys to new stores to people who had never managed a store before. Their bench was so weak that many stores didn't even have a store manager or assistant manager.

Yet that strategy was keeping analysts and investors reasonably happy, even if it might be slowly wrecking the company.

Such lack of discipline in growth, good as it may look in the moment, will of course hurt in the future. Those companies' leaders know that, at some point, the music will stop. They just hope it won't stop while they are still at the helm.

Discipline in Doing the Right Thing: Making Integrity a Habit

Of all the discipline that good jobs leaders demonstrate, it's the integrity and good ethics they maintain that most surprises many observers. In business, it's easy to allow ethical slips that you find ways to justify ("No one will notice" or "Others do worse") or, worse, to operate in a way that lacks integrity simply because it's profitable and not illegal. To leaders pursuing excellence, a small compromise is just as dangerous as a big compromise. Sharp told me that small compromises are even worse because you don't notice them. He spoke of Enron and Arthur Andersen, two companies that collapsed due to unethical business practices. "Instead of asking, 'Is this decision acceptable from an accounting point of view?'" he noted, "they should have asked, 'Is this the right thing to do?'"

Sinegal wanted to help build a company that would be around for the next fifty years and become an American institution. "You don't do that by selling out when things get tough."

Over the years, he has shared several examples of when Costco did "the right thing" according to their values, even though doing so came at the expense of short-term profitability:

- Costco discovered one year that employees had paid 1.5 percentage points more in health insurance than the company said they would, so the company gave every employee a refund—several million dollars in total.

- Both Costco and one of its landlords overlooked a clause that guaranteed the landlord rent increases. After ten years, someone at Costco realized they owed the landlord more than $1 million plus reasonable interest. He asked Sinegal what he thought. "Why are you coming to me?" Sinegal asked. "The answer is obvious. You pay it." The landlord was astounded to receive a check he hadn't even realized he was owed.

- When Covid-19 hit the United States, many retailers, including supermarkets, were designated "essential" businesses. They remained open when the country shut down. During this period, many companies began paying frontline employees $2 an hour extra as hazard pay. By June 2020, companies such as Kroger had ended the hazard pay, but Costco kept it going until March 2021 and then raised starting pay from $15 an hour to $16 an hour in March 2021 and then to $17 an hour in October 2021.[17]

Doing the right thing for customers and employees may seem obvious. But why do you pay the landlord when he has no idea you owe him anything? Sinegal and the management team wanted everyone at Costco to act with integrity 100 percent of the time. They also didn't want employees to see their leaders as hypocrites. According to Costco's code of ethics, all employees—at all levels—have to:

1. Obey the law.
2. Take care of our members.
3. Take care of our employees.
4. Respect our suppliers.

If we do these four things throughout our organization, then we will achieve our ultimate goal, which is to:

5. Reward our shareholders.

Todd Miner, the Costco meat manager, told my students about the time a customer had bought regular chicken but was charged for the more expensive organic chicken because of a labeling mistake. Todd called her to let her know that Costco would be reimbursing her for the difference. She told him she never would have noticed such a small error—why was he bothering to correct it and even to call personally? Todd told my students—with pride—what he told her: "Because we are Costco and that's what we do."

Obviously, you can't just tell people to act with integrity. You have to prepare the conditions to enable them to act with integrity. Todd wouldn't have noticed that mistake with the chicken if his store operated with high turnover and he was too busy fighting fires to go over old accounts. He wouldn't be able to call a member and offer a refund if he wasn't empowered to do so or given enough time to do his job. Even if he thought calling the member was the right thing to do, he might not have done it had he worked at a company whose executives made decisions that demonstrated that they cared more about financial performance than about taking care of the customer or doing the right thing.

The Golden Rule

Most of the leaders we've discussed here will at some point mention the Golden Rule as a guiding principle for their companies. Treat others as you would like to be treated. Progressive's CEO Tricia Griffith told my students that the Golden Rule was not just words, and that Progressive's ability to stick to the Golden Rule was what had kept her at the company since she joined as a claims manager trainee in 1988. (Notice that Progressive, like other companies pursuing excellence, emphasizes internal promotion.)

When Progressive's leaders went to New Orleans after Hurricane Katrina and saw how much sewage had gotten into the water that flooded so many of their customers' cars, they made a decision to crush every car. "We were the only company that did that, and we lost millions on it because you can sell that for salvage," Griffith said. "But we wanted to do the right thing and make sure that those cars were never refurbished and driven by your sister, my mom, their daughters."

During the first few months of Covid-19, as the frequency of accidents declined dramatically, Progressive's profit margins increased—*a lot*. Griffith said, "It wasn't right. People were driving less. They should be awarded for that. So we gave them 20 percent of their premiums back." It cost Progressive more than a billion dollars.

The power of the Golden Rule in service industries is that it spreads to customers and increases their affection for the company. One of the best examples of a company that follows the Golden Rule is H-E-B. Like Costco, H-E-B did not stop Covid-19 hazard pay for its workers. Instead, they permanently increased pay for everyone—more than $2 an hour for those who have been at H-E-B for a year or more and accelerated merit pay increases for everyone else. "Texans count on H-E-B, and that means depending on our great Partners, who are the heart and soul of our business," H-E-B said in June 2020. "We believe this crisis will be around for an indeterminate amount of time and our goal is to reward our Partners for their hard work and dedication with more than temporary bonuses." Craig Boyan, H-E-B's president, told me, "Our pay strategy that we talk about with our team is 'Pay as much as we can, not as little as we can.'"

Eight months later, on February 16, 2021, Tim Hennessy, a Texas resident, posted a message on Facebook titled "The Heart of America."[18] Texas was having record low temperatures, snow and ice made roads impassable, and millions of Texans lost their electricity. Hennessy and his partner had gone to H-E-B to stock up on groceries before the next snowstorm hit. The store was packed. Halfway through their shopping, the power went out. They kept shopping and by the time they got to the checkout, there were long lines, which didn't seem to be moving. But then suddenly the line started moving quickly—much more quickly than normal. When they made it to the cashier, she asked if they had any alcohol. They said no. She then said, "Please go ahead, but we can't bag anything up for you." Hennessy and his partner were confused. How were they supposed to pay? The cashier said, "Just go ahead and be safe driving home."

They couldn't believe the generosity of H-E-B. "This is the America I know," wrote Hennessy. "I salute H-E-B for the kindness they showed us, the thoughtfulness they showed us, the generosity they showed us, and the caring that they showed us (along with the other hundreds of fellow Texans in the store at that time)."

H-E-B's kindness spread to customers, too. People were helping each other. Being kind to one another. Treating people with respect and dignity is contagious.

Measuring Success

When we work with public companies at the Good Jobs Institute, we often hear resistant executives say things like, "We have an obligation to maximize sales and EBIT." I want to be clear that as inspiring as the leaders I've discussed in this chapter are, their approach does *not* mean they care less about their investors than the "profit maximizers" do. They just maintain a different mental model for how to create value for their shareholders. (They think different.) For them, the best way to do that is to focus their efforts on continuously delivering more value to customers, and that's not possible without a stable and motivated workforce.

Adopting this customer-centric approach and hence prioritizing employees and the work they do enabled leaders like Sinegal, Sharp, Griffith, and Chester Cadieux to create outsize returns for their shareholders—in both the medium term and the long term. They knew that keeping a disciplined focus on the customer, paying attention to doing the fundamentals well, and creating a system that leverages frontline employees would confer not only profits but also continuous improvement of performance and strong differentiation. When I spent time with QuikTrip's store managers, they all told me the same thing: competitors can copy what QuikTrip sells but they can't copy QuikTrip's consistency in serving customers quickly, offering a friendly and clean environment, and having the best prices. The fact that these capacities reside in a *system* means that they cannot easily or quickly be copied.

However, adopting this customer-centric approach may be scary because customer loyalty is more difficult to measure than current profit. But remember the discussion in chapter 5; there's nothing "scientific" about ignoring or underweighting variables that are incredibly important but difficult to measure.

It's a virtuous side effect that these leaders can produce such results while also knowing that they are doing the right thing for their customers, employees, and society. The late Clay Christensen tells us—in his book, *How Will You Measure Your Life?*—that the measure he would use to evaluate his own success is the individual people whose lives he's touched. "I came to understand that while many of us might default to measuring our lives by summary statistics, such as number of people presided over, number of awards, or dollars accumulated in a bank, and so on, the only metrics that will truly matter to my life are the individuals whom I have been able to help, one by one, to become better people."[19] According to Christensen, management is among the most noble professions if it's practiced properly. As a manager, not only do you determine whether someone can put food on the table and a roof over their heads, you are also in a position to make a difference in their life eight hours a day. You have the opportunity to frame each person's work so that, at the end of every day, they go home energized and fulfilled. This isn't just a nice thought; leaders like Sharp and Sinegal and others make it their job.

It isn't lost on these leaders that their decisions affect the lives of workers and their families and the prosperity of the communities in which they operate. When they talk about employees, you hear them use words like duty, responsibility, or obligation. Chet Cadieux, CEO of QuikTrip since 2002, told my students that his father, the cofounder of QuikTrip, wanted QuikTrip employees to live the American dream, which included owning a nice house and a car. Jim Sinegal, too, felt a responsibility for the people he led: "If you understand that people have to pay for food and lodging and everything else and you try to make it possible for people to buy a home and to be able to send their kids to good schools, then you look at your business a little differently."

When you visit a Costco warehouse with Sinegal, employees want to come over and say hello. If my students are with us, Sinegal will tell them that this behavior indicates that morale is good—it's when people's heads are down that you need to be worried. Customers who recognize him stop him and thank him for creating Costco. Employees and customers want to take a picture with him. I've twice seen employees cry after thanking him for their life-changing job at Costco.

But these visits are not all hugs. Sinegal expects the warehouses to manage and display products well and the managers to be on top of the numbers—how much they sold of each category, how much inventory they have, and so on. But everyone knows that these expectations are an expression of care, not a display of power.

Over the years, students who have joined a Sinegal warehouse visit have told me that it was one of the MIT Sloan experiences they will never forget. One student told me it had been the second-best day of her life, topped only by her wedding day! For recent classes, I've been asking students who took the tour to write about their experience and share it with their classmates. Most talk about Sinegal's humility and attention to detail. Some marvel at how much Costco workers at any level know about the business and how much they care.

Many students remembered what Michele Rivera, a front-end manager at Waltham who had been with the company for twenty-six years, said: "Costco takes care of me, and I take care of Costco." It's that simple.

Wellsprings of Courage

If you are a founder and are now sufficiently inspired that you can over-come fear and doubt to pursue a good jobs strategy, you're lucky. You're building something from the ground up, so you can create good jobs and operational excellence from the start. But if you're a professional man-ager in a company already operating in mediocrity, then making system change probably seems like a risky bet. You can't ignore profitability, even in the short term. A drop in the share price could cause a drop in morale. A few quarters of poor performance could cost you your job.

Even if deep inside you know your company needs to turn its vicious cycle into a virtuous one and even if you are inspired by the leaders we've just heard from, you might conclude that this process would take too long. Why should you be the one risking your own reputation when you weren't the one who caused all that mediocrity? The vicious cycle was put in place long before you got there.

There is indeed plenty there to fear, but remember that courage is not the lack of fear. Rather, it is the capacity to do something risky or hard because—even though you are afraid—you see that it's the right thing to do. What this book—and the next four chapters in particular—can do is give you the courage it takes to move forward. To make you a little *less* afraid. We will hear leaders from retail to health care to hospitality to manufacturing explain what gave them the courage to pursue system change—specifically, the big bet on people. We will see that the benefits to be gained are greater than you might expect and the risks, though real, are less than you might expect. Much as I admire these leaders, I want to assure you that you don't have to be a superhero to join their ranks.

John Furner at Sam's Club

John Furner became the CEO of Sam's Club in 2017, when the retail chain was in need of a turnaround. Some of the stores were struggling financially. Satisfaction with products and prices was too low—a big problem given that members pay a fee to shop there. Between 2014 and 2016, same-store sales growth (not counting fuel sales) averaged 0.7 percent while for Sam's Club's biggest competitor, Costco, it averaged 5.7 percent. Employee turnover was high. Productivity was low, for some of the very reasons we've discussed (searching for items, putting out fires).

When I first met Furner in 2017, along with his COO and CHRO, he asked good questions about the good jobs system. It was clear that he understood how the elements of the system worked together to drive performance for customers, employees, and investors. When he talked about how inventory problems were just as much employee turnover problems as they were logistics problems or how inconsistent schedules resulted from inconsistent deliveries, I tried to hide my enthusiasm! Furner also believed in the importance of frontline work at the stores. His father had worked at Walmart, and he himself had started there in 1993 as an hourly worker in the gardening department. When the music career he hoped for didn't take off, he stayed at Walmart. He took on many roles, including store manager, district manager, and buyer. He served as chief merchandising officer at Sam's Club and executive vice president of merchandising and marketing at Walmart China.

As I was driving home from our dinner, I thought to myself, "Wow, he seems serious about this!" But then, I kept thinking about a comment he had made. It didn't take him more than five minutes into our dinner to recognize my admiration for Costco and Jim Sinegal. Furner pointed out that Costco and Sam's Club were both founded in 1983 and, since then, Costco had had two CEOs while Sam's Club was now on its fourteenth.

History, then, suggested that Furner would likely hold his position for about three years. Would it make sense for him to attempt a system change? Given where the company was and how many things had to be different, Sam's probably couldn't make all the necessary changes in that time span. Someone else would either have to finish the job or just abandon it as a predecessor's mistake. Could there at least be reasonable progress within a few years—enough to show he hadn't been wrong? And what about all those below him? With CEOs changing all the time, would they embrace system change or just put their heads down and wait him out?

Furner was under performance pressure. Whatever he did during his tenure as CEO would determine how people would perceive him as a leader. It would likely determine what his next job would be. He could make big investments in people and make the needed operational changes, but he was under pressure to improve sales and earnings in the short term. He could instead focus solely on digital transformation, something I could tell he was serious about, something that would take less time and meet less resistance than a good jobs strategy. He could have a clear path to success.

Furner had plenty of reasons to be afraid of pursuing system change. He went for it anyway.

Why Furner Pursued Excellence

Furner's changes included raising pay. Others in the company had cautioned him against investing in employee pay. The finance team said a pay raise was not in the budget and wouldn't pay off. HR said they had raised pay before, but it hadn't reduced turnover. Furner thanked these advisers for their feedback and then went ahead and raised pay, starting with key positions such as team leads, meat cutters, and bakery specialists.

Their pay increased by $5–$7 an hour, more than a 30 percent increase. Furner told his team, "This is what we're going to do. And the person who is accountable for it is me and if it doesn't work, please tell the next person, 'Don't do this.'"

Furner didn't simply spurn the data on pay raises, but he also knew that siloed decision-making was a barrier to making system change. He also didn't think historical data analysis would provide the answer to the question he was really asking: *How can we get turnover under control so we can create a strong membership proposition?* He and other executives were convinced that employee turnover was at the heart of many of their problems—especially inventory management and customer service.

Reducing turnover was strategic because Furner and his team were committed to making Sam's Club member focused. They started with a simple question: Why do customers choose Sam's Club in the first place? What did Sam's Club offer that would make someone pay to join as a member and then renew? A team of behavioral scientists found that what brought and kept members was getting high-quality products at low prices, being able to find what they were looking for, getting fresh food that was really fresh, and getting help from knowledgeable workers. NPS data verified these findings. For example, members' NPS rating of Sam's Club dropped by more than 30 points—a huge number—when they couldn't find an item.

Turnover hurt product availability, value, and member experience. In fresh food, turnover also hurt the products themselves—lettuce wilted, bananas rotted.

Turnover also mattered for Sam's Club's ability to adopt and scale digital technologies that would improve both the customer experience and employee productivity. Creating a seamless omniexperience, for example, required accurate inventory data, which—as we've seen—depends on a stable and motivated workforce.

Sam's Club would need help from its employees to improve and scale technology investments that would improve their own productivity. Say you are creating a system to schedule bakery production based on anticipated demand. If you do it without involving the bakery staff, it probably won't be as accurate, and the staff will resent or even resist it if it has been foisted on them rather than created with them.

Everything kept coming back to how at the heart of many challenges was a stable, motivated workforce. It kept coming back to turnover.

Furner didn't think they could reduce turnover just by raising pay, but he didn't think they could reduce it without raising pay. People were leaving for jobs that paid several dollars more an hour. Nothing management could do would ever keep people working for less than they could make elsewhere doing essentially the same job. So pay had to go up. Then it was up to Furner and his team to make that investment worthwhile by maximizing productivity and employee contribution. That, he believed, was within his and his team's power—that's what they got the big bucks for.

When Furner and COO Dacona Smith came to my MBA class in 2021, the students wanted to know how these leaders knew their strategy would work for sure. Furner didn't answer in financial terms. He didn't talk about the ROI on raising frontline pay. True to the customer-centric essence of the good jobs strategy, he talked about customers. "Customer loyalty in retail is the absence of something better," he acknowledged. But Sam's Club couldn't be anybody's "something better" without strong operational execution and a motivated and capable workforce; it could only keep customers who had nowhere better to go—not a viable long-term competitive position.

The key to being customer centric is being frontline centric and, sure enough, Furner also told the students about his belief in employees and the work they did. I don't know if he would have been that comfortable making his big bet on excellence had he not himself worked in the front lines. He *knew* the importance of that work and the difference between doing it well and not so well. He didn't need anyone like me to convince him of their value and the difference between a motivated frontliner and an unmotivated one—he'd seen it all for himself. No team of analysts with data could convince him that what he had seen in the trenches wasn't real. In January 2020, Furner told a crowd of over two thousand people at the National Retail Federation's Big Show: "I had such a belief in the team that was in the field, specifically. These were the people that work

in fulfillment centers. They cut meat. They bake bread. They run registers up front. . . . I had so much belief in the enthusiasm they had—if we
could take a bet on them—that they would do everything they could to
make it worth it for us."

Furner's bet turned out to be a good one for Sam's Club's performance
and for his own career. Later, we will look at *what* changes he and his
team made at Sam's Club and *how* they made them. Furner had confidence, but it was never a sure thing. It was a bet. Which means it took
courage.

Conviction That Investment in People Will Pay Off

Instead of asking the kind of question we saw in chapter 5—"Does investment in people pay off?"—leaders like Furner ask a more far-reaching
question: "Can we be a strong and lasting company—one that wins with
our customers and adapts to changes—if we don't invest in our people?"
The answer, in their view, is "No." How could they serve their customers
well with the corporate disabilities we saw in chapter 4—that is, if they
couldn't hire the right people, train them well, and empower them to solve
customer problems? If they couldn't even match labor supply to customer
demand? So, in their eyes, the bet on people and operations wasn't even
too risky a bet. It was a solid investment. Yes, they still had to take a leap
of faith—even solid investments carry some risk. But that leap of faith
was rooted not only in their belief in their workers, but also in their belief
that the investment would pay off, even if they couldn't quantify it
precisely.

Remember (from chapter 1) the executive who said that investment in
people is "a little bit like trying to quantify the net present value of buying a laptop. It's hard to do, but you know it's positive having a personal
computer versus not. So, it's a little bit of a leap of faith, but intuitively
you just know that some of these things will pay off." That was PayPal's
then-CFO, John David Rainey (he's now CFO at Walmart). He had worked
at Continental Airlines and recalled the CEO there, Gordon Bethune,

talking about how quickly a happy mechanic could fix a plane versus one who was mad. "So, I think," Rainey continued, "it is penny wise and pound foolish to focus just on what you're paying employees and try to make it that bare minimum to kind of get by. I think if employees are proud to work for a company that's mission-driven and they're paid appropriately, then they're going to stay a lot longer and it becomes more of a career versus just a job."

Dan Schulman, president and CEO of PayPal, had the same belief: "I believe very strongly that the only sustainable competitive advantage a company has is the skill set and passion of its employees. You show me someone who believes in the company, is financially healthy, who is passionate about what we are doing, and I think our attrition will go down—which has happened. Our training costs will go down—which has happened. Our Net Promoter Score will go up—which has happened. Eventually, that investment will pay back."

When Aetna's Mark Bertolini took his company through an exercise of "What would we need to believe to make this investment?" most of his team believed that Aetna would realize bigger benefits than the $10.5 million investment they were planning to make. The exercise helped them see that even the worst-case scenario was not bad at all.

To be fair, Aetna and PayPal both have high profit margins and their low-wage employees make up only a small portion of their overall costs. Quest's call centers also make up a small portion of Quest's overall costs. Taking a leap of faith was therefore easier for these companies. They didn't have to bet the farm. But how about retailers or restaurants, for whom profit margins are in the single digits and low-wage employees make up the biggest operating cost? For a retailer whose labor costs are, say, 10 percent of sales and whose profit margins are 3 percent—fairly ordinary numbers in that industry—a 30 percent raise for frontline employees, like the one at Aetna, could wipe out profitability in the short term. The patient could die before the medication kicked in.

Yet even the leaders in that industry with whom I've worked don't consider the bet too risky. First, the business case is clear for them. They can all imagine the upside. As with Rainey's example of buying a laptop, these

CEOs couldn't precisely quantify that upside, but it was obvious to them that they would be able to increase their sales, reduce their costs, and achieve higher productivity—a very big upside indeed. And they could already see companies like Costco and QuikTrip thriving with good jobs.

Mud Bay, a pet products chain in the Northwest, didn't need much data to justify a good jobs system. Co-CEOs Lars and Marisa Wulff didn't even believe that one *could* quantify the benefits. As Lars Wulff explained:

> I grew up in business loving Excel. At the same time, [my sister Marisa and I] both understand very clearly that the business we're in is a business of human beings and that those human beings are making decisions every second that affect what shows up or doesn't show up in Excel. So, I think when you look at something like the cost of pay raises, there is no way that we could say, "It's going to cost us this and we can be confident that we will make it up with this, this, and this." What we had to do is say fundamentally, "We're not paying people enough. If we want to be the sort of company that we want to become, if we want a retention rate of 80 percent or 90 percent, if we want people to love their job, we're going to have to pay more." Ultimately, we will have to make the bottom line work, but the truth is that a bottom line is composed of a few hundred lines on an income statement. Although it may be appealing at some emotional level, the reality is that it's very difficult to say this moved 14 basis points in one direction and I made it up with 8 basis points here, 5 basis points here, and 1 basis point there. It's not reality. It's fiction.

Professional managers of public companies, however, do not have the luxury of saying, "Numbers be damned. This is the right thing to do and we'll make it work." Answerable to their board and investors, most have to be able to make the case in advance with numbers. Let's look at how one CEO did it.

At the end of a workshop with FastMarket, a convenience store chain with more than two hundred stores, the participants were pumped up.[1]

Their stores operated with more than 100 percent employee turnover and more than 40 percent manager turnover. Most of their full-time employees were not making a living wage. Their stores were full of problems. They knew they could do much better for their customers and employees if they invested in their people and strengthened their operations. But the company was already profitable. So would the board and their owners let them do this, especially given the pay raises that would be needed? "Will we be allowed to take this journey?" they asked. "Can we afford to invest in people?" The CEO answered: "I turn that question around and say can we afford not to? We are trapped in a vicious cycle." He pointed out that they were spending the money anyway—in turnover, in errors, in lost sales. Better to spend a pile of money on success than on eventual failure. What if a stronger competitor entered their market? he asked. Could they even survive?

But they couldn't just tell the board that they had to get out of the vicious cycle. "To simply say 'We want to be the best-in-class retailer' is probably not good enough," said an executive who was leading the implementation team. The board would want to know what return management expected to generate from this investment. They would want to know some of the key measures of progress along the way.

To articulate the business case for making system change, quantifying the direct cost of turnover is critical but not sufficient. If your company is like most other companies with low-wage workers, you won't be able to justify the investment by just showing how it lowers the direct costs of turnover. In many companies, direct turnover costs are around 10–25 percent of total payroll costs. So even cutting direct turnover costs by half would only amount to 5–12.5 percent of the payroll costs. So far, the Good Jobs Institute has worked with only one company whose turnover costs were so high (45 percent of payroll costs, because employees had to be licensed) that cutting those costs by a quarter would be enough to justify bringing all full-timers to a living wage.

But for FastMarket—and for any company operating in mediocrity—the potential upside was much higher than just lowering direct turnover costs. As we saw in chapter 3, the costs of poor operational execution are much higher than the direct turnover costs. Benchmark data from the National Association of Convenience Stores allowed FastMarket to compare itself with top performers in their industry. How much could they reduce the gap between themselves and these top performers? Even a small increase in sales would pay for much of the investment they wanted to make. They knew their own costs of overtime pay and cost of goods sold—but how much could they reduce those costs by moving from mediocrity to excellence? Even by *starting* to move from mediocrity to excellence? And then there were all the productivity gains that could be expected from a well-paid, well-motivated, carefully empowered workforce.

Higher sales, lower costs, and higher productivity from better operational execution are the three benefits that companies can estimate that affect profitability *now*. But having a stronger company with stable employees, strong operations, and better customer service also provides benefits beyond immediate profits. In fact, most of any company's market value is based on the expectations for how it will perform in the future, not on current profitability. And that's where the biggest benefit of this journey really is. Remember from chapter 4 that when you operate with high turnover, there are many things you can't do—you can't hire the right people and train them well, you can't empower or create trust, you can't manage capacity, you can't have strong unit managers, you can't have high expectations. That weak system may be profitable now, but it is less competitive. If you're operating in excellence rather than mediocrity, you create confidence among your investors (and your own management team). They will see how you adapt to change. They will see new levels of same-unit growth. They will reward you with an improved price-to-earnings ratio. Maybe not right away, but soon.

Raffaella Sadun and her colleagues' research cited in chapter 4 also highlights competitive benefits. Companies with operational excellence not only outperform their competitors in terms of operating profit and productivity, but also are more innovative, with more patents per employee, higher R&D expenditures, and higher output growth.

Operations Reduce the Riskiness of People Investment

There's another reason why the leaders even of low-margin businesses could feel reasonably safe taking a leap of faith on people investment. The four operational choices of the good jobs system—focus and simplify, standardize and empower, cross-train, operate with slack—fundamentally changed the risk profile of people investment by improving employee productivity and contribution. Low margins make it difficult to consider higher pay, especially when you know that the benefits won't come right away. But if you can raise pay and simultaneously improve employees' work so that each unit of labor would, by design, generate more output, then you've solved the problem. The leaders who make the bet reason that if those four operational choices work in companies as varied as Costco, Four Seasons, In-N-Out Burger, Shouldice Hospital in Ontario (dedicated to repairing hernias), and the mighty Toyota, that's plenty of evidence that it can work at their company.[2]

It can. And in fact, it always could have. You see, I didn't invent or even discover any of those operational choices. They have long been considered best practices in management—as long as you can trust your workers! Scholars from strategy to operations to psychology have been talking about them for decades. Have you ever heard a strategy professor argue that companies should be all things to all people? Of course not—strategy is choice—but it takes courage to choose. Have you ever heard anyone in the business world say that the path to higher labor productivity and customer satisfaction is increasing operational complexity? Of course not—people have been talking about the costs of complexity for decades! Have you ever seen a business book argue that you should *not* empower people or cross-train them so they can do a variety of tasks and feel ownership of their work?

The most counterintuitive of the four operational choices is to operate with slack, but in fact, any operations management professor will tell you that in an environment with variability, the optimal strategy *is* to operate with slack. In that field, there is one theory that works almost like the laws of physics: queuing theory, which shows that as capacity utilization increases the average queue size and the average waiting time, both increase in a highly nonlinear fashion.[3] Running near 100 percent capacity in a volatile system inevitably leads to slowdowns and poor performance. The more variability there is in the system, the more extra capacity you want available. Put in ordinary terms: when there's a lot going on, you shouldn't rely on nothing going wrong.[4]

That theory is ignored *constantly* in practice because most managers believe in being "lean" when it comes to labor. That's why we see "optimized" schedules with four-hour shifts, processes that assume employees can finish a ten-minute task in ten minutes and never be interrupted by customers, and performance management systems that punish managers if they assign more hours than they are budgeted.

We saw in chapter 3 how the four operational choices played out for the call centers at Quest Diagnostics. Although Quest was now paying more for each unit of labor, each unit of labor was now generating much more value than the increased wage. Pay went up, but call volume went down *19 percent*. Most important, as Quest invested in people and implemented the four choices, its corporate disabilities became abilities. Now they could hire better. Now they could create trust. Now they could manage capacity. Now they could really focus on the customer. Now they could have strong managers and hold their people to high expectations.

Leaders Who Had Conviction That the Good Jobs System Would Drive Strong Results at Their Companies

Skepticism from executives and leaders is inevitable, but since 2014, when my first book came out, I've been surprised that I haven't gotten *more* pushback about the good jobs strategy. Instead, many leaders reached out to tell me they were living in the vicious cycle I described—but now they could see a way out. They could see themselves making specific changes that would help them create a stronger company. And they came from industries expected and unexpected: retail, of course, but also health care, food services, financial services, senior living, and manufacturing. I heard from the CEO of a two-unit restaurant, a hotel/casino, and a paint business.

If you aren't sure yet that this book really applies to your company or your industry, this sampling of some of those interactions might change your mind.

Lars Wulff, co-CEO of the pet products chain Mud Bay, emailed me in 2014 that the leadership team had read *The Good Jobs Strategy* and had been talking about its application at Mud Bay's thirty stores. "We've all admired Costco and Trader Joe's for years," he wrote, "and we're all equally motivated by a love of operational efficiency and a drive to do right by the people we work with and for." From 2014 to 2017, Mud Bay raised its average hourly wage by 24 percent and increased the percentage of people who worked more than thirty hours a week—and hence received benefits—from 69 percent to 82 percent. That's massive for a company with 2 percent profit margins and store-level labor costs that were more than 10 percent of sales. If it hadn't worked, the expenses would indeed have sunk the company. But, like Quest, Mud Bay simultaneously made changes to improve employee productivity. So, just as at Quest, labor became more expensive but also became even more productive and valuable.

Greg Foran, CEO of Walmart in the United States from 2014 to 2019, reached out to me, and we spent a day touring stores in the Boston area and talking about the four operational choices and the investments he and his team had begun making at Walmart. Foran told *Harvard Business Review* that the concepts in the book were

> so blindingly obvious: If you simplify operations, standardize work processes, and empower your employees, you will get better results. I particularly liked the empower process. Just standardizing isn't good enough. . . . I've been working in retail for forty years. If you don't give people some surety around how many hours they will be given and what their schedules will be like, you create problems. I've watched businesses I've been associated with

do things like cut people's jobs back so that they get three hours here on Tuesday and four hours there on Wednesday. You can address that through cross-training so that when there's downtime in one type of job, people can perform another.[5]

That conviction helped Foran make many courageous changes at Walmart—including increasing pay, improving schedules, and simplifying the business. He left Walmart US stronger than he found it, before going back home to lead Air New Zealand.

JaNessa Bumgarner, the CEO of Lucky Eagle Casino and Hotel, said in an interview that after reading *The Good Jobs Strategy*, she started shopping at Costco and Trader Joe's more and could see for herself how different their service was. That gave her confidence to begin raising pay and making operational changes at Lucky Eagle. Bumgarner was convinced that getting on this journey was the right thing to do. "The tribe has always wanted to be a good partner in the community. The best way to be a good partner is to provide jobs that are economy boosters. . . . We shouldn't be offering less than a stimulus check. We should have people who are committed to us."[6]

Investors who have conviction in the good jobs system

During the last six years, many investors have reached out to me and to the Good Jobs Institute. I was surprised to hear from Charlie Penner, then at Jana Partners, an investment company that engages in shareholder activism. I had always associated activist investors with short-term value creation for shareholders, often at the expense of customers and employees. That might mean cutting investment in people or R&D, stock buybacks, capital restructuring, or selling parts of the business. To me, this approach was exemplified by the famous activist Carl Icahn's hostile takeover of Trans World Airlines and then selling its assets, or Eddie Lampert buying Sears and underinvesting in everything from store renovations to people. Why would someone like Penner be interested in the good jobs strategy?

But as I got to know Penner, I came to appreciate how his approach has evolved toward long-term value creation for shareholders. He is interested in finding opportunities where citizens' and shareholders' concerns overlap. When he came to my class, he told my students that he found good jobs compelling because it made companies stronger and more adaptable in the long run. My students were as surprised as I had been to hear Penner talk about cross-training and operating with slack. He had even identified a retailer that could benefit from the good jobs strategy and had worked to make a case for shareholders. Sadly, another activist approached that same company and that one may not push for people investment.

In 2022, Fred Lynch, an operating partner at AEΛ, a private equity group, asked me to present to their portfolio companies. Lynch was exposed to the good jobs strategy when he was the CEO of Masonite, a door manufacturer, where he had seen the combination of higher pay with strong operations succeed. At the end of my talk, he told the participants that it could look scary to raise pay but encouraged them to consider it as part of a system. He asked the group, "Did you ever think that an operating partner at a PE firm would be advocating for higher pay?" But it wasn't just higher pay he was advocating for; it was fixing the whole system.

The private equity arm of Two Sigma Investments that's focused on impact investing is putting its money where its mouth is. Right before the pandemic, the Good Jobs Institute started working with them to improve frontline jobs and operations. The pandemic delayed our work, so as I write this book we are still in the early stages. But our hope is that within a few years we will create case studies for other private equity companies showing that they can create value within a reasonable time by improving jobs and operations.

Reasons You're Afraid to Bet on People

Leaders take risks and pursue large-scale change initiatives all the time. But somehow, it seems easier to take risks on capital investments or on deals than on people. Why is that? My colleagues at the Good Jobs

Institute and I have asked many company leaders and investors that very question. Keep in mind: these are ambitious people who are not risk-averse. Here are the biggest reasons they gave us for being afraid to bet big on people.

1. You can't quantify the benefit

Leaders are generally more comfortable estimating the benefits of technology, marketing, or even R&D investments than the benefits of people and operations investments. It's much easier to invest in changes that you think will improve specific measures, all else being constant. For example, when you invest in automating a process, you may think you have a good sense of the savings from reduced labor hours. When you invest in systems to improve forecasting or managing inventory, you may have a good sense of how much sales will increase or inventory holding costs will decrease. When you invest in digital marketing, you can estimate how much sales will increase. In all these cases, looking analytically at the effect of a given investment on performance *in isolation* could give you enough confidence to make that investment. What is more, some of these investments have short payback periods, measured in months.

But with people investment, such analysis is a slippery realm in which all else *isn't* constant. In companies like Sam's Club, where profit margins are thin and frontline employees make up a large portion of expense, you can't just raise pay or increase hours—you need to make the operational changes that improve productivity and contribution, which is what pays for the increase in labor costs. (That's not *all* it does, of course.) There are too many variables to make numerical predictions; you have to imagine what the benefits could be, like leaders at Aetna and FastMarket did, and *believe* it will work. No matter how much data someone like me serves up, it still requires a leap of faith that system change is possible and will be worthwhile.

By now, though, I hope you have more conviction concerning near-term benefits to the bottom line (the sales lift, cost savings, and productivity improvements) and concerning the longer-term benefits that come from increasing the earnings multiple by creating a stronger company that can adapt to changes and differentiate in the eyes of customers. So that leap of faith is rooted in strong evidence, logic, and even in some numbers.

2. Investors and the board aren't interested in good jobs

The second reason for fear is *institutional isomorphism*.[7] That is, organizations end up adopting certain practices not because they are efficient but because they have legitimacy in the eyes of outside stakeholders—for example, the practice we saw in chapter 2 of benchmarking wages against other mediocre players in the industry. Technology investments or even mergers and acquisitions tend to have more legitimacy—in the eyes of investors and the board—than people investments do. Such investments are easier to justify, even without rigorous data analysis, and the board and investors may even be pushing for them. Growing quickly generally has legitimacy in the eyes of investors.

When people are unsure about how they or their firms should act, they fall victim to a powerful force described by psychologist Robert Cialdini—social proof. That is, they imitate what they see others doing, especially organizations similar to them. In retail, for example, a lot of company leaders blindly imitate Amazon because they are constantly challenged: "Amazon is doing this; why aren't you?" During the pandemic, when analysts kept asking Costco's leaders why they weren't doing things others were doing, such as same-day delivery from stores and allowing customers to buy online and then pick up at stores, CEO Craig Jelinek and CFO Richard Galanti kept talking about Costco's model. It didn't make economic sense for them to pursue those options, successful as they might be for some other company. When analysts pushed them on why Costco doesn't open more units when there are so many opportunities, they responded that their hands-on model requires them to grow more slowly and that they feel good about it and feel no urge to mess with it.[8]

Jim Sinegal tells my students that a business shouldn't imitate others' success, but rather embellish its own strengths. "I think the worst thing you can do is to try to run your business the way someone else tells you that you should run it."

Given the demographic trends and tight labor markets that are expected to continue, investing in people may become more legitimate. As investors get more savvy about operational mediocrity, they may begin seeing the risks of investing too little in people and start asking for data related to turnover and pay. It is telling that there was so little pushback from investors when Costco continued its $2 Covid-19 frontline wage premium after others stopped it or when it permanently raised pay. Investment in people may also be more legitimate if leaders have credibility and can clearly explain why they are making the investment. Mark Bertolini told me, "When I announced our wage increase at the J. P. Morgan conference in 2015, we had over two-thirds of our shares sitting in the room. And nobody gave me a problem with it. Nobody."

3. Accounting systems disfavor it

When companies invest in technology or R&D, they can capitalize the investment. People investment is recognized as an immediate expense on the income statement. The tax code that favors technology investment also increases the incentive to invest in "so-so" technologies. This is one area where a change in policies could help.

What's more, people investment seems irreversible. Wages are sticky. Once you increase them, it's hard to go back. On the other hand, rewards like bonus programs and tuition reimbursements, which cost less, allow those in the compensation department to sleep at night, thinking they *are* investing in workers, regardless of whether employees have enough money in their bank account when the water bill comes due. But, as we'll see in chapter 9, you don't have to make the whole investment at once. Just as there is a vicious cycle, there is a virtuous cycle. Once you get that going, it becomes easier to continue making investments.

4. Implementation risks seem too high

Leaders have heard too many stories about "lean" implementations that failed or that took too long or were difficult to sustain. Adopting a good jobs system can look equally daunting. Any CEO would have to wonder: "Will my company be able to make the changes in a reasonable amount of time? What will my board or investors say?"

Other types of investment seem easier and faster. And it's true, they are—but they don't fix your problems. They don't make you more than mediocre. In fact, they often make your core weaker. The "Implementation" part of the book addresses this fear.

5. You might look naive

Some leaders fear that the workers may take advantage of them or, in the end, won't justify the investment made in them. What if they don't work hard even with higher pay and better jobs? Wouldn't you look naive if you raised everyone's pay and still got the same low productivity and high turnover you had before? That's not a risk when you make capital investments. Interestingly, there's less of this fear when it comes to investing in pay or benefits for higher-level employees, which are treated more as "real investments" versus expenses. Time to ask again: Could it be that you are a Theory X manager who fundamentally discounts the value of frontline work and distrusts workers' ability and motivation?

The examples in this book should help you overcome this fear. The principle of reciprocity has been widely documented; your employees are not likely to take you for a ride. Besides, companies that operate in excellence have—and enforce—high expectations. The workers who don't measure up don't keep their jobs.

Results

Even if I have convinced you that the leap of faith these leaders took was justified, you might still ask: Was the leap sufficiently rewarded? Yes, it was.

The companies that began their excellence journey saw significant improvements in employee turnover. At Quest Diagnostics call centers, turnover dropped by more than 50 percent within eighteen months. Absenteeism dropped from 12.4 percent to 4.2 percent. At PayPal, turnover at call centers dropped from 19.4 to 7.3 percent in a year, a 62 percent decrease. Mud Bay's turnover dropped 35 percent in three years, from 48 to 31 percent. Turnover of team leads at Sam's Club decreased substantially after their pay increased and their job design improved. Within two years all hourly turnover (excluding the first ninety days) decreased by 25 percent and store manager turnover decreased by 29 percent.

All these companies saw higher sales, lower costs, and improved productivity. At Quest, despite spending more money on reps, overall costs decreased by $2 million. Improvement ideas, most of which came from the reps, saved the company $1.3 million a year, or about $1,400 per rep. Call transfer rates dropped from 12 percent to 9.5 percent, so customer satisfaction increased. Within two years, Sam's Club's NPS increased 7 percent and sales grew by $15 billion—almost 15 percent—without opening new stores. And Sam's began closing the gap with Costco. From 2019 to 2021, Sam's Club's same-store sales growth averaged 7.4 percent, while Costco's averaged 9.3 percent. Productivity, measured as units sold per labor hour, increased 16 percent. In summer 2021, about two and a half years into Sam's Club's journey, Doug McMillon, the CEO of Walmart, who had served as Sam's Club's CEO from 2005 to 2010, talked about the record growth in membership: "Nineteen years ago, I got the opportunity to become chief merchant at Sam's. And I can confirm there hasn't been a time in the last nineteen years when Sam's has had this much momentum."[9]

In three years, sales-per-square-foot at Mud Bay increased from $317 to $394—a 25 percent increase—compared to a 9 percent increase in the industry during that time. Sales per labor hour increased from $133 to $149—that's $128 more in sales for every worker's eight-hour shift. Mud Bay online reviews averaged 4.8 or 4.9 on a scale of 1 to 5. During this period, profit margins dropped from 2.2 percent to 2 percent, but a big reason for that drop was a reduction in prices and an increase in home office staff from thirty-six to fifty-six people.

I have more examples to share with you, including a one-unit restaurant, a two-store nonprofit retailer, and a factory. I am saving those for chapter 9. We will see similar results: lower turnover, higher customer satisfaction and sales, lower costs, and higher productivity.

Remember: reduced direct turnover costs and better operational execution are just the outcomes that one can demonstrate with data. There are competitive benefits that emerge from a good jobs system that are harder to quantify—such as a company's ability to adapt to change and its ability to differentiate itself from competitors in the eyes of its customers and employees. During Covid-19, Sam's Club quickly devised curbside and concierge services. In October 2021, when so many retailers were having trouble staffing their stores, Sam's Club CEO Kath McLay said the retailer had had full employment for months. The turnover reductions noted above are even more impressive when one considers what was happening in the labor market. That was a period of record quit rates in the United States.

For Mud Bay, the less quantifiable benefits were essential, such as connection with customers in a highly competitive market. During its implementation, as Mud Bay's business was thriving, I asked my MBA class if anyone shopped there. One student immediately raised her hand. She loved Mud Bay because the staff had been so helpful and empathetic to her through a string of cat problems. This was extremely valuable for that class of ambitious future business leaders to hear, as were Lars Wulff's own words, when he said, "The good jobs strategy has made us the sort of organization that is much more likely to be here—healthy, growing, and profitable—ten and twenty years from now than we would be otherwise."[10]

These companies are stronger and in a better position to adapt to changes. But, since the beginning of the pandemic, things haven't been all roses for their employees—even at companies that have always pursued good jobs and operational excellence. Those whose companies were considered essential businesses during the early months of the pandemic kept working while risking their health. They were the ones who got yelled at by customers who didn't want to wear masks. Higher demand, some of which came from other businesses that couldn't keep their doors open due to worker shortages, significantly increased their workload. At the same time, hiring became harder when there were more jobs than people willing to take them. (So much so that QuikTrip raised pay significantly. In 2022, full-timers could start at $50,000. Part-time hourly pay was up to $20 an hour.) Then came supply-chain problems in the form of long lead times, unpredictable deliveries, and out-of-stocks followed by too much inventory. These days, inflation has made customers increasingly frustrated and ill-tempered, another hardship for frontline employees.

Despite all the hardship, these workers kept showing up. It's a good time to invest even more in them.

Summon Your (Well-Founded) Courage

Leaders of many kinds of companies—public and private, large and small, competing on low cost or on differentiation—have been able to start off on an excellence journey and make great progress. Even the world's largest company by revenue—Walmart—is taking steps in this direction. I hope the financial and competitive benefits these companies have achieved in a reasonably short time will encourage you—which means *give you courage*—to begin the journey in your own organization.

Remember that what all these leaders have in common, from Mary-Ann Camacho at Quest to John Furner at Sam's Club to JaNessa Bumgarner at Lucky Eagle Casino, is a belief in their frontline workers. Furner and Bumgarner both started in the front lines. Bumgarner was a busser, cleaning tables. She knew jobs on the front lines were not easy: "You are dealing with people, germs, cups, and the whole time, people are expecting the front line to provide amazing service."

Escaping mediocrity and getting to excellence requires designing a system based on trusting workers. That doesn't automatically mean you have to trust everyone. We saw that at NUMMI, after implementing the Toyota Production System, most of the former GM employees ended up doing just fine. But about 4 percent of them didn't make it. At Quest, almost all reps thrived in the new system, but about 3 percent didn't. As McGregor argued, building a system assuming trust enables trust.

And for a while, it may cost more money than it delivers to make this change. How do you get over that hump? In the next chapters, we'll see how these companies and others have been able to implement system change without breaking the bank.

From these brave leaders, I've learned that implementing system change is not as daunting as it may seem. Yes, excellence is harder to achieve than mediocrity. It requires discipline. It's like maintaining a healthy body—you need to eat right, exercise, limit bad habits, and sleep well; and you need to keep doing those things as long as you want to stay healthy. But if you have the courage to prioritize this journey to excellence and are thoughtful about what changes to make first, other tactical steps of implementation are not that different than any other change.

Actually, there is one clear difference. This change, unlike many in business, appeals not only to people's heads but also to their hearts. People know it's the right thing to do and want to feel good about what they do. At a convenience store chain—one month into their journey—we asked, "How can you create urgency around the good jobs system across the company?" An executive was quick to reply, "We don't need urgency. We all want to do this so badly."

IMPLEMENTATION

Make the Case

Let's get down to work. I can't give you a step-by-step playbook for how to adopt the good jobs system in your own organization. The right moves will vary from company to company. But I can give you the essential ingredients you need to make the right moves. My biggest lesson in "implementation" during the last eight years has been that there are three essential ingredients without which successful adoption is unlikely. We will go through these one by one in this and the next two chapters.

The first essential ingredient is aligning the organization—especially the upstream functions that affect frontline work—to prioritize this system change. The second is making the right changes first so that you get on a virtuous cycle as quickly as possible. The third is learning how to maintain momentum and sustain the good jobs system. By understanding these ingredients—and why they matter—you can identify the specific elements of system change needed in your company that best fit your situation.[1]

* * *

In 2015, the CEO of a large retailer reached out because he was interested in adopting the good jobs system. He was confident in his company's ability to make investments—even before they were necessary—in technology, supply chain, store renovations, and so on. And he saw investment in people as something his company could easily do. Our first project was to quantify the cost of the status quo to develop urgency and alignment. My students and I collected, cleaned, and analyzed data from hundreds of units and tens of thousands of employees. We quantified the direct cost of turnover and the costs of poor operational execution. When we presented the total financial costs of mediocrity to the leadership team—including the CEO, CFO, and COO—they cared enough that a year and a half later, when we started the Good Jobs Institute, they became our first company partner.

A few years later, the CEO of a financial services company reached out because he was interested in creating more good jobs in America. After hearing more about the good jobs strategy, including the examples you've read about here, he empowered his team to identify how they could profitably make their call center jobs good jobs.

Yet neither of those two companies got much further on adopting the good jobs system, because neither could prioritize it. Yes, they could see that the investment could pay off financially, but in the eyes of the C-level leaders, it didn't seem like it was something they *needed* to do to thrive or survive. It wasn't solving a particular business problem related to growth or increasing margins. In short, it was seen as worthwhile, but not essential—not a matter of corporate life or death. As a result, there was insufficient urgency in making the necessary changes.

Leaders have to choose how to divide their time and attention among many potentially good investments. Even if you've run the numbers and quantified all the costs of mediocrity, some other investment—say, acquiring a company, implementing a new technology, focusing on pricing, or adding a new sales channel—will always be competing with it, and those other investments could bring a higher return with less time, effort, and risk.

For companies that did make progress, investment in people and strong operations were more than a nice-to-have, long-term goal. Leaders who do take it on have been convinced—and they say out loud—that the status quo is intolerable, and a system change is necessary in order to grow and compete (or to keep growing and competing).

They arrive at that conclusion because the change is framed in terms of solving a business problem and in terms of winning with customers— rather than as an investment of X dollars with such and such expected return. It's the difference between running because it's good exercise and running for your life.

None of this is surprising. Change management experts will tell you how important it is to make the status quo unacceptable. John Kotter's eight-step change process starts with "establishing urgency."[2] Kotter argues that all of a company's top executives and most of its managers have to believe that change is necessary. Michael Beer, who has studied organizational change for decades, argues that successful change must solve an important business problem and that most of the executives have to believe that the cost of not changing is higher than the cost of changing.[3] In *Good to Great*, Jim Collins talks about the importance of "confronting the brutal facts of your reality."[4]

To speak of "making the status quo intolerable" might suggest some kind of con job to convince people of an emergency that may not really exist. Not so. In fact, both individuals and organizations are quite capable of finding a dangerous or even deadly status quo tolerable. Diabetics keep eating ice cream, alcoholics keep drinking alcohol. So what I'm talking about is convincing a management team to stop treating a truly and demonstrably dangerous threat to their company as tolerable. Here are some ways to do it.

Hold Up a Mirror

A powerful way to make people uncomfortable about the status quo is to show them what their performance actually looks like and how different it is from how they perceive themselves. This is where you should let the data speak. Look at data related to customers (satisfaction and loyalty), operational execution (quality, productivity, safety, cost), and employees (turnover, take-home pay, schedules, internal promotion). Compare yourself against the best (not the norm) in your industry. Weakness in any one of these data points suggests trouble in the future.

In 2001, pulmonologists working in the cystic fibrosis area at Cincinnati Children's Hospital Medical Center (CCHMC) believed that theirs was among the best hospitals in the country. But patient outcome data on lung functioning and nutritional status (as measured by body mass index) collected by the Cystic Fibrosis Foundation showed that they were in the twentieth percentile—that is, near the bottom. Clinicians couldn't believe it. Some were close to tears when they saw the data. The evidence of their poor performance convinced them that the status quo was unacceptable.[5] (You may wonder how they could have failed to know how poorly they were doing. Recall the study cited in chapter 4 showing that most business leaders think they are doing better than they actually are.)

Within seven years, CCHMC rose from the twentieth percentile to the ninety-fifth. Then, in 2019, the leaders at CCHMC turned their mirror to the sterile processing unit. Again, they didn't like what they saw. Employee turnover was too high, which was a costly barrier to improvement and reflected poorly on CCHMC and its values. A core value at CCHMC is respect for everyone. But the high turnover in this department was in part due to low starting pay—$11 an hour. In addition to sterile processing, employees in other areas, including environmental services and food services—about three thousand people—were in low-wage job classifications. Many faced food insecurity. "Here we were talking about social determinants of health for children and equities for our patients and families and yet we weren't paying wages and benefits that were allowing our employee to live with dignity," said CEO Michael Fisher. "When we looked in the mirror, we were not living that value."

Indeed, there's a growing body of literature that finds low wages associated with child neglect and low-birthweight babies.[6] Conversely, a predictable monthly unconditional cash transfer given to low-income families may have a clear benefit for infant brain activity.[7]

CCHMC was one of the largest employers in its metropolitan area and therefore felt an obligation to set an example in its community.

CCHMC cared about racial justice. Fisher said, "When it comes to children's health and being an employer of choice, mediocrity is not acceptable."

How to hold up a mirror when it comes to employees

For customer satisfaction and operational execution, holding up a mirror is often straightforward because many companies have their go-to metrics for each. When it comes to employees, things get tricky. As we've seen in chapter 2, too many high-turnover companies have executives who believe they are already offering good jobs. They often rely on engagement surveys, which don't help them see the truth. Some aren't even interested in the truth.

Start with employee turnover and tenure. How many people are you losing per year in each of your frontline roles? How much does it cost to replace each? What's the total direct cost of turnover? What's the tenure of employees within each role? Do you have a stable team? What's the percentage of frontline employees who have been with you for more than a year, two years, and three years?

To know whether your turnover and tenure is healthy or unhealthy, don't compare yourself to other mediocre companies in your industry. Look at the company with the best jobs. Full-time turnover in convenience stores averaged 80 percent in 2019. Is 80 percent anything to shoot for or be proud of? Not really, because QuikTrip's was 20 percent that year. That's the benchmark if you're in the convenience store business, and other industries will likely have similarly low marks to aim at.

Then look at data related to the basic needs we've covered in chapter 2 such as pay, schedules, and career paths. Rather than asking people how they feel about their pay or benefits, look at objective data. What percentage of your hourly employees are enrolled in the company's health-care plan? Mark Bertolini of Aetna was shocked when he found out that his workers couldn't afford the company's own health plans. For pay, look at hourly employees' take-home pay—not just hourly wage because, as we've seen, many so-called full-time workers don't get forty hours a week. Look

at the full range of workers doing work for the company, including con-
tract workers. Their numbers will be even worse.

Again, don't benchmark other mediocre companies. First examine
whether your employees—especially full-timers—make enough to be able
to focus on the job by comparing monthly or annual take-home pay with
the living wage in their area.[8] MIT's living wage calculator is a great
resource for this. Because the official "living wage" is just subsistence
wage, leaders like Dan Schulman (PayPal) and Mark Bertolini don't
have the heart to use it as a benchmark. PayPal targeted 20 percent net
disposable income (NDI) after taxes. Aetna under Bertolini reached
over 27 percent personal disposable income for most employees. Those
are more realistic indicators for whether one is paying people enough
to live on.

If you are running a frontline service business, you should also examine employees' schedules. How far in advance do they know their schedules? How much fluctuation is there from week to week? Do they actually
work their scheduled hours or are there last-minute changes all the time?
Finally, examine what percentage of your frontline managers are promoted
from within and, if possible, review that data by race and gender. As we've
seen in chapter 6, targeting nearly 100 percent internal promotion makes
it a career—not just a job—for employees. For the company, commitment
to internal promotion doesn't just change certain metrics; it changes the
whole system—from hiring to training to developing people.

Bring people together to discuss the data

Once you collect all this data, one of the best ways to use it is to bring
people from the home office and your strongest frontline managers
together and discuss the data—starting with customers and operational
execution and ending with employees. Are they surprised? Are they
shocked?

Then move from the outcome data to the system that produces those
outcomes. Evaluate your company along the four operational choices and
investment in people. Are the mental models and specific choices consis-

tent with the "bad jobs system" or the "good jobs system" we covered in chapter 1? How are decisions made by various home office functions contributing to those outcomes? Are they aware of the full impact of their decisions? Providing a safe space for people to discuss the system, including the corporate disabilities we talked about in chapter 4, can be eye opening for home office leaders. Seeing how much even the strongest frontline managers suffer creates an emotional reaction—an urgency to make things better.

Make the Status Quo Unacceptable Competitively

It may be easier to make the status quo unacceptable when, as at CCHMC, lives are in danger (though it's amazing how few pharmacy chains and senior living organizations are doing so) or when the company's leaders find the status quo with unlivable wages unacceptable ethically.

But not all companies will see an unacceptable status quo when they hold up a mirror. So another tool in creating the urgency to change is to connect your troublesome data and the system that produces that data to a current or future threat. Sure, poor operational execution can be profitable, *but what happens when a competitor can offer lower prices or better service because they can execute better?* Yes, workers can tolerate poor pay and unstable schedules—because they need a job—*but what happens when they have other options and no longer will work for you?* Okay, you're growing quarter after quarter and the stock market loves you, *but what happens when customer needs change or the minimum wage increases significantly and you are not able to adapt to these changes as quickly as your competitors?* Walmart's CEO, Doug McMillon, carries with him a list of the top ten retailers in the United States over the last few decades to remind himself how many have come and gone.[9]

When I began studying Borders in the late 1990s, it was a highly successful retailer of books and music. I spent untold hours at the stores, at headquarters, and analyzing data. This is where I first synthesized the idea of the vicious cycle—what happens when companies do not invest in their people and how much those seemingly small operational problems can hurt sales and profits.

And yet, honestly, the vicious cycle didn't seem all that vicious at the time. Despite high turnover and operational problems, Borders experienced high profitability growth. Their big-box "category killer" model was so popular with customers that operational mediocrity was okay for a long time.

I can't remember anyone thinking that they might not exist a decade later. I don't think anyone—inside or outside the chain—thought of Borders as mediocre. What Borders hadn't done was to look in the mirror and ask, *What would happen if people had an easier way to find and buy a book?*

When profitability growth is the measuring stick, it is easy to think a company is performing well even when it's ignoring customers, employees, or operational execution. So look hard at the inputs that produce profitability—and imagine competitive pressures on them.

Sometimes, those competitive pressures aren't even imaginary; they're a real, present crisis. Quest Diagnostics, for example, was losing important accounts, getting angry calls from their own commercial team about unhappy customers. The direct cost of turnover at the call centers—$10.5 million—hurt Quest's ability to provide low prices. The good jobs system was a way to solve an urgent business problem, and that's why it was prioritized.

If there is no crisis, you can still use the future potential scenarios described above and you can link a good jobs system to your company's central competitive challenge, be it differentiation, growth, or adaptation.

For Progressive Insurance, the impetus to invest in people and operations came from two places. First, they wanted to grow in a mature industry that grew only at the same rate as GDP. Second, they faced new legislation. Proposition 103 in California, passed in 1988, forced insurance companies to roll back escalating rates. Twenty percent of Progressive's business was in California, and the company paid out $60 million in refunds. Peter Lewis, who was CEO at the time, later called it "the best thing that happened to this company. I decided that from then on, anything we did had to be good for the consumer or we weren't going to do it."

For Dewey Hasbrouck, owner of two restaurants in the Moe's Original BBQ chain, the urgency for change came from the pandemic. Like most other restaurants at that time, his suffered from low traffic, higher costs, and difficulty attracting and retaining employees. To bring customers back, he decided he had to "fix his business." That meant paying his employees more and helping them work better. Hasbrouck's two restaurants already tended to pay better than other restaurants, but even full-time employees were making only $30,000. "It was so eye-opening to think that when you compare your wages against other restaurants, it looks like one thing, but when you compare them against the actual cost of living, it looks completely different. So I knew the model was broken."

Tell Stories: You Can't Beat Competition without Doing Fundamentals Well

In the mid-2000s, many people thought Amazon would put Best Buy out of business. It didn't. Hubert Joly, the CEO who turned Best Buy around, has said many times that the problems with Best Buy were internal, not external. Over time, they had forgotten why customers would come there. They had underinvested in people, stores, systems, and supplier relations. Joly focused on fixing those fundamentals and left Best Buy a stronger company.

Mud Bay faced a similar competitive threat. For pet products, e-commerce was growing much more quickly than the brick-and-mortar business. Mud Bay therefore had to provide a compelling reason for customers to come into their stores. That meant their stores had to be inviting—irreplaceable—places for pet owners (and even for pets themselves) to visit. But that required knowledgeable and motivated employees who can focus on customers and solve their pet problems. That wasn't going to happen—not reliably, anyway—with 48 percent employee turnover.

Russ Rose at Penn State

Prioritizing fundamentals may not be perceived as cool these days. New technologies, mergers and acquisitions, and new products and services can be more exciting than running the core business well. But have you ever seen a winning team that doesn't do the fundamentals well? I learned this lesson many years before I began studying how businesses work—from a volleyball coach. I came to the United States from Turkey on a volleyball scholarship to Penn State. Our coach was Russ Rose, and I can see now that he embodied much of what I later learned from companies that pursued excellence. For example:

- He focused on the fundamentals of our "business" and didn't get distracted by cool coaching fads. We didn't do a lot of different drills. We did a few drills focused on fundamentals. We did them over and over, and we kept getting better. Every practice was a competition. He prepared detailed analysis of our competition before every game. And he knew what data mattered most. While everyone else focused on statistics that are easily measured, such as how many digs or kills a player had in a game, Rose tracked—in his notebook—how many digs or kills the player missed.

Sadly, the fate of Borders was different. Borders, too, had a strong competitive challenge as Amazon started taking away book sales and digital music took away CD and record sales. Keep in mind that, at the time, Amazon wasn't profitable and it wasn't clear that it ever would be. Yet, it had enthusiastic support from investors and did everything possible to give customers what they wanted. If the company couldn't deliver that kind of service profitably—it delivered it anyway.

While Amazon bent over backward for customers, Borders responded by doing everything possible to please its shareholders, not its customers. Pleasing customers would have required fixing operational execution.

- He held us to high standards (having created a training program which enabled us to meet them). High expectations started from recruiting. Rose made it clear that he wanted his players to commit to working hard and getting better at every practice. Your spot in the starting lineup was never guaranteed. You had to keep earning it or you'd lose it. (You could, of course, earn it back—by playing well.)

- He had a stable team. Seniors graduated, obviously. But, except for one person who stopped playing volleyball due to an injury, I don't remember anyone transferring to another school during my four years. Rose knew our individual strengths and weaknesses and created a system that leveraged our abilities. He even knew almost everyone's parents (mine, sadly, were too far away). Each of us could perform at a much higher level on his team than we would have somewhere else—so why would we want to transfer?

And what were the results of this "old school" pursuit of excellence? When he retired in 2021, Rose had seven NCAA championships under his belt and was the winningest coach in the National Collegiate Athletic Association Division 1—that is, the winningest in all NCAA sports!—with a record of 1,330–229.

With 69 percent full-time and 112 percent part-time employee turnover, Borders stores were full of problems. Eighteen percent of customers who asked a Borders employee for help experienced a phantom stockout—the product was in stock, according to the inventory system, but no one in the store could find it.[10] Customer frustration, lost sales, and high inventory and labor costs aside, these phantom stockouts made it impossible for Borders to integrate bricks with clicks.

Instead of fixing what was broken and offering customers a compelling reason to visit stores, as Best Buy did, Borders pursued growth by opening more stores. But each store was selling less, so Borders cut costs more. It increased its share of part-timers. It cut staffing levels and eliminated community relations coordinators, whose job was to create special in-store events to bring in potential customers. In 2005, Borders did a stock buyback for $250 million when its stock price was at the highest it had been in years.

Borders could have done many other things, of course: fix operational execution, improve the customer experience, and offer more live events (something Amazon couldn't do).

You might think this is a situation bigger than Borders, that the entire book business simply lost to Amazon. Not true. Research shows that while Borders was dying, independent bookstores grew 49 percent from 2009 to 2018 because they offered customers things that online shopping couldn't duplicate: community (promoting the idea of customers supporting local communities), curation (personal and specialized customer experience), and convening (book signings, lectures, game nights, reading groups, and birthday parties).[11]

One of the reasons the four low-cost retailers I studied for my first book are all still thriving is that they never lost their focus on the customer or their discipline in running their business well. During the pandemic, one of the few large retailers that didn't offer delivery from its stores or curbside pickup was Trader Joe's. Yet, their customers kept lining up outside the stores. Why? Referring to all the things Trader Joe's doesn't do, founder Joe Coulombe wrote, "We violated every received wisdom of retailing except one: we delivered great value, which is where most retailers fail."[12]

Appeal to Different Motivations

Committing to a good jobs system requires thinking in a customer-centric way rather than a primarily financial way—quite a change for many executives and managers. You won't get everyone to change their thinking right away. To get leaders whose motivation to win is largely financial excited about this journey, you can make a somewhat different version of the case for a good jobs system. Here's how it goes:

Our company has been on a vicious cycle of low pay, high turnover, understaffing, and poor performance. It is not sustainable.
Look at what happened to Borders, Sears, and even General
Electric. Companies that focus on the customer and prioritize
running their business well, such as Four Seasons, Costco, and
Progressive, have done well for their shareholders, without making
shareholders the top priority, and we want to do the same. So we
will drive sales and earnings growth by winning with our customers. We will continuously improve our products and services,
which will also make us a stronger, more resilient company. But we
can only do this with an empowered, motivated, experienced
workforce. And we can't have that workforce unless we pay them
well and design their work for high productivity and high customer service. So that's what we have to do because everything
else depends on it.

That's the type of story that someone like Charlie Penner, the activist
I mentioned in the previous chapter, tells so well. That's how Penner, when
he was working at Jana in 2017, pushed Apple to introduce controls to
prevent kids from getting addicted to iPhone and iPad screens. That's how
in 2020, while at the investment firm Engine No. 1, he led a campaign to
push Exxon to treat climate change as a threat to the planet *and* to its
bottom line. He was able to make a strong case to shareholders, including BlackRock, State Street, and Vanguard. But would that approach work
for the good jobs system? Penner told my MBA students in 2021 that the
case for the good jobs system would be easier to make to shareholders
than the case that Exxon should treat climate change as a threat. Even
shareholders who don't care at all about how people are treated could be
brought on board for the good jobs system because of its long-term financial upside. And if someone looking at a company from outside, as he
does, could make the case, imagine what a strong case you could make
after examining your own company's system.

But you don't have to rely solely on a financial and competitive case.
You can also (and should also) appeal to the ethical imperative for good

jobs and the connection of ethics to your company's purpose and values.

So many frontline employees I've met working in call centers, senior living facilities, retail stores, and elsewhere are frustrated because their job doesn't allow them to properly take care of the customers. Helping others is motivating.[13] Workers want to do the right thing, but they are not given enough time or latitude to do a good job.

People higher up are increasingly rethinking whether they want to work for a company that's driven solely by financials. No one wants to be part of a company hiding sick people to increase sales or paying employees below subsistence levels to meet a near-term financial target. It doesn't take gross lapses in ethics to feel like what you're doing is not entirely good.

You can appeal to most executives' natural inclination to be ethical and to use teamwork, camaraderie, and a sense of purpose to drive results. One of my students who had served as an airborne infantry officer for eleven years was struggling to find in the nonmilitary world the camaraderie and sense of purpose he found in the Army. His Costco store visit convinced him he could reclaim that sense of purpose by being part of— and someday driving—a good jobs company.

When appealing to motivations, you also have to address the fears that come with the change. Even when we're motivated, we can be afraid of what this thing we want will mean. For example, a participant in an executive education course challenged me when we were talking about the first operational choice of the good jobs system: focus and simplify. "You mention eliminating things that don't add value to the customer, and I hear layoffs."

She had a point, and if you are proposing a good jobs system for your company, this fear needs to be addressed. The Toyota Production System Support Center (TSSC)—which works with companies trying to implement lean manufacturing and which therefore deals with many of the strategies and issues of the good jobs system—has a rule: any company with which they work must make a commitment that no one will lose their job as a result of the intended improvements. You can make a similar pledge when adopting the good jobs system. Given all the negative effects of lay-offs on the people who are laid off and on the people who keep their jobs but suffer from survivor guilt, doing everything you can to avoid layoffs—from cutting elsewhere to using natural attrition to keeping a strong balance sheet—is sound advice. And if you have to eliminate some jobs, detail which jobs, why, and how the company will help those people find new jobs, and try to ensure that remaining employees do not live with fear or feel guilty.

Provide the Right Conditions

You may be surprised how much people at all levels will be excited about this change. But when people in various corporate functions learn about the good jobs system and what it entails, they are often afraid that their own incentives—pay and promotion—and their siloed structures won't let them make the decisions that they now see are the right decisions—for the customers, employees, and performance.

These people are often used to "optimizing" for their own silos and expect the frontline employees to deal with the consequences of their decisions. Logistics, for example, focuses on minimizing logistics costs. If that means unpredictable deliveries to restaurants, so be it. Marketing focuses on sales. If a last-minute change to promotions means higher workload or unpredictable schedules, so be it. In a good jobs system, everyone would recognize that the most important work is done at the front lines. The functions are there to make it easier for the frontline staff to serve the customer. As a result, some departments' costs may have to increase so that overall corporate costs can decrease or customer satisfaction and sales can increase. But if logistics keeps being measured on minimizing logistics costs, they can't be frontline focused. If marketing keeps focusing only on sales, they can't be frontline focused. Only a committed leadership team can help provide the right incentives and bring people together to do what's right for the company.

Keep in mind, though, that the problem isn't always resistance or counterproductive incentives. Sometimes, even obvious changes aren't made simply because no one has time to make them. At the financial services company call center that couldn't make progress, for example, almost a third of the call volume concerned confusing bill-payment procedures. Fixing that so that the reps could be more productive wasn't hard but was never prioritized. It was never prioritized because frontline work wasn't seen as essential to win.

Set and Communicate Targets

In October 2015, Doug McMillon, the CEO of Walmart since 2014, announced that it would cost Walmart $2.7 billion over two years to raise the minimum wage of associates from the federal minimum wage of $7.25 an hour to $9 an hour in 2015 and $10 an hour in 2016. Wage investment along with building the e-commerce business would reduce short-term profitability. As a new CEO, McMillon initially got some pushback. Walmart's stock price took a 10 percent hit that day. Although the hit to the stock price didn't even last long, a lot of executives at Walmart still remember it. It must have been demoralizing to see investors punish you for doing what you think is the right thing to do. When CNBC's Jim Cramer asked McMillon why shareholders should trust him that this was the right investment to make, he replied, "If we don't win with customers, we don't have a business." Walmart's executives told Wall Street, "If you give us a breather on the bottom line, we'll deliver an improved top line. But it won't happen in a year; it's going to take three years."

But don't make people wait three years to see results! Your sales may not improve in a year, but you can promise progress on the metrics related to employees, customers, and operational execution that you used when you held up a mirror to your company. Provide short- and medium-term targets for improvement (e.g., offering living wages, reducing turnover, increasing customer loyalty) and hold yourself accountable. Just because you made a change doesn't mean it has been successfully implemented in the front lines, so process-related metrics may be a good way to show early signs of success. One company, for example, started with measuring whether unit managers were actually offering predictable and consistent schedules. If the changes are not being implemented in the front lines — you know there's a problem.

Explaining where you want to go and why and painting a picture of progress help both externally—to get investors and analysts on board— and internally—to create faith among the skeptics by showing early success.

Center the Journey around Customers

You know by now the core benefits of a good jobs system, and you will be highlighting them as you make your case: lower turnover costs, better operational execution, higher customer service and sales, and so forth. Centering the journey this way—around winning with customers—has several important benefits.

1. It helps clarify your value proposition and makes strategic trade-offs easier

Framing good jobs and strong operations around customers enables companies to articulate their value proposition early on. What can your customers count on you to be the best at? And what will you give up to accomplish that?

When Mud Bay started its journey, staff suggested reducing the store's hours. Mud Bay was open from 9 a.m. to 9 p.m. Monday through Saturday and from 10 a.m. to 7 p.m. on Sundays. Staff often had to stay a half-hour more to close the place up, and they didn't like staying that late, especially on Saturdays. They reported that the stores were "dead" near closing time anyway. But when a Mud Bay team analyzed sales data over a six-week period, they saw that the last-hour sales were significant enough that if they lost those sales, the payroll savings would barely make up for it.

In many companies, that would have ended the discussion. But for Mud Bay's leadership team, analysis of historical data and strict financials weren't the only consideration. Closing earlier could improve employee satisfaction and possibly reduce turnover. Having the store open eleven versus twelve hours would also increase the overlap between the morning and afternoon shifts and enable staff to serve the customers better. And after all, that's how Mud Bay was hoping to win with its customers—offering consultative selling at low prices in a friendly environment. Giving up some convenience—important, but not their particular value proposition (as it would be for, say, a convenience store)—would strengthen their real value proposition.

Okay, but what about those lost sales? "I was really scared of inconveniencing customers and losing all the sales," Lars Wulff told my students. His sister, co-CEO Marisa Wulff, thought differently. They wouldn't lose most sales if they managed the transition well with their customers and changed customer behavior. They could explain to their customers why they were reducing hours. They could close the doors and still let customers in during the first few weeks to train them on the reduced hours. She was thinking of it like Costco's intelligent loss of sales.

So they bit the bullet and reduced their hours, opening a half-hour later and closing a half-hour earlier on weekdays. On Saturday, they closed an hour and a half earlier. The overall sales loss was—zero. Same-store sales growth was at a healthy 13.2 percent compared to the previous year. Since 2017, Mud Bay has reduced hours even more—a total reduction of 16 percent—with, according to what the co-CEOs told my students, no drop in sales (see figure 8-1).

2. It encourages systems thinking

As we've seen before, in many large organizations, leaders at different levels can tell you about previous changes that didn't work. "We've empowered people before and lost a lot of money." "We've increased staffing levels

FIGURE 8-1

"All else equal" thinking versus system thinking

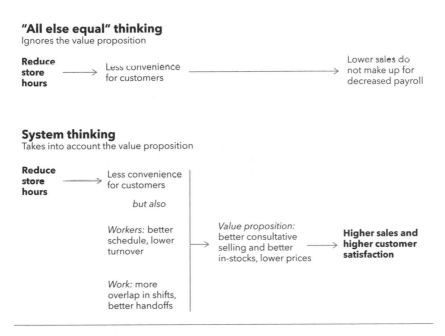

"All else equal" thinking
Ignores the value proposition

Reduce store hours → Less convenience for customers ────────→ Lower sales do not make up for decreased payroll

System thinking
Takes into account the value proposition

Reduce store hours → Less convenience for customers

but also

Workers: better schedule, lower turnover

Work: more overlap in shifts, better handoffs

→ *Value proposition:* better consultative selling and better in-stocks, lower prices → **Higher sales and higher customer satisfaction**

and it only increased our costs." "We've reduced sales promotions and lost sales."

With a focus on the customer, the questions to ask are:

- Can we create a winning customer experience if our frontline workers aren't empowered to solve customer problems or if they don't have time to take care of the customer—say, because we waste so much of their time with sales promotions?

- Why haven't our previous attempts worked? What else would we need to do to get it right this time?

The power of the second question is that it helps people take the system perspective. The reason previous attempts didn't work is likely because of what we saw in chapters 4 and 5. The vicious cycle results in a system with corporate disabilities. You can't hire and train well, empower people, manage capacity, and set high expectations. Changing any one element in isolation won't produce strong results—with so much else still working against it, it just can't. Therefore, what happened in the past in your own company is not a reliable predictor of what will happen in the future if you make the leap to thinking about the system, not just the siloed change.

Getting it right this time requires understanding the interconnected elements of the good jobs system. We have to empower people—what do we need to do to make that work? We need to give people enough time to take care of the customer—what do we need to do to make that work? At the end of our workshops, we often hear some version of this statement: "We have to make sure we don't come out of this workshop and just try a few tactics. We've done that before. We need a whole new system."

3. It helps involve and align people upstream who drive the work

Focusing on customers also helps managers look at their processes end to end and understand what gets in the way of delivering value for customers.

In April 2022, Mary Gundel posted on TikTok about what it is like to manage a Dollar General store. Gundel was a top manager—she was given a pin that read "DG: Top 5%." She knew she was risking her job by posting, but she was undeterred. "Whatever happens, happens. Something needs to be said, and there needs to be some changes, or they are probably going to end up losing a lot of people," she said on her first TikTok post.[14]

Her posts went viral, and she was fired.

Dollar General is rated among the worst large employers in retail. According to data collected by Danny Schneider and his colleagues at the Economic Policy Institute, 92 percent of employees at Dollar General made below $15 an hour in 2021. Fifty-seven percent made less than $12 an hour and 22 percent made less than $10 an hour.[15] There's no publicly available data on Dollar General's employee turnover, but in April 2022, the company had 78,284 openings posted on Glassdoor. That's nearly 50 percent of its total workforce. About one-third of the openings were for management positions, including store manager and district manager. To be clear: job openings do not represent exactly how many people a company is looking to hire. Maybe the company hadn't updated its postings lately. But these numbers do suggest a high turnover. For comparison, at that same time, QuikTrip—a company with 24,000 employees and stores similar in size to those of Dollar General—had 138 job openings (0.6 percent of the workforce). Costco, with nearly 200,000 employees in the United States, had 365 job openings -0.2 percent of the workforce. (And Costco stores are much larger, so one cashier posting might actually be seeking five cashiers.)

In her first TikTok video, Gundel highlighted how corporate decisions showed disrespect for frontliners and made it impossible for them to serve the customers. Here are a few examples:

- Unexpected deliveries that meant aisles full of boxes. This made it not only unpleasant but also unsafe for both customers and employees. It also caused lost sales because customers couldn't get to the shelves with boxes in the way.

- Corporate mandates such as "You can't touch truck deliveries until Thursday," which made no sense when a large delivery arrived on Tuesday.

- Understaffing. Gundel's own store went from 198 hours of labor per week to about 130. This meant long hours and burnout for her and angry customers yelling at her for lousy service. Gundel is an example of why mediocre companies can't hold on to managers.

Note that she wasn't complaining much about how hard she works, but rather about the corporate decisions that make it hard for her to do a good job and serve customers. She used hashtag #PutInATicket for her videos to highlight how the home office avoids problems by burying them in bureaucracy. "You know what they tell you? 'Put in a ticket.'"[16]

In every company, the work done by the frontline employees—its amount, its timing, its design—is significantly determined by people who do not themselves do or even manage that work. For Gundel, staffing was likely decided by Finance, delivery schedules by Logistics or Supply Chain, and rules about unloading a shipment by Operations. That alone is three or four functional groups making decisions for the front lines without involving the frontline workers themselves—and possibly not even in concert with each other. If Logistics knows shipments come on Tuesday while Operations is mandating Thursday unloading, it's pretty clear they aren't talking enough (if at all) to each other, never mind to the frontline workers.

In a restaurant chain, the menu, the suppliers, and decisions concerning digital service—Do we offer takeout? Home delivery? Are the online and in-store menus different?—all come from headquarters. But they have a lot to do with the minute-to-minute work that the kitchen staff, waitstaff, and front-of-house staff do. So you might have a fantastic unit manager, but if the deliveries are coming at different times or are unreliable ("Where are those eggs we ordered?") or the menu is so complex that it takes forever for customers to figure out what they want or if fulfilling digital orders is screwing up table service—well, there's only so much the frontline workers can do to deliver a great customer experience, and leaning on them to somehow do better isn't going to help. In fact, it will make things worse, because people don't take well to being blamed for what they know isn't their fault. Even less so if the fault is with the very people who are blaming them.

Making the case for a good jobs system means making sure those who make decisions can see things from the frontline perspective by spending time on the front lines. Better yet, if those decision-makers are so convinced of the importance of frontline workers, then they ought to seek and take those frontline workers' input and involve them in decisions on a regular basis.

What decision-makers seeking to achieve excellence do not do is fire top managers pleading for help.

Start the Virtuous Cycle

You're ready to prioritize system change. Now it's time to start executing. Your first job is to know where you'll invest and what you'll take away and *when* you'll do these things—in what order—in order to start the virtuous cycle.

If your company is like the dozens of companies we've worked with, there will be strong alignment on what changes have to be made to become a customer-centric and therefore frontline-centric company.

But you'll realize that you have to make a lot of changes within each of the four operational choices and investment in people. Some of the changes will cost a lot of money (e.g., increasing pay or adding more hours). Some will take a long time to implement (e.g., standardizing processes). Some changes can be done within each unit (e.g., improving hiring or attendance policy). Some require alignment with corporate functions (e.g., simplifying product and information flow). You can't make all these changes at once, yet you can't just make them one at a time, because many are interdependent.

Then where to begin? Should you start with investing in people by raising pay to create a capable workforce? That's expensive. And there are probably employees who should not have been hired in the first place—do you raise *their* pay, too? In any case, raising pay without changing the work employees do won't be enough to make the job a good job or to drive performance. A jockey on an injured horse isn't going to win just because you doubled his pay. Okay then, how about starting with standardization and empowering staff for continuous improvement? That might not seem like it requires any investment at all—just change the rules and let 'er rip. But how long will it take? Even the Employee of the Year isn't going to contribute much improvement if he or she is busy clearing boxes out of the aisle from a shipment that conveniently arrived on the busiest day of the week.

First, Triage

At most companies, there are certain high-leverage points that show results early and create momentum. To understand those high-leverage points, we will now need to change gears—from strategic and ethical discussions to operational details.

In the successful journeys we've seen, leaders first applied triage. They attacked the vicious cycle by stabilizing the workforce, meaning reducing turnover, understaffing, and low ability. At most companies, stabilizing the workforce required a few core steps:

- raising pay

- improving schedules

- raising expectations

- creating clear career paths

- giving employees enough time to do their jobs

But these changes—especially raising pay and giving people more time—cost a lot of money. How do you break the vicious cycle without going broke? (See figure 9-1.)

Sometimes, the only way to add is to subtract. So instead of adding more labor hours, which costs a lot of money, companies reduced employee

FIGURE 9-1

The vicious cycle

workload. They examined the biggest drivers of workload in the front lines and asked themselves: Which of these labor-intensive activities produced outcomes that really mattered to their customers? What could they take out of their customer offering to deliver more to their customers? What made employees' work needlessly tedious, unproductive, and unpredictable? All these forms of simplification made it possible to raise pay, because fewer labor hours were needed when fewer were being wasted. Simplification also improves customer service, reduces costs by reducing errors, and makes employees' work better.

Subtraction is seldom considered a big change lever. In large organizations, people know they'll be noticed for what they add, not for what they subtract. Subtraction also doesn't come naturally to most people. The authors of a study in which participants were asked to make various changes to LEGO constructions found that people were much more likely to do so by adding pieces than by removing them, even if removing them was a simpler and more effective solution. The researchers even speculated that "defaulting" to adding rather than subtracting "may be one reason that people struggle to mitigate overburdened schedules [and] institutional red tape."[1] I would say their laboratory findings are well— though not strictly scientifically—borne out by decades of observation of how companies go about their business.

This is one reason that simplification requires input from the frontline employees themselves. They will find obvious opportunities to subtract that headquarters execs would never see.

By investing and subtracting, you can lay a foundation on which to build. As we've seen in chapter 4, when there's high turnover, there's tremendous disconnect and distrust between the home office and frontline staff. Once your workforce and the work they do are stable, everything else—including training, standardization, and empowerment—becomes easier. As performance improves, you'll be able to invest more in people. (Remember, the virtuous cycle is a *cycle*.)

Another big benefit of starting with investing and subtracting is that those are the two changes that require the most courage. If you can make some of those big and possibly irreversible changes quickly, you can build momentum and make it more likely that the next leader will build on your changes rather than abandon them.

Ensure Stable Workloads and Stable Workforces before Adding Hours

The minimum requirement for being customer centric is to have enough capable people who can serve the customers without making mistakes and making folks wait too long. Yet, from the Starbucks baristas to pharmacists at large chains to nurses at hospitals to caregivers at senior living organizations, we hear a persistent complaint: there isn't enough time to do the job and serve the customer or care for the patient. Employees— and this includes frontline managers—are burned out. That's wrong in itself, but it's also a big problem for corporate performance. (There may be some people who thrive on overload, but for most of us, it creates anxiety. Anxiety is *tiring* and that takes its own toll on how effective, productive, and engaged your workforce will be.)

One reason this problem of overwork and burnout persists is that many of the executives of companies whose employees and managers complain about understaffing believe they are allocating *more* than enough hours.

They've created elaborate labor models that estimate the workload. How many customers do we expect to serve? How long does it take to serve them? What are all the other tasks that need doing—such as cleaning at a hospital, processing deliveries at a restaurant, and shelving merchandise at a retail store—and how long do they take? If management finds, for example, that the average workload on Mondays is 100 hours, they may even budget 110 hours to provide some slack. So how can frontliners complain so much about understaffing?

Do you want to hear a dirty little secret? Companies make all the same mistakes we do. Just like us, they take on too much, underestimate how long it will all take, waste time, and schedule as if nothing will go wrong. Their models are wildly optimistic and don't account for the actual way work gets done. When they budget hours, they don't think about something as simple as correcting a mistake on price labels. They don't build in the time it takes to take down a promotion and put it back up due to a last-minute change from headquarters. Or various uncoordinated requests from headquarters. Or technologies that are supposed to save time but actually waste it. Or an indecisive customer. Or interruptions from customers. Or the time it takes to fix a broken piece of equipment. These models are not particularly accurate about demand and the effect of sudden rushes—say, at a restaurant after a high school sporting event. You may think that the workload distribution looks like the one on the left in figure 9-2, whereas it actually looks like the one on the right, with a higher mean and quite a bit more variation. In the end, models make executives feel good because they're data driven. But when the data is as inaccurate as I've indicated, the models can't be anything but misleading.

For staffing, it's not just the workload distribution that's different from what the labor model assumes. Instability in the workforce, in terms of attendance and ability, is also a problem. Labor models tend to assume that people who are scheduled will show up, but sometimes they don't—and what happens then? The models also assume average skill, but with high turnover and low pay, that's likely to be a false assumption. Newer people take longer at a task than others and are more likely to

FIGURE 9-2

Two workload distributions (assuming Gaussian/normal distribution)

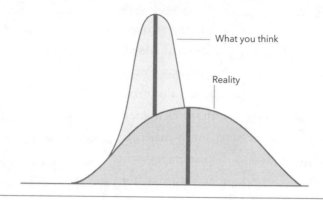

What you think

Reality

make mistakes, which then have to be corrected—possibly by someone else. (Or left uncorrected, which is just shifting the problem from staffing to customer satisfaction and thus to sales, growth, and other things that do rather matter.) HQ often assumes that employees are trained on the standards, but with too many standards in the first place and then high turnover, you can be sure those standards won't always be followed—if they're even known. At companies where employees are not cross-trained, you may have the "right" number of labor hours, but they may not be used if the individuals' skills don't match what needs to be done during their shift.

In sum, at companies operating in a vicious cycle, there's tremendous variability in both demand for labor and supply of labor. Such companies are constantly bouncing between overstaffed and understaffed, both of which are expensive. So, yes, getting on a virtuous cycle requires having enough capable people to do all the work and serve the customer. But you don't want to solve this problem just by adding more hours. First, you want to examine the workload and see where you can subtract tasks, smooth workload, and stabilize people. And never forget—it's the frontline workers who know what would help most.

Subtract to Improve the Customer Offering

Companies that succeed in breaking the vicious cycle simplify in a way that makes their customer offering stronger. They remove all the products and services and deals they had added over time—for financial reasons or through lack of discipline or encouraged by social proof—that ended up hurting their customer value proposition and making life more annoying or difficult for both the customers and the employees.

Obviously, simplifying is much easier if you have clarified the reason you exist in the eyes of your customers—why your customers come to you in the first place. Recall that Mud Bay, for example, reduced its hours, recognizing that customers came to them for consultative service, not convenience. (A convenience store or a gas station along the highway would rightly make a different decision.) But even if you haven't yet clarified your reason for being, you'll still find a lot of opportunities for simplification. In fact, simplification could even help you clarify your reason for being. If you focus on what your business is *not* and eliminate that, it might become clear to you what your business *is*. (You might recall that this is how Sherlock Holmes claimed to solve his cases. "Once you eliminate the impossible," he tells Watson, "whatever remains, no matter how improbable, must be the truth."[2])

Pull the Biggest Levers First

In almost every workshop we hold, when participants list what their company can stop doing and what changes they can make to reduce and smooth workload so as to improve customer service, it's a *long* list. Be careful, therefore, about tackling too much all at once. It's important not to make the simplification itself too complicated.

The companies that made the most progress began by pulling the biggest levers first.

For Quest, the biggest lever to pull was reducing call volume. Quest centered this change on the customer: they surveyed physicians and found that they would rather get normal test results by fax than by phone anyway: "Don't bother me with normal results!" By subtracting the work of reporting normal results, Quest reduced outbound calls by 16 percent—a huge gain just for eliminating something that almost no one wanted anyway! Then they subtracted having to get up from your desk to go use the fax machine—by installing fax capability on the reps' computers. That saved even more time—and equipment fees.

Quest also reduced inbound calls by 7 percent by improving its online portal to show doctors the status of shipments and have test results sent to their cell phones. The result of these and other subtractions was a decline in the number of calls that needed to be transferred, which meant higher labor productivity and better customer service. (And eventually, more time supervisors could spend on training and process improvement.)

Sam's Club did a lot of subtraction to improve the member experience and reduce workload. Chad Donath, who led the company's operational transformation, explained to me: "We looked at the entire club to understand: What was work? When did the work need to be done? How do you structure the club in the right way so that it can get all the work done? Historically, we had looked at one area, not understanding the unintended consequences [for other areas]."

When they examined work in the front lines, they found that managers were buried with requests from the home office. Donath had been with the company for three decades and had been an assistant manager and a store manager himself. He knew very well what managers at those levels went through. He told his colleagues, "No more communication directly to stores." Instead, communications that used to go right to managers went first to a gatekeeper (they called it "ATC"—air traffic control). If HR or logistics or merchandising wanted to put in a new initiative, introduce a new tool, or pilot a new program, they had to discuss it and get permission during a Monday all-department meeting. This freed up time store managers had been wasting dealing with confusing, often mixed messages from corporate.

When it came to the workload of Sam's Club employees, the biggest lever for reduction involved merchandising. Over time, Sam's Club had added more and more products, so it was taking a lot longer to organize them on the shelves. "The massive SKU elimination and moving to pallet-driven shelving made a big difference to reduce workload," said Tim Simmons, who led the technology transformation. (Mud Bay also reduced its assortment by more than 10 percent largely by eliminating redundant products; for example, carrying two rather than three sizes of a brand of dog food.) Another time waster was frequent price changes. Sam's Club eliminated many of them.

But what about the impact of those changes on the members—the shoppers? At clubs that reduced SKUs, members began giving Sam's Club higher marks on breadth of assortment. When presented with less, shoppers perceived that clubs had more items.[3] When John Furner came to my class he gave the example of a member thanking the manager of a club for finally stocking a particular electric toothbrush. Actually, Sam's Club had been carrying that item for ten years, but it had always been difficult to find amid the clutter. At both Sam's Club and Mud Bay, reducing variety ended up improving customer satisfaction and sales. In addition to reduced clutter, fewer products meant higher in-stocks (due to both better forecasting of demand and better operational execution) and lower prices for customers.

Sam's Club reduced workload in many other ways, from streamlining the membership signup process—by cutting the nine types of membership down to two—to removing the photo centers from the clubs.

New technologies that augmented associates by saving their time and enabling them to serve the members better were another significant source of simplification.[4] For example, an app allowed the store's Tire & Battery Center to find the right tire for a member in under five minutes, whereas it used to take twenty minutes or more. Another app, called Ask Sam, allowed associates to easily access store information, from product prices and locations to who was working what shift that day. Another app produced production plans in the fresh food departments. Christopher Shryock, the chief people officer, told me that "the message we give our associates is, 'The technologies we introduce will make your work simpler so that you can be in front of a member.' Associates see that and they resonate with it." Hearing associates' voices was a key design principle. All apps had a field in which associates could make suggestions.

Let me point out here that smaller, more symbolic moves can sometimes be useful by making it clear that you are listening to employees and that you do care. At Quest, the reps—each serving patients all over the country—often got mixed up about what time it was for the people they were talking to. So Quest put in clocks showing the time in different time zones. Doing so didn't solve any major problems, but it relieved a daily aggravation and that means a lot to people. At the two Moe's Original BBQ restaurants, customers often interrupted kitchen staff to ask where the utensils were. So utensils were put out where customers could easily see them. That quick win showed the staff that their voice was heard. Small changes can make a huge impact over time. Nevertheless, you can't just settle for a string of quick wins.

Smooth the Workload

Smoothing workload is one of the most effective ways to improve productivity and quality, increase the percentage of full-timers, and offer more stable schedules. Toyota, for example, practices *heijunka*, or "level production." Instead of producing according to actual fluctuations in customer demand, Toyota smooths its production using inventory as a buffer. Service can't be inventoried like products, but service companies can smooth workload in two ways: scheduling non-customer-facing tasks when traffic is low or altering customer demand.

One of my favorite examples of smoothing workload comes from Zara, a fashion retailer known for its fast and responsive supply chain. Zara can produce new items and deliver them to its stores in less than three weeks versus an industry average of six months. Such a short lead time lets Zara read demand early in a season and then adjust its offerings. Each store orders merchandise twice a week, based on what's selling or not selling. Zara stores in Europe receive deliveries within twenty-four hours of ordering; others within forty hours.

This ordering and delivery cycle proceeds like clockwork. Stores know exactly when to order, when they will receive the goods, and how much workload (unloading and stocking) there will be. The cycle is designed for workload smoothing, with deliveries on days when customer traffic is low.

To smooth workload at Costco, buyers coordinate product introductions so that new items are brought out at staggered times. In addition, to even out holiday sales, they begin displaying holiday items well in advance of the holiday season.

Workload smoothing can also be done within the day. At Mud Bay, for example, before 2015, two employees arrived at the store at 5 a.m. to make sure all overnight deliveries were shelved before the store opened at 9 a.m. Then field leaders pushed for a new approach: Two employees would arrive thirty to forty-five minutes before opening and shelve the largest, heaviest deliveries, storing the rest in the back room. Then, throughout the day, all employees would shelve the rest during lulls. Of course, this required employees who had been cross-trained in both shelving and customer service. And it meant giving up on an outcome that mattered to one of the founders but turned out not to matter much to customers: stores being perfectly organized before turning on the "Open" sign. As it turned out, having more employees working during customer hours increased both employee productivity and the level of customer service. With enough people on deck, it made sense to leave much of the shelving to be done during store hours—making very efficient use of their time.

Moe's Original BBQ franchisee smoothed workload by altering customer demand. They used their nacho special to boost traffic on typically low-traffic days. They also ended up closing on Sundays. In fact, when Dewey Hasbrouck first opened the restaurant, it was closed on Sundays. But then, with business slow, he thought, "How can I afford to be closed fifty-two days a year?" He later regretted that decision, because staying open seven days a week was tough on his staff. The pandemic provided the perfect excuse to close on Sundays; customers proved willing to accept it.

Stabilizing workload helps stabilize schedules

Stabilizing workload by smoothing it and making it more predictable is a key to stabilizing schedules, which, in turn, is a key to reducing turnover and the many ills associated with it. At Mercadona, all store deliveries are made in the morning—a relatively quiet period. The same truck driver brings deliveries to the same store in a fifteen-minute delivery window, which significantly reduces variability in workload. In the same vein, all changes to products and processes are made on a low-traffic day. Meanwhile, cross-training helps Mercadona handle customer peaks— employees can shift between customer-facing and non-customer-facing tasks depending on traffic. All this smoothing enables the company to operate with 85 percent of its employees being full-timers working regular shifts.

Sam's Club adopted a policy of block scheduling—that is, predictable, consistent shifts—and the proportion of full-time employees grew 13 percent in two years. Those improvements could not have happened without smoothing workload—specifically, by changing the times of deliveries, by eliminating the night shift so that associates working overnight would instead work during the days when members were in the clubs, and by simplifying job codes and introducing cross-training so associates could shift between tasks in their area. (Over time, Sam's Club had kept adding job codes. They cut them from eighty-four to thirty-two and created work groups, with cross-trained associates in each group.)

Companies that can't stabilize workload can't provide stable schedules— even when they know how much good it would do them. An experiment in twenty-eight Gap stores found that improving schedule stability increased store productivity by 5.1 percent.[5] Yet, Gap was still limited in how much it could improve the consistency and predictability of employees' schedules, because it couldn't change merchandising and delivery, which was where the instability came from.

That's the reason why the retailer cited in chapter 8 couldn't adopt the good jobs system even though senior leaders saw good jobs as a good investment. The leadership approved a pilot but only gave the implementation team permission to change what happened within the four walls of the store. The team could make small improvements, but the biggest workload drivers were decisions made by corporate-level merchandising and logistics. Frequent promotions and constant display changes—often last-minute—caused unpredictable schedules. Deliveries arrived at stores on Fridays, one of the busiest days. So the workload was heavy Friday through Saturday and then very light during the week. That, in turn, meant that more than 80 percent of the hourly employees were part-timers who were assigned too few hours (most worked less than fifteen hours a week) to make a decent living.

The mindset of those in merchandising was that delivering on a Friday morning would help them best match supply with demand during busy periods. Had they taken a more customer-centric, systemic approach, like Zara—one of the best when it comes to matching supply with demand—they would have seen the full impact of their decisions. Big spikes in workload hurt store operations and caused mistakes. Often, boxes would remain in the back rooms because there wasn't enough time to process them all. With so few hours assigned to them, employees never became experts in selling or in managing displays, so of course their sales productivity was lower. Unstable schedules drove turnover, which led to inexperienced employees making mistakes in displaying merchandise and serving the customer. All these unintended consequences ultimately hurt the company's ability to deliver the products customers wanted and serve them well.

This company was not able to move from siloed decision-making to customer-centric decision-making. As a result, it never saw good jobs and operational excellence as necessary to differentiate itself. A good investment, yes, but that wasn't motivation enough to change their mindsets. (See figure 9-3.)

FIGURE 9-3

"All else equal" thinking versus system thinking

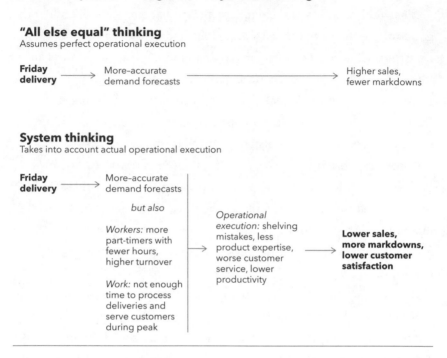

"All else equal" thinking
Assumes perfect operational execution

Friday delivery → More-accurate demand forecasts ⟶ Higher sales, fewer markdowns

System thinking
Takes into account actual operational execution

Friday delivery → More-accurate demand forecasts

but also

Workers: more part-timers with fewer hours, higher turnover

Work: not enough time to process deliveries and serve customers during peak

→ *Operational execution:* shelving mistakes, less product expertise, worse customer service, lower productivity ⟶ **Lower sales, more markdowns, lower customer satisfaction**

Invest in People as Early as Possible

Another big lesson to learn from successful journeys is to invest in higher pay as early and as much as possible. Of course, the companies that do so also improve schedule stability, career paths, and expectations—the other investments in people—as quickly as possible. But raising pay early was crucial.

Low pay *guarantees* turnover—and all the bad things that come with that. Hasbrouck of Moe's Original BBQ recalled: "Before we raised pay, we had tried different things. We tried profit sharing during Covid-19 when we had some good months, but it rang very hollow. We tried to create a protective bubble around our staff with pizza nights and little perks. And it just never really improved their lives. You have to pay people and offer good benefits . . . and then you can expand out from there. But if you're just trying to do a few things around the edges, you can't expect too much."

The Wulffs at Mud Bay had always wanted their company to be a great place to work. But they had been paying at or below the market wage. After reading Jack Stack's *The Great Game of Business*, a popular book for leaders of employee-owned companies and practitioners of open-book management, low wages seemed reasonable. "Keep your wages below market," wrote Stack, "so you can keep your overhead below your competitors and keep sharing profits." But profit sharing doesn't help much when pay is lower than subsistence level.

Given limited resources, you'll need to choose whose pay to invest in first and how much you can invest. As you consider *whose pay to invest in first*, ask yourself:

- Which roles have the highest turnover (and lowest pay)?

- Which of the lowest-paying roles are the most important for company success?

As you consider *how much to raise pay*, ask:

- How much can you afford in order to get as many employees as possible—especially the full-timers—up to a living wage?

- How much do you need to pay to attract and retain the talent you need?

Now let's see how several companies handled this important step.

Whose pay to invest in first?

Many successful journeys start with pay raises for all hourly workers. For Mud Bay and Quest Diagnostics, the reason was simple. These workers met both key criteria: they had the highest turnover *and* they were the ones interacting with customers and solving—or not solving—their problems. At both companies, frontliners' experience and knowledge were key. High turnover, of course, is the enemy of experience and knowledge.

Aetna and PayPal started their pay investment specifically with whichever employees were considered financially insecure. Most were working in call centers and they, too, met both criteria: turnover was high, yet these were the public face of their companies.

At Sam's Club, the first pay raises were for positions with the largest impact on company success and member experience—team leads, meat cutters, and bakery specialists. Team leads owned specific sections. Corporate leadership had noticed that clubs with long-tenured team leads—who really knew their communities and clubs—performed better. Sam's Club concluded that if it took good care of its team leads and got them to stay with the company longer, those employees would take care of everything else. Experienced employees in fresh food departments such as meat and bakery were critical for member loyalty. They wanted to make these positions destination roles for other associates to get promoted to. The message given to all other employees was that they would be next. Once Sam's Club got into a virtuous cycle, it could raise pay for other positions, too. And they did. In 2021, the minimum wage at Sam's Club rose from $11 an hour to $15 an hour. Starting with team leads was successful enough at Sam's Club that Furner then implemented it during his first year as CEO of Walmart US.

How much to raise pay?

It would be great to at least make sure that the company's minimum wage for full-timers is a living wage; it would be even better to ensure that every employee has some disposable income. But that may not be possible immediately, especially for companies whose profit margins are low and whose low-wage employees account for a big portion of overall costs. In that case, you may consider making incremental improvements or complementing a small increase in minimum pay with frequent tenure-based increases.

For Mud Bay, the pay increase was about what they could afford given their 2 percent profit margins. In 2014, they began to raise their hourly wages twice a year in fifty-cent increments along with raises tied to annual performance reviews. In this way, the average hourly wage increased from

$11.50 in 2014 to $15 in 2017. Hourly wage increases along with providing more hours per employee (the percentage of employees who worked more than thirty hours a week went from 69 to 82 in three years)—thanks to efforts to smooth workload—made a big difference in take-home pay.

By 2022, Mud Bay was financially healthy enough to pay every worker a living wage, as calculated by MIT's living wage calculator. It took a while, but they got there, whereas raising pay that much from the start could have sunk the company.

Daily Table, a nonprofit grocery chain based in Boston that sells healthy food at low prices in low-income neighborhoods, began with raising pay for hourly employees from $12 an hour to $15 an hour in February 2019. The chain's first two locations were in Dorchester and Roxbury, two sections of Boston with high poverty and high food insecurity. Initially, wages at Daily Table were the minimum wage in Boston and the market wage for retail there. The founder, Doug Rauch—formerly president of Trader Joe's—thought that, as a nonprofit and a startup, Daily Table couldn't afford more than the market wage.

But five years on, he realized that they couldn't afford *not* to pay more. Staff with constant money and health worries found it hard to focus on the job and to get along with customers. Rauch learned that several full-time employees were homeless. Turnover was 200 percent. The $3-an-hour pay increase—what Daily Table could afford—brought wages close to MIT's living wage for one adult and set Daily Table above the competition in terms of pay. Rauch explained: "We were paying minimum wage and getting a minimum response. What if we went to $15 an hour and reduced turnover and raised the standard of accountability? We said, 'We want to provide you with a better outcome and we think you will lean in and provide us with a better outcome, too.'" Within a year, turnover dropped 40 percent and sales per hour improved.

Aetna and PayPal combined raising pay with reducing health-care costs to enable everyone to have sufficient net disposable income. PayPal had a target of 20 percent net disposable income after taxes. Aetna raised its minimum wage from $12 an hour to $16 an hour in 2016. Why exactly $16 an hour? Bertolini told me that even the labor activists were calling for a $15 minimum wage at the time, so he decided to top that. A minimum wage of $16 an hour plus lower health-care costs for employees who were under 300 percent of the federal poverty line meant financial security—a world of difference for those who hadn't had it.

At Sam's Club, initial raises in 2019 were between $5 and $7 an hour, from a base of $15. Furner told my students that they had complicated spreadsheets with cost-of-living differences in various cities and regions. It proved possible, using these spreadsheets, to justify doubling pay to $30 an hour or to justify not raising pay at all. If those were both answers to the same question, he figured, they must be asking the wrong question. So instead of asking what pay raise could be justified financially, they asked how much they had to pay to make those positions the best ones in retail in every part of the country. After all, the real goal was not a specific bottom line but rather to attract and retain strong talent to reduce turnover and all its attendant ills. That was bound to be good for the bottom line, even if they couldn't predict exactly how good.

While Quest raised starting pay by only $1 an hour—from $13 to $14—in 2016, they rewarded tenure by providing predictable raises at three months, six months, and twelve months. They also created clear career paths for reps, which hadn't been the case up until then.

It's hard to overstress the importance of tenure-based pay and career paths for frontline workers and for companies' ability to keep them. When I studied Costco, Trader Joe's, QuikTrip, and Mercadona, I found that they all rewarded tenure through higher pay and through targeting 100 percent promotion from within. They have predictable and significant pay raises annually or biannually, usually up to a certain cap. At Mercadona for example, if you were a fruit and vegetable specialist, your pay would grow annually for four years, by which time you would be making 35 percent more than what you made in your first year.[6] At Costco, the median pay is almost 50 percent higher than the starting pay. These companies know that employees are more valuable to them as they gain experience and become more productive. So they want to do what they can to keep them.

In 2018, Eric Mason, a Chick-fil-A owner-operator in Sacramento, California, raised the minimum pay of his staff to $17 an hour and transitioned to more full-time employees. But, in his view, the most effective people investment he made was to establish a clear "roadmap for advancement." Each promotion comes with a set pay raise on a scale from $18 to $30, and Mason thinks the set pay rates are important. "Before it was just me walking around going, 'Hey, John, you're doing a really great job, I'm going to give you a 25-cent raise' or 'Sarah, gosh, your salads are amazing. I'm going to give you a 75-cent raise.' But I didn't like that because it was so inconsistent. Now the model is very stable and everybody in the house knows what to expect." Mason believes that the road map for advancement—combined with continued feedback—is the real glue that holds together a living wage model. "It's a key in their brain like, 'Okay, I see the future of this work,'" he says. "I always say they come for the pay, but they stay for the culture."[7]

Expect Issues

As you see, there are many ways to go about raising pay. Be warned that all of them will pose problems with fairness and compression. (Compression happens when starting pay reaches what long-term employees are making.) I haven't yet seen an example where everyone was happy with the changes in pay. If you have to start with certain positions, others will of course find it unfair. Longer-tenured employees may also find it unfair. When the minimum wage was raised at Moe's Original BBQ, some longer-term employees felt it was unfair that new employees were starting at much higher pay than they had received in their day. At Aetna, where the minimum wage increased from $12 to $16, people who were already making between $16 and $20 were unhappy. How come they didn't get a raise? Bertolini told them that he understood, but the objective for now was not so much to reward this or that group but to ensure that *everyone* had the financial security that, up until then, only some had enjoyed.

What about Employee Ownership?

A common question related to pay and benefits is, "What about employee ownership?" Giving a stake to workers can align their interest with those of management and shareholders and make them more engaged. The upside for workers can be big. Employees who are given stock in the company where they work can see their assets appreciate and build wealth over time. Some companies such as QuikTrip effectively use employee ownership to build wealth for their employees. When the private equity firm KKR bought CHI Overhead Doors, they gave stock to hourly employees, shared company data with them, and involved them in improvement. Productivity and profitability improved dramatically. When KKR exited within seven years, the checks to workers ranged from $2,000 for a new employee to $800,000 for the most-tenured hourly employees and truck drivers.

Employee ownership can work if you are already operating with low turn-over. One company with which we worked had an employee stock ownership plan (ESOP). But it had a vesting period of four years and the company had 90 percent annual turnover, so most workers ended up with little or no equity. In fact, most of the workers we spoke to there couldn't tell us what an ESOP was, even though the company had T-shirts that read: "ESOP: Ask us about it!"

If you start your pay increases with hourly employees but not their direct managers, you may have compression issues. If you have multiple locations with cost-of-living differences, you may have people complaining if they're all paid the same no matter where they live. Or you could have people complaining about being paid differently (in different places) for the same job. Mud Bay initially raised pay equally for the whole chain, but a lot of people didn't think it was fair that employees living in expensive Seattle earned no more than employees doing the same job in much-cheaper Olympia. By 2022, when the company had strong enough financials to bring everyone to a living wage in their own area, some complained that it wasn't fair to base pay on the cost of living where the store is. After all, you could be working at a store in a suburb but actually living and buying your groceries in a much more expensive downtown area.

On this issue, all I can say is: You can't make everyone happy—just do your best. But in any case, involve the frontline employees in the decision as much as possible and then explain—with no equivocation—why you made your final choice. At least some will accept a decision they wish had been different. No one will accept finding out you hadn't been straight with them.

Involving frontline employees and explaining the why should be your guidelines for how to make all changes. As we've seen in earlier chapters, many ills result from disconnects between the home office and the front lines. The more you can spend time on the front lines, get to know their perspective, involve them, and be transparent with them on how the changes will affect their lives and their work, the better. There are many ways to involve the frontline staff. Quest included reps as part of their centralized implementation team. Sam's Club had "change champions" who were all from the field: assistant managers, club managers, market managers. (Centralized implementation teams at these companies as well as at Mud Bay also had representatives from key HQ functions whose decisions affected frontline work.)

Go beyond Raising Pay and Creating Career Paths

You can also raise expectations.

It is sometimes said that 90 percent of success is just showing up. There's some truth to that, so companies including Sam's, Quest, Moe's, and Daily Table began raising expectations by creating a robust attendance policy. Previously, at Quest, a rep could be absent for up to five days in a row and have it counted as a single absence. When MaryAnn Camacho explained to a group of reps that, from now on, every day you

Stabilizing People at a Manufacturer

Deublin is a manufacturer of rotating unions—complex sealed bearings used in machine tools, paper mills, wind turbines, and other industries. When the company's president, Ron Kellner, read about the Toyota Production System (TPS) and visited factories that had implemented it, it was clear to him that it was superior to Deublin's batch production system. Even though Deublin was a profitable "smooth sailing" company, as he told me, there were many problems under the surface. Batch production led to mistakes, delivery problems, long lead times, and costly inventory. Kellner made the case to his board that if Deublin stuck with the status quo, they would lose competitiveness.

Deublin's production line was down 31 percent of the time. Although that was partly due to instabilities in materials, machinery, and methods, there was also a lot of people instability. The line's complexity required highly trained employees who knew the product and the process, could consistently follow standardized work, were attentive to detail, and could quickly identify what was going wrong and think of ways to solve it. Deublin did not have a steady supply of such workers.

Workforce and workload stability is a prerequisite for operational excellence. When Toyota executives describe the technical elements of TPS, they use the house image.

Notice that the figure is a house with a foundation. The two pillars cannot stand without that foundation. You can't do just-in-time (JIT) production if your equipment keeps breaking down, if the quality or delivery of your supplies is unreliable, if your work processes depend on exceptions and workarounds, or if you have high employee turnover, attendance problems, or low ability. So, any company that wants to adopt TPS must address people stability early on their journey. You also can't do JIT production without *heijunka*—that is, level production. A predictable and smooth workload is a prerequisite for the pillars.

At Deublin, the biggest problem was high turnover among temporary workers brought in to deal with seasonal variability in demand. Temps often proved inadequate and had to be replaced. Those who could do the work often left for companies that offered clearer career paths and better pay. Before Deublin could improve its production process, it had to address its turnover.

It did so by creating a process designed to systematically hire the right people rather than just hiring and waiting to see who worked out and who didn't. This process included a standardized dexterity test and a behavior assessment test. Deublin also changed its training procedures to provide new hires with mentors and to do a better job helping them master crucial skills. This helped cut the time needed for temps to secure full-time assembly-line positions from twelve months to six months. Deublin raised starting wages 25 percent and offered a 20 percent raise and increased benefits after six months. The company also explicitly laid out how one could progress to machinist, supervisor, and mid- and upper-level management roles.

Turnover among temps dropped 50 percent and Deublin found itself with a much more stable and productive workforce.

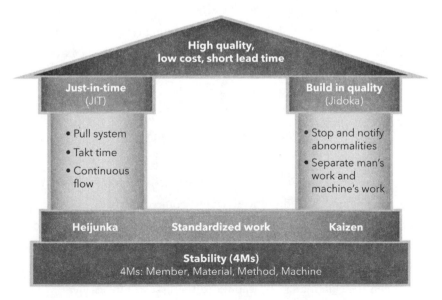

Source: © 2022 Toyota Production System Support Center, Inc. ("TSSC").

didn't turn up counted as one day you didn't turn up, one rep stood up and started clapping. "The employees who had been coming to work had been picking up the slack for everybody else," Camacho explained, "and they were sick of it." Supervisors, she hoped, would now spend less time managing absences and more time coaching, developing the team, and contributing to continual improvement. "You cannot let a nonperformer continue," she explained, "because it becomes cancerous for the entire team."

Once Quest was able to reduce turnover and attendance problems, they raised expectations further by improving hiring and training. Previously, they used to look for call center experience. But just because you have worked in a call center for Verizon doesn't mean you would do well at a diagnostics company. So now they identified the *attributes* that mattered to the job: empathy, skill in personal interactions, and familiarity with medical terminology—which might well be found in people who hadn't already worked in a call center. The first phase of hiring was now done by a talent acquisition team that screened candidates, a process that not only produced better candidates but also reduced the workload for call center managers; they no longer had to spend their time going through piles of résumés instead of focusing on managing their teams. Once candidates were screened, the call center managers would conduct structured interviews to do final selection.

Effect of the Initial Changes

Higher pay can be life changing for the people who get it. Bertolini told me that employees he didn't know would come up to him and say, "Oh, my God, thank you. Now I can send my kids to college" or "Now I don't have to go talk to bill collectors on break anymore" or "Now I can work just one job instead of two." Simmons at Sam's Club told me he was at a club when the club manager announced the first pay investment.[8] "I saw tears. It was a big deal. It was really an emotional day," he said. There were many stories Simmons and his colleagues heard. For example, a meat cutter informed of his pay increase responded: "I need to call my wife. I don't have to work two jobs anymore."

Psychologist Robert Cialdini describes reciprocation as a widespread and basic norm of human culture and a powerful principle of persuasion.[9] At Mercadona, reciprocity is considered a universal truth. In successful adoptions of the good jobs system, this norm is in action. You give by investing in pay and making the employees' job better, then you receive their commitment and hard work.

Creating a more manageable workload creates pride in one's work. I am amazed at how frequently I see in social media groups frontliners proudly sharing photos of the store displays they've just set up or a picture with a customer they helped or some other example of a job well done. You could say the secret of the good jobs system is all right there: most people *want* to do a good job and will appreciate whoever gives them the chance to do so.

When Sam's Club reduced workload, they started getting letters from customers thanking them for hiring the additional associates. They hadn't done any such thing, but it seemed like they had because the associates could spend noticeably more time helping customers. They also had time to become more knowledgeable about products.

Investing in people and simplifying work produce many other benefits. Training is quicker and easier with simpler processes to learn and fewer products and services to learn about. Offering stable rather than chaotic work schedules also does wonders for training. Fewer people to hire means you can now take the time to do the training right. If you've reduced your employee turnover by 30 percent, you can now spend at least 30 percent more per employee in training without increasing your budget.[10] On-the-job training can now be done by more-experienced people. And managers are less likely to feel dispirited at the prospect of training someone who probably won't be there long anyway.

Standardization, too, is easier. Taking out all the nonessentials—the clutter of nifty but unnecessary products, tools, discounts, reports, communications, and processes—means there are fewer things to standardize and fewer things that one needs to be trained in. Stability in people means you can now involve employees in creating and improving standards and empower them to make decisions and contribute to continuous improvement—because now you have a solid core of people who really know the job and the customers, who care about the company and their careers in it, and who have time in the day to think, plan, and experiment.

Perhaps the most important impact of these changes in stability is that you have a much better chance of keeping your managers, because their job is better. Although pay is frequently the reason that frontliners quit, it is rarely the primary reason their managers quit. In companies with high frontline turnover and rampant operational problems, managers are generally paid fairly well but they burn out, both from stress and from the sheer number of hours. They'd love to spend their time developing people but, as we've seen, a system of mediocrity hardly lets them do that.

Remember Eric Mason, the Chick-fil-A owner-operator who raised the minimum pay and transitioned to more full-time employees? One reason he did that is that he just couldn't take the chaos anymore. He was in his forties and was at work Monday through Saturday until two in the morning. High turnover meant he couldn't build anything lasting. "You set out a game plan, but things weren't getting done because there were so many things going on in each person's life." In 2018, his restaurant sales had been around $5 million a year. By 2021, they were over $11 million, but he was healthier, living a better, less chaotic life.

We've covered a lot in this chapter, but remember, this was only about how to get your journey to excellence off to a good start. There's still a ways to go, so in the next chapter, we'll discuss how to make sure you don't lose your momentum or get sidetracked.

Ride the Momentum

When Kath McLay became the CEO of Sam's Club in November 2019, the chain had just simplified its customer offering, simplified work, and invested in its frontline workers. As at other companies, simplifying and investing started a virtuous cycle. Workers whose pay and work improved stayed longer and were able to serve the customers better. Simplification helped reduce prices—a big reason why customers chose Sam's Club. All this drove higher sales, which allowed McLay to invest more in pay and in technologies that simplified associates' jobs even more. From 2020 to 2022, Sam's Club increased hourly pay by 18 percent. McLay and her team reduced product variety, reduced opening hours, and cut down on one-day promotions that did drive traffic but also drove the associates crazy and increased supply chain variability.

That's the thing about the virtuous cycle. From a restaurant to a factory to a call center to Sam's Club, the pattern is the same. Once you invest and see performance benefits, you can afford to invest further and see further performance benefits. That's momentum!

In this chapter, we will focus on three things that companies can do once they have created a virtuous cycle for themselves that they couldn't do before:

- Develop strong managers

- Empower employees to solve customer problems and be customer advocates

- Develop a capacity for adaptation and continuous improvement by developing standards and routines and making small incremental changes with frontline input

Now You Can Develop Strong Managers

Companies that operate with excellence spend time and resources on manager development. Their managers know how to grow their employees and the business. They learn about coaching and giving feedback. At Toyota, for example, managers learn about situational leadership—adapting their management style to their goals and circumstances, including the particular people they have on their team. At Costco, everyone understands that 90 percent of a manager's job is teaching, so managers learn how to ask questions and coach instead of giving orders and checking off boxes. Managers in companies operating in excellence also learn the business; they know what drives performance and how to improve it. Remember in chapter 6 how Todd Miner at Costco could tie the fat trim on the rib eye to how much his department would lose in shrink? At Toyota, there are daily huddles focused on performance metrics for quality, cost, and productivity. At Mercadona, one of the first things store managers do in the morning is check the numbers from the day before and then go to each department to talk about performance and how to improve it. Every day.

Given how important managers are, it is tempting to want to start the change effort with manager training. It is easy and comforting to point to gaps in your managers' or employees' competence as the problem and thus to training as the solution. This is especially so because, at mediocre companies in which the whole system is designed for inconsistent operational execution, there are nevertheless pockets of excellence. Company leaders, as we saw in chapter 4, look at those units and wrongly conclude that competent unit managers can solve their system problems. Those exceptional managers can be extremely helpful in teaching other managers how to lead. But as Michael Beer—a leading authority on change management—has found from decades of research and real-world advising, training as a change strategy doesn't work.

Why not? Because even well-trained and motivated employees can't apply their knowledge and skills in a system that doesn't let them. Even worse, those employees who try and fail become cynical. Beer and his colleagues observed that "corporate leaders may fool themselves into believing that they are implementing real change through corporate education, but others in the organization know better."[1] One company spent $20 million on a state-of-the-art center for safety training yet saw little improvement in safety.[2]

So first you need to improve the system so that training can work. Start by giving your managers what they don't have now: time. That's a key reason why you start with subtracting workload and workload variability in the frontlines, as we outlined in chapter 9: it frees up the managers to excel rather than put out fires, fill in for missing workers, or manage unnecessary complexity. Instead of that supermarket manager we met in chapter 4 spending so much of his time filling in for missing cashiers, he would be mentoring cashiers so that they might eventually become store managers.

You should also think about redrawing the duties of your managers, removing parts of the job that have defaulted to them but could easily be done by others. For example, managers don't need to be involved in the initial phases of hiring (advertising the job, initial screening) or in the paperwork involved in onboarding.

Once Sam's Club set the conditions to protect managers' time, it made sense to invest in leadership development. Sam's Club developed a six- to eight-week training program for team leads which exposed them to all areas in the club (membership, merchandising, fresh food, curbside service, and so on) and taught them about financial acumen, strategic thinking, and coaching. Quest invested in coaching programs to teach supervisors how to lead people, provide feedback, and hold crucial conversations.

Once you get turnover and understaffing under control, it is also possible to have a strong talent pipeline. In the first two years of its journey to excellence, Quest's internal promotion rate tripled; more positions than not were being filled from within. From 2019 to 2022, the time to fill an open position at Sam's Club had dropped by 74 percent. Manager turnover decreased by 29 percent. And promotion of hourly employees to salaried positions increased 117 percent.

Over the last two decades, I've spent time with hundreds of frontline managers. One thing I hear repeatedly is how much pride they have in developing people and watching a protégé's career grow and how much pride they have in improving their unit. Sean Mckendry, a warehouse manager at Costco, put it nicely: "I started out twenty years ago as a baker in the bakery department, not thinking that one day I'm going to run a $150 million business. But I had people around me that took the time to teach me different parts of the business to help me further my career and now I just want to do the same thing [for others] and further their careers."

When you commit to promoting from within and create the conditions for managers to develop promotable people, you're going to have a reliable supply of strong managers who can't wait to grow your business.

Now You Can Empower Employees

Stability in people and workload also enables empowering frontline workers to solve customer problems, become customer advocates, and create real differentiation. Here's how it played out at Aetna's call centers.

The manager running the Jacksonville, Florida, location told Mark Bertolini that his team had an idea to empower frontline reps. Customers often called to complain about being denied something important, such as a prior authorization, a pharmacy prescription, or an out-of-network provider. Reps were not always allowed to resolve the matter. A member might tell the rep that the pharmacist at Walgreens said her insurer won't cover the drug her doctor had prescribed. Let's say the member's employer had accidentally left her off the eligibility list, but of course she doesn't know that and neither does her employer or the pharmacist. As things were, if the rep saw in his system that this caller was not eligible, he would simply tell her she had to find out from her employer why not. Reps were eager to keep the call short because they were evaluated and paid partly on how quickly they handled calls.

The Jacksonville team had something quite different in mind, which they called "service without borders." A rep would have the flexibility to reach out to other parts of the company (such as pharmacy, clinical care, eligibility, and network providers) to resolve the member's issue while the member was still on the line. So, in this example, the rep would put the member on hold and call whoever in Aetna is responsible for eligibility, who would then call the member's employer and find out about the mistake, have them correct it, and share the accurate information with Walgreens so the pharmacist could fill the prescription—all while the member is on the line with Aetna. In addition, the reps would be allowed to use their judgment to grant one-time exemptions for products or services that Aetna was not obligated to cover. If the reps thought there had been an honest mistake, they would grant the exemption, pay the claim, and educate the customer.

Impressed, Bertolini invited the manager to present this idea to the executive team—but the team pushed back at what they viewed as a radical change. Senior leaders thought the reps would "give away the farm." Bertolini thought otherwise. He believed reps would be able to tell which customers had legitimate claims and which might be trying to rip off Aetna—after all, they talked to customers all day. He explained: "We get calls from customers who go to the pharmacy, for, say, a $4 antibiotic and for whatever reason, the pharmacist tells them that they are not eligible. Regardless of eligibility, we should cover it, because no one is trying to steal a $4 antibiotic and the last thing we want to do is to lose a customer over so small an item."[3] In fact, it was cheaper to pay for the item than to spend the resources to manage a complaint.

Bertolini piloted the proposal for six months with a group of reps who served less than two percent of Aetna's members. The reps were told that if the costs exceeded a certain threshold, they would have to go back to the leadership team and explain what's working and what's not. Bertolini wanted to make sure the executives would not interfere with the reps. "If you have people standing around watching all the time, they'll blow it up. They'll pick at it like a scab," he said. "So you put a budget around it and say, 'If the scab becomes infected—if it goes over the budget—we'll look at it again. Otherwise, leave it alone and let them do their work.'"

The reps put their heads together and created work groups for specific issues. They created a central operation so that when a customer complaint came in and they didn't know the answer, they knew where to get it. They created support groups to discuss tough cases. They held each other accountable. Although it was a lot of work, this program made their own jobs much better. Reps had always wanted to help the customers and now they had much more power and ability to do just that. After a year, the reps had spent less than 20 percent of their budget. Member satisfaction increased. The program eventually went companywide.

When I asked Bertolini what gave him the conviction that he could trust the reps to make good decisions, he said, "You can't just sort of turn on the trust switch. 'So okay, now we're going to trust you. Now we expect it all to work.' Because first of all, the employees are going to say, 'What are they up to?'" You first had to gain their trust. "Trust begets trust." It was crucial, he said, that empowerment came *after* Aetna had invested in higher pay, better benefits, and employee well-being programs. Employee turnover had already dropped. The way people thought about their jobs had already changed; there was more pride in working at Aetna. That's the kind of workforce that can—and *should*—be empowered.

Having already created the right conditions for empowerment became a serious advantage for companies during Covid-19. Things were changing all the time, which meant that you needed adaptable people who could solve problems promptly, come together as a team, and get a lot done quickly. Unempowered employees are almost by definition not adaptable—the system they're in won't let them be. At Mud Bay and Sam's Club, both designated as essential businesses during the first few months of the pandemic, a capable and motivated workforce enabled them to follow safety processes and come up with new ways to serve customers. It took Mud Bay just a few days to create curbside delivery. When Sam's Club found out that some of their members were nervous about getting out of their cars, it took them only six days to set up a concierge service, even though that involved the product team and store operations team.

It should come as no surprise that empowerment can help you adapt and can improve customer and employee experience and company performance. But remember—as Bertolini said—that you can't just decide "We're going to empower our people." You can't do it if you are operating with workforce and workload instability. Set that foundation first.

Now You Can Create a Culture of Continuous Improvement

Apart from empowering employees to serve the customers and solve their problems, you now have the muscle for continuous improvement. There aren't so many different things to do—you've simplified and subtracted—so it's easier to standardize processes. You have stability in people—because you've invested in them—so you can involve them in standardization and improvement, which is not merely a good idea, it's essential.

This is exactly what happened at Quest. Once they reduced turnover, reduced understaffing, and raised expectations, MaryAnn Camacho—who was leading the call centers—thought it was time to standardize call center processes and begin building a culture of continuous improvement.

Camacho knew that effective standardization would require frontline input and buy-in. She also wanted everyone to learn how to identify problems, design solutions, and take part in implementing change. To get there, she decided to select two pods to be "model pods." Supervisors who wanted their pod to be selected had twenty-four hours to come up with a five-minute presentation explaining why they should be a model pod. The presentation was dubbed "Shark Tank," after the reality TV show. Supervisors came up with catchy names for their pods, like the Wicked Tunas, the Go-Getters, and the A-Team. One supervisor turned up in galoshes and waders with a fishing pole and said, "We are going fishing. We're going to catch the big one as far as employee engagement, redoing our stats, and getting control of our organization."

The two model pods were introduced to quality management and continuous improvement tools and began holding daily nine-minute huddles. Members discussed performance metrics, ideas for improvement, and current projects, much of which was written up on a huddle board, which helped them monitor how they were doing. Huddles were also a chance for pods to celebrate recent wins.

Within weeks, reps began carefully observing each other's work and finding ways to reduce waste and improve efficiency. One idea, for example, was dubbed the "Spanish whisper." While a caller could select English or Spanish when calling in, the bilingual rep who answered did not know beforehand that the caller was a Spanish speaker and lost twenty-three seconds per call finding that out. With the Spanish whisper, phones were programmed to whisper the word "Spanish" into the rep's ear before he or she picked up the call. Another idea was to include patient account numbers when paging physicians. Reps who couldn't get physicians on the phone to communicate critical results would have them paged. Before the change, that page included only a callback number, not any identifying information about the patient. Often, a different rep answered the physician's callback and wouldn't know whose results to provide.

Every week, the model pod supervisors shared their progress with all the other pod supervisors and with members of other groups such as training and workforce management. Soon, standardized processes and improvements from the model pods were being replicated. For example, after a few months, all the pods held daily huddles. "That weekly meeting became a very hot ticket," said Camacho. "People . . . wanted to see how their peers were doing because we show our scorecards. Furthermore, they wanted to hear about the standardization projects that would be implemented across the [call center]." When other pod supervisors saw the improvement in work and performance and the recognition their "model" peers were getting, they, too, wanted to be one of those teams. By February 2017, there were twenty-two model pods.

To further involve frontline employees in improvement, Quest introduced Frontline Idea Cards (FICs) to help collect, evaluate, and implement ideas from reps. Anyone who submitted a card received a thank you card, signaling that management was listening. Each week, the Friday huddle was dedicated to evaluating and ranking FICs. High-impact, easy-to-implement ideas were often referred to as "just do it" ideas. For example, have a board visible that showed all the equipment used in labs so that reps would know what tube or container the caller was asking about. FICs were a big boost to rep morale. "Before the FIC, you never felt like your ideas were being heard," one rep said. "You could say something to someone, but it didn't go anywhere." In eighteen months, over fourteen hundred ideas were submitted and more than half were adopted.

Small Changes, Big Changes

Small changes are beautiful, and the positive momentum creates faith in the organization. Companies like Four Seasons, Mercadona, and Toyota, which have a culture of making small improvements every day, end up putting a healthy distance between themselves and the competition. Compounding is powerful.

But for companies operating with high employee turnover, understaffing, and a lot of firefighting, small changes can never be enough by themselves. In one of the Good Jobs Institute's earliest partnerships—with a supermarket chain—we started with small changes in two areas: the deli section and the checkout lines. There was a strong business need in both areas. The long lines were so bad they became a meme. High shrink at the deli reduced profitability. We worked with the deli and front-end managers to identify the most important metrics and how to display them in a way that would make sense for them and their teams. Every day, there would be a huddle in which the team would go over what was coming up that day, performance metrics, and what had been getting in the way; suggest solutions; and celebrate small wins. Within six weeks you could see the beginnings of a culture change. Neither the frontline staff nor their managers had ever been empowered this way. They enjoyed contributing their ideas and were proud to see them implemented.

But department managers were skipping the huddles when there were attendance problems they needed to deal with, and no one had time for a huddle when the deli shelves were messy and they had to prepare the store for customers. After some employees left, their managers shifted their focus from improvement to hiring and onboarding. Then there was a new store opening. Because this supermarket chain, like most others that operate in a vicious cycle, did not have a strong talent pipeline, the district manager and the store manager were pulled in to help get the new store going. The management support required to implement the changes was no longer there.

The lesson here is that making small changes can work *if* you have a reasonably stable system. If you are dealing with high turnover and a workload that is too heavy and too variable—driven by decisions made upstream—you just won't have the time or capabilities to leverage small changes into a virtuous cycle. That's why it is so important to make those *big* changes discussed in the last chapter—investing in people and simplifying their work—as early as possible.

When I share Quest's FICs with executives, they get excited about leveraging the knowledge of their frontline employees. Then I tell them, "Don't try this at home if you don't have a stable workforce and don't have clear mechanisms to act on their ideas." What enabled Quest to continue their huddles and FICs was the stability of the reps and their work and the organizational capability to implement new ideas. The biggest enabler, of course, for everything we've talked about in the last two chapters was the decision to become customer centric and therefore frontline centric, prioritizing the work frontline workers do and continuously improving it to better serve the customer.

Pilot or Just Fly?

We've talked about what to do first as you embark on your journey to excellence. Another important question is: What changes do you pilot before rolling them out? What changes do you just go ahead and implement across the company? This turns out to have less to do with research and best practices than with the conviction and courage we discussed in chapters 5 through 7.

Running pilots has become so prevalent in large organizations that at times managers don't stop to think things through—they just run pilots! As we saw in chapter 9, pilots often suck up frontline time, so be careful. What's more, there are circumstances in which the results of a well-constructed experiment will be dangerously misleading. For example, if Costco ran A/B tests—considered a best practice—to see whether adding a promotion or more SKUs would increase sales or even if raising prices a little would increase profits, they would most likely find that, yes, each of these would. But if Costco took to making decisions this way, soon enough they would drift from their strategy and begin to damage the trust they've built with their customers and even their employees.

Other complications with using pilots for testing elements of the good jobs system include interdependence and time. As we've seen before, many changes won't work in isolation. Pilots are also much better at capturing short-term effects than long-term ones. And as we know, with system change, things are likely to get worse before they get better.[4] At Quest, some employees left after expectations were raised with the new attendance policy. At Sam's Club, some employees left after the company moved to consistent schedules. If you're remodeling a section of your restaurant, you know you'll lose some customers during the remodeling and even for some period after.

I keep coming back to conviction and courage. It is one of the most important things I've learned—and one of the most inspiring things I've witnessed—during the eight years I've been working with business leaders to adopt the good jobs system. What does this have to do with piloting? You may be surprised to learn that none of the companies in the last chapter ran a pilot to test if raising pay would improve performance, although that might seem to be the riskiest of the changes they had in mind. They weren't making an incremental change to their existing system. They were changing the way they operated because they had become convinced they:

- Had to be customer centric

- Couldn't be customer centric without improving operational execution

- Couldn't improve operational execution without reducing turnover and improving employee ability

- Couldn't reduce turnover and improve ability without increasing pay

It wasn't a matter of whether they would increase pay. It was a matter of how much they could afford to increase and what else they had to do to make the pay investment work. You'll recall from chapter 6 that the supermarket chain H-E-B's pay policy is to pay frontline employees as much as they can while still offering customers great value and making a good profit.

Once you decide whose pay you'll raise and how much, making the actual change is not that hard. But for many other changes, these companies ran pilots (a) to learn *how* to make the change and (b) to bring others along.

Mud Bay, for example, knew they would add in-store weigh-in stations for dogs to help pet owners keep track of their pets' weight. (Yes, it's an issue for animals, too.) Rolling out the weigh stations required collaboration between the marketing, store development, and store operations teams at headquarters and the stores themselves. They piloted the program in a few stores, tried different scales, put the scales in different locations, got feedback from employees and customers, tweaked it, and then rolled it out.

At Quest, MaryAnn Camacho knew that creating a continuous improvement culture within each pod was important. Quest used a group of model pods to learn how best to do it and then leverage success in those pods to convince the others that this was worth doing.

Thus, they limited the inevitable initial mistakes and failures to a few particularly dedicated and well-led pods and accelerated acceptance and success in the rest.

Similarly, Bertolini knew that empowering Aetna's reps was the right thing to do for the business. The pilot run of "service without borders" in Jacksonville was conducted in a way that increased its likelihood of success, giving that group of reps the resources—including six months' time—to figure out how best to do this new thing. Once executives saw that empowerment improved member and rep experience without increasing company risk, they felt comfortable rolling it out in that particular form. So in this case the pilot here accomplished both goals: to learn how to do it and bring others along.

John Furner at Sam's Club also knew that reducing product variety was the right thing to do for their business. But that was a tough sell for people in merchandising. Merchandisers are good negotiators who don't like being told what to do. So Furner, like Bertolini, carefully created the right conditions for the pilot to be successful. They first piloted the SKU reduction at a club where they knew that the manager would handle it well. They went pretty extreme, reducing the variety by nearly 25 percent in that location! They told the club manager that if the SKU reduction hurt sales, they would adjust his bonus. But if it worked out, he might get to shape Sam's Club. They did the pilot only for a few weeks to show that sales didn't decrease and that member satisfaction with the assortment went up. Was this a long enough period to prove anything? Hardly! If sales had gone down during that period, would they have piloted longer? Probably!

Of all the companies I've mentioned in part 3, Sam's Club probably went through the most and biggest changes. They were a $60 billion company that had been around for thirty-five years—thus, hard to move—and they really did need a turnaround.

Chad Donath said this journey to excellence was the biggest and most complete change he's been through during his thirty-three-year career at Walmart. Donath joined Walmart at a store in Kewanee, Illinois, in 1989. His first job was pushing carts and cleaning bathrooms. He moved up in the organization and came to Sam's Club to lead the operational part of the transformation.

In 2019, Sam's Club rolled out many changes we covered in chapter 9 across the organization. Some changes were "piloted to test" whether they should be made (e.g., technology); some were "piloted to learn" how to make the change (e.g., implement block schedules) and to bring others along (e.g., SKU reduction); and some were "just done" (e.g., pay raises).

In the "pilot to learn" category, they piloted each of the big changes in a separate location. Once they learned how to do it, they layered those changes together in a few locations to see how the combination worked. For example, Sam's Club used to have an overnight shift to receive and stock merchandise. That shift often had high turnover—it wasn't a very desirable job—and there was little overlap between the night and the morning shifts, which made for a sloppy handoff. Early in the morning, when the morning shift would begin arriving, overnight shift staff would have to keep opening the door and then locking it as well as turning the alarm in the receiving area on and off. Talk about wasting time! So the company wanted to eliminate the overnight shift and decided to pilot the change. It was a logistical dance. Deliveries into the store would need to change: they had to decide which parts of the club to stock in the morning shift versus the evening shift, and they had to identify which crew would drop what pallets during the day versus in the evening. They also had to learn how to talk about the change with associates, how to train the associates, and how to help them understand why this would improve their jobs for them. They ended up piloting this approach for more than five months before rolling it out across the network.

As much as piloting helped Sam's Club learn how to make changes like these, there was no guarantee that the changes would work, and they weren't waiting for one. They had a theory for what they had to do to become the membership club that customers would love the most. "We went all in," Donath said. Everyone warned them against making such big changes. When they asked consulting companies for help in project management, every proposal they got back offered the same strategic advice: don't do this. Making that many big changes is too risky. This advice, though paid for, was ignored. "This organization has a lot of courage muscles," said Tim Simmons, who led the technology part of the transformation. "We believed we were doing the right thing. We just stuck to our guns. We knew what we had done and what we could do. . . . I've lived through twenty-eight years of piecemeal changes. So, we said, 'We're going to do this.'"

You Are Not Done!

Let's imagine that you have implemented all four operational choices of the good jobs system. You have invested in people. You have strong managers and high expectations. You could say you've done it, but that doesn't mean you're done. Now you have to stay the course. Professional managers, in particular, can find it hard to resist doing things that improve short-term performance at the expense of long-term performance. Psychologists have a name for this: present bias. What matters *now* matters most. As we saw in chapter 5, there will always be temptations to violate—let's say, temporarily suspend—the good jobs strategy for the sake of short-term performance. Top-line growth pressure, earnings pressure, or just reaction to noise (rather than a valid signal) can motivate you—it may seem they're forcing you—to add more to the customer offering at the expense of hurting your value proposition or to raise prices because of margin pressure or to cut labor costs during a downturn or to grow units more quickly than you can staff them with strong managers. But "temporary suspensions" don't tend to stay temporary. They can put you in a vicious cycle. How do you resist these dangerous temptations?

One way to do it is to put in place what psychologists call "commitment devices" that deliberately limit what you can do in the future. Costco's 15 percent maximum markup, having been made very public, is a commitment device to retain its pricing authority and trust with customers. Targeting 100 percent internal promotion is a commitment device for focusing on developing people. Mercadona's explicit ranking of its stakeholders—customers first, then employees, then suppliers, then society, and then investors—and a history of making decisions consistent with that ranking is a commitment device. Sam's Club now regularly reviews the number of sales promotions to make sure they are not giving in to the temptation to add. That's a commitment device. At Texas Road-house, a steakhouse with one of the highest net promoter scores in the restaurant industry, adding a new menu item requires subtracting an existing one. That's a commitment device.

The hardest pressure to resist is growing more quickly than you should, given your operating system and your management bench. I've seen too many companies do destructive things just to meet their growth targets. We've seen how Isadore Sharp at Four Seasons, Tricia Griffith at Progressive, and Craig Jelinek at Costco were all careful about growth. Sharp stopped unit growth when the chain didn't have enough strong hotel managers to run new units. Jelinek didn't give in to analyst pressure to open more stores—its model, dependent on strong managers, requires careful growth. Progressive won't grow unless they hit a 4 percent profitability target. The commitment device that Mark Bertolini at Aetna used was to underpromise earnings growth, so as to nip certain kinds of investor/analyst pressure in the bud. If you are starting a new company, your commitment device could be to keep your valuation low or to raise as little money as possible.

Find your own commitment device for growth and let your shareholders know that the point is to run the business in the best way for the long-term health of the company—yes, even at the expense of possible short-term gains. Then they are free to take it or leave it.

Don't these commitment devices limit innovation as well as risky growth? They don't. In fact, they fuel it. When Jim Sinegal comes to my class, the students always ask him two questions: Doesn't 100 percent internal promotion result in complacency? Aren't you nervous that someone will beat you because of your limited offering? And Sinegal always gives the same answer. He talks about how much Costco has evolved since its founding. The warehouses are completely different. Pharmacy, meat department, produce, hearing aids, bakery, optical, deli, and the food court didn't exist when Costco first started. "We didn't even have the hot dogs. Imagine, the world was deprived of our dollar-fifty hot dog!" So how do you innovate and evolve while sticking to your core? At Costco, sticking to the core never meant refusing to do anything new. It meant that there are three questions to ask before considering a new service or product (Mercadona and Trader Joe's have very similar questions):

- Can we do it well?

- Can we save our customers money?

- Can we make a profit on it?

If Costco thinks the answer to all three is yes, then the company is willing to give it a try. They think before they pilot. These questions impose discipline on experimentation—but certainly don't prohibit it—and make it easier to resist the temptations that arise constantly from competitors or investors.

One way to look at staying the course with a good jobs system is that, like the good jobs system itself, it requires a good deal of subtraction. One stays the course by removing from consideration those options which, though advantageous in some immediate way, would diminish the company's ability—its operational capacity or its dedication—to be as customer centric (and frontline centric) as possible.

EPILOGUE

It might have occurred to you that this book advocating some pretty big changes in corporate behavior is really about old-school principles of good management: Focus on creating real value for customers. Prioritize the work of those who serve the customers. Take care of your employees' basic needs to allow them to focus on their work and have dignity. Design the work so that employees are both motivated and able to be productive and to shine in front of the customers. Involve the people who do the work in improving that work. Make it a habit to do the right thing.

These old-school principles have been hijacked for some time by too much focus on short-term financial decision-making and on pursuing fast growth at all costs. When I was a doctoral student in the late 1990s at Harvard Business School, Jack Welch's management practices and business philosophy were revered. Almost everyone was in awe of how well GE could meet its earnings targets with amazing precision. We learned about stacked ranking and firing the bottom 10 percent of your employees every year as good management practice. GE almost made focusing on the core business uncool. Why would you do that when there are easier and faster ways to grow your valuation? Instead, Welch popularized a focus on dealmaking. GE moved away from manufacturing and into industries ranging from media to financial services—all via mergers and acquisitions.

One person who was not so impressed was Kent Bowen, a professor at Harvard Business School who was on my thesis committee and has remained my mentor.[1] He told me, "One day, someone is going to write a book about how much value those GE principles destroyed."[2] I didn't fully grasp what Kent meant until I studied how Home Depot fell into a vicious cycle in the mid-2000s. One of Welch's protégés, Bob Nardelli, almost killed the company's successful—customer-centric and frontline-centric—culture by applying the GE philosophy. (Another GE alum who worked under Welch for eighteen years, Jim McNerney, went on to be the CEO of Boeing and oversaw the development of the disastrous 737 MAX.)

During a presentation by an operations management scholar who was studying "revenue management" at airlines, Kent asked (although I don't remember his exact words): Shouldn't the airlines focus on running a good operation and serving the customers instead of overbooking and playing pricing games with their customers? Again, I didn't fully grasp what he meant until I began to understand the difference between being customer centric and financial centric.

Now I do. I sometimes find myself repeating Kent's questions to entrepreneurs and students who come to see me for advice. Just the other day, an entrepreneur told me about the growth pressures at his nine-year-old company. Even 30 percent growth, he said, was considered unacceptable. He then described the toll such high growth took on the mental health of his team—including his own anxiety. He acknowledged that there was no good reason to push for such rapid growth—there weren't even any network effects in his business. It all came down to investor expectations. "Why are you letting high growth drive your decisions?" I asked. "Why don't you focus on serving your customers, creating trust with your employees, and pursuing operational excellence?" He replied, "I feel like we have been worshipping the wrong god."

But you've now seen that there is an excellent alternative to that kind of anxiety and exhaustion. You've seen what that alternative requires and what it offers in return—and that the return is well worth the investment. You've seen that it takes courage and conviction to make the necessary system change, but you've also seen that the change is not quite as risky as at first it seems.

Let me conclude with one more piece of encouragement. You've seen this, too, throughout the book, but I'm going to make a special point of it here. Whatever the obstacles to your journey to excellence, you're going to have a lot of wind at your back. That wind will be your own people. Over and over in the last eight years, I have been startled and touched by how badly people in all parts and at all levels of the organization want to make this kind of change.

In workshop after workshop with one company or another, I've seen people from various functions—logistics, marketing, product design, finance, HR, and so on—genuinely upset to learn how much trouble they sometimes make for their frontline employees. They are genuinely anxious to begin a journey to become customer and frontline centric . . . *if only their leaders will allow them.*

Leadership sometimes means leading people where they don't at first want to go. Yet leadership can also mean leading people where they *do* want to go but need strong leadership to get there. For CEOs and other executives, then, this is a chance to exercise that kind of very satisfying leadership and to leave a most enviable legacy.

NOTES

Introduction

1. The US Bureau of Labor Statistics has been collecting quit rates since 2000 via the Job Openings and Labor Turnover Survey. The rate was lowest in 2009 and, in 2021, the quit rate reached a record high. "Job Openings and Labor Turnover Survey News Release," US Bureau of Labor Statistics, March 9, 2022, https://www.bls.gov/news.release/archives/jolts_03092022.htm.

2. Sarah Butler, "Amazon Offers $3,000 Sign-on Bonuses to US Delivery and Warehouse Workers," *The Guardian*, September 14, 2021, https://www.theguardian.com/technology/2021/sep/14/amazon-offers-3000-sign-on-bonuses-to-us-delivery-and-warehouse-workers.

3. Marcela Escobari, Ian Seyal, and Michael J. Meaney, "Realism about Reskilling: Upgrading the Career Prospects of America's Low-Wage Workers," Brookings Institute Report, November 2019, https://www.brookings.edu/research/realism-about-reskilling/.

4. Ruth Igielnik, "70% of Americans Say U.S. Economic System Unfairly Favors the Powerful," Pew Research Center, January 9, 2020, https://www.pewresearch.org/fact-tank/2020/01/09/70-of-americans-say-u-s-economic-system-unfairly-favors-the-powerful/.

5. Anne Case and Angus Deaton, *Deaths of Despair and the Future of Capitalism* (Princeton, NJ: Princeton University Press, 2020).

6. Even Rhodes Scholars! See Noam Schreiber, "Why a Rhodes Scholar's Ambition Led Her to a Job at Starbucks," *New York Times*, June 19, 2022, https://www.nytimes.com/2022/06/19/business/starbucks-union-rhodes-scholar.html#:~:text=They%20are%20motivated%20by%20a,U.S.%20locations%20had%20a%20union.

7. "U.S. Workers' Organizing Efforts and Collective Actions: A Review of the Current Landscape," MIT Institute for Work & Employment Research, June 2022, https://mitsloan.mit.edu/institute-work-and-employment-research/new-report-u-s-workers-organizing-efforts-and-collective-actions.

8. Sarah Anderson and Sam Pizzigati, "28th Annual IPS Executive Compensation Report," Institute for Policy Studies, June 2022, https://ips-dc.org/report-executive-excess-2022/ (accessed December 2022).

9. I'm grateful to my MIT colleague, David Autor, for sharing with me his analysis on why labor markets are expected to remain tight.

Chapter 1

1. For example, a 2006 study found higher customer satisfaction, as measured by the American Customer Satisfaction Index, associated with higher excess returns *without* higher stock market risk; see Claes Fornell, Sunil Mithas, and M. S. Krishnan, "Customer Satisfaction and Stock Prices: High Returns, Low Risk," *Journal of*

Marketing, vol. 70, issue 1. In his latest book, *Winning on Purpose* (Boston: Harvard Business Review Press, 2021), Fred Reichheld, creator of the Net Promoter Score, a widely used customer loyalty metric, shows that in a wide range of industries—grocery retailing, financial services, utilities, airlines, auto, telecom—companies with the highest Net Promoter Score show the strongest returns.

2. In *Winning on Purpose*, Fred Reichheld draws a very useful distinction between good growth and bad growth: Good growth comes from creating loyal customers. Bad growth comes from either attracting new customers by tempting them with deals or discounts or from taking advantage of existing customers through hidden fees.

3. In my previous book, *The Good Jobs Strategy* (Boston: New Harvest, 2014), "focus and simplify" is called "offer less."

4. Mercadona's market share went from around 15 percent in 2008 to over 20 percent in 2012. See Deborah Ball and Ilan Brat, "Spanish Supermarket Chain Finds Recipe," *Wall Street Journal*, October 23, 2012.

Chapter 2

1. Zeynep Ton, Cate Reavis, and Sarah Kalloch, "PayPal and the Financial Wellness Initiative," MIT Sloan School of Management case 21-002, August 1, 2022, https://mitsloan.mit.edu/teaching-resources-library/paypal-and-financial-wellness -initiative.

2. Mark Bertolini, *Mission Driven Leadership: My Journey as a Radical Capitalist* (New York: Currency, 2019).

3. "Winning the Juggling Act," The 2020 Compensation Best Practices Report, PayScale, https://www.payscale.com/content/report/2020-Compensation-Best-Practices -Report.pdf.

4. Leslie Davis and Hannah Hartig, "Two-Thirds of Americans Favor Raising Federal Minimum Wage to $15 an Hour," Pew Research Center, July 30, 2019, https://www.pewresearch.org/fact-tank/2019/07/30/two-thirds-of-americans-favor -raising-federal-minimum-wage-to-15-an-hour/.

5. A list of companies that have committed to at least $15 an hour can be found at the Good Jobs Institute website: https://goodjobsinstitute.org/companies-committed-to -raising-wages/.

6. MIT Living Wage Calculator, https://livingwage.mit.edu/.

7. Stephanie Kramer, "U.S. Has World's Highest Rate of Children Living in Single-Parent Households," Pew Research Center, December 12, 2019, https://www .pewresearch.org/fact-tank/2019/12/12/u-s-children-more-likely-than-children-in-other -countries-to-live-with-just-one-parent/.

8. Ken Jacobs, Ian Eve Perry, and Jenifer MacGillvary, "The Public Cost of a Low Federal Minimum Wage," UC Berkeley Labor Center, January 14, 2021, https://labor center.berkeley.edu/the-public-cost-of-a-low-federal-minimum-wage/.

9. Jonathan Morduch and Rachel Schneider, *The Financial Diaries: How American Families Cope in a World of Uncertainty* (Princeton, NJ: Princeton University Press, 2017), 11.

10. Daniel Schneider and Kristen Harknett, "Consequences of Routine Work Schedule Instability for Worker Health and Well-Being," *American Sociological Review* 84, no. 1 (February 1, 2019), https://journals.sagepub.com/doi/10.1177 /0003122418823184.

11. Board of Governors of the Federal Reserve System, "Economic Well-Being of U.S. Households in 2021," May 2022, https://www.federalreserve.gov/publications/files /2021-report-economic-well-being-us-households-202205.pdf. A year earlier, the number

had been 40 percent. According to the Fed report, the improvement is partly due to Covid-19 relief funds.

12. Schneider and Harknett, "Consequences of Routine Work-Schedule Instability for Worker Health and Well-Being."

13. Sean F. Reardon, Rachel A. Valentino, Demetra Kalogrides, Kenneth A. Shores, and Erica Greenberg, "Patterns and Trends in Racial Academic Achievement Gaps among States, 1999–2011," Stanford Center for Education Policy Analysis, 2013, https://stanford.io/326CPL9.

14. Stig Leschly and Stacey Childress, "Note on Student Outcomes in U.S. Public Education," Note 9-307-068 (Boston: Harvard Business School, 2019).

15. "Percentage of High School Dropouts among Persons 16–24 Years Old (Status Dropout Rate), by Income Level, and Percentage Distribution of Status Dropouts, by Labor Force Status and Years of School Completed: Selected Years, 1970-2016," *Digest of Education Statistics*, https://bit.ly/3em0kVu.

16. Greg J. Duncan, Kathleen L. Ziol-Guest, and Ariel Kalil, "Early-Childhood Poverty and Adult Attainment, Behavior, and Health," *Child Development* 81, no. 1 (January–February 2010): 306–325, https://srcd.onlinelibrary.wiley.com/doi/10.1111/j .1467-8624.2009.01396.x.

17. Anandi Mani, Sendhil Mullainathan, Eldar Shafir, and Jiaying Zhao, "Poverty Impedes Cognitive Function," *Science* 341, no. 6149 (August 30, 2013): 976–980, https://www.science.org/doi/10.1126/science.1238041; Sendhil Mullainathan and Eldar Shafir, "Freeing Up Intelligence," *Scientific American Mind*, January–February 2014, https://scholar.harvard.edu/files/sendhil/files/scientificamericanmind0114-58.pdf.

18. Supreet Kaur, Sendhil Mullainathan, Suanna Oh, and Frank Schilbach, "Do Financial Concerns Make Workers Less Productive?" NBER working paper 28338, January 2021, https://www.nber.org/system/files/working_papers/w28338/revisions /w28338.rev0.pdf.

19. Mahdi Hashemian, Zeynep Ton, and Hazhir Rahmandad, "The Effect of Unstable Schedules on Unit and Employee Productivity," MIT Sloan Research Paper No. 6056-19, May 5, 2021, https://papers.ssrn.com/sol3/papers.cfm?abstract_id =3839673#:~:text=Unstable%20schedules%20may%20reduce%20employee,develop%20 employees%20can%20be%20challenged.

20. Alana Semuels, "Poor at 20, Poor for Life," *The Atlantic*, July 14, 2016, https://bit.ly/3mQxW0Y.

21. Katherine Schaeffer, "6 Facts about Economic Inequality in the U.S.," Pew Research Center, February 7, 2020, https://www.pewresearch.org/fact-tank/2020/02/07 /6-facts-about-economic-inequality-in-the-u-s/.

22. "Income Inequality in the United States," Inequality.org, https://bit.ly/2I20LrU.

23. Aaron De Smet, Bonnie Dowling, Bryan Hancock, and Bill Schaninger, "The Great Attrition Is Making Hiring Harder. Are You Searching the Right Talent Pools?" *McKinsey Quarterly*, July 13, 2022, https://www.mckinsey.com/capabilities/people-and -organizational-performance/our-insights/the-great-attrition-is-making-hiring-harder -are-you-searching-the-right-talent-pools.

24. Jennifer Calfas, "'I Didn't Really Have a Choice.' Meet the Teachers Quitting Their Jobs Due to Low Pay and Dwindling Benefits," *Money*, May 21, 2018, https:// money.com/teacher-pay/; Matthew D. Hendricks, "Does It Pay to Pay Teachers More? Evidence from Texas," *Journal of Public Economics* 109 (January 2014): 50–63.

25. Amanda Silver, Sarah Day Kalloch, and Zeynep Ton, "A Background Note on 'Unskilled' Jobs in the United States—Past, Present, and Future," MIT Sloan School of Management, June 23, 2021, https://mitsloan.mit.edu/teaching-resources-library/a -background-note-unskilled-jobs-united-states-past-present-and-future.

Chapter 3

1. Zeynep Ton, Cate Reavis, and Sarah Kalloch, "Quest Diagnostics (A): Improving Performance at the Call Centers," MIT Sloan School of Management Case #17-177, May 1, 2017.

2. Ananth Raman, Nicole DeHoratius, and Zeynep Ton, "Execution: The Missing Link in Retail Operations," *California Management Review* 43, no. 3 (Spring 2001), https://journals.sagepub.com/doi/10.2307/41166093.

3. Aine Cain, "Home Depot Founder Arthur Blank Says Pushing Out Full-Time Workers to Cut Labor Costs Will Backfire on Retailers—a Lesson the Home-Improvement Giant Learned the Hard Way," *Business Insider*, August 31, 2020, https://www.businessinsider.com/home-depot-arthur-blank-good-company-bob-nardelli-workers-2020-8.

4. The information on the changes under Bob Nardelli and their impact on customer service and sales are from Zeynep Ton and Catherine Ross, "The Home Depot, Inc.," Case 608-093 (Boston: Harvard Business School, 2008), https://store.hbr.org/product/the-home-depot-inc/608093.

5. One of my MIT Sloan students, Matthew Kilby, did his thesis, "Creating Good Jobs in Automotive Manufacturing" (2021), at Nissan's Smyrna assembly plant, https://dspace.mit.edu/bitstream/handle/1721.1/139565/kilby-makilby-mba-mgt-2021-thesis.pdf?sequence=1&isAllowed=y.

6. Jodi Kantor, Karen Weise, and Grace Ashford, "The Amazon That Customers Don't See," *New York Times*, June 15, 2021, https://www.nytimes.com/2021/06/15/briefing/amazon-warehouse-investigation.html?.

7. James P. Womack, Daniel T. Jones, and Daniel Roos, *The Machine That Changed the World: The Story of Lean Production* (New York: Free Press, 1990).

8. Net Promoter Score is derived from asking respondents to rate the likelihood that they would recommend a company, product, or service to a friend or colleague.

9. Zeynep Ton and Ananth Raman, "The Effect of Product Variety on Retail Store Sales: A Longitudinal Study," *Product and Operations Management* 19, no. 5 (October 2010): 546–560, https://onlinelibrary.wiley.com/doi/10.1111/j.1937-5956.2010.01120.x.

10. Zeynep Ton, *The Good Jobs Strategy* (Boston: New Harvest, 2014).

11. Clara Xiaoling Chen and Tatiano Sandino, "Can Wages Buy Honesty? The Relationship Between Relative Wages and Employee Theft," *Journal of Accounting Research* 50, no. 4 (2012): 967–1000, https://onlinelibrary.wiley.com/doi/abs/10.1111/j.1475-679X.2012.00456.x.

12. Malin Knutsen Glette, Karina Aase, and Siri Wiig, "The Relationship between Understaffing of Nurses and Patient Safety in Hospitals—A Literature Review with Thematic Analysis," *Open Journal of Nursing* 7, no. 12 (2017): 1387–1429, https://file.scirp.org/Html/3-1440916_81018.htm.

13. Anita L. Tucker, "Workarounds and Resiliency on the Frontlines of Health Care," Patient Safety Network, August 1, 2009, https://psnet.ahrq.gov/perspective/workarounds-and-resiliency-front-lines-health-care.

14. Hazhir Rahmandad and Zeynep Ton, "If Higher Pay Is Profitable, Why Is it So Rare? Modeling Competing Strategies in Mass Market Services," *Organization Science* 31, no. 5 (September–October 2020): 1053–1312, https://pubsonline.informs.org/doi/10.1287/orsc.2019.1347.

Chapter 4

1. Laura Amico, "Clocking In: What It's Like to Work a Bad Job," *Harvard Business Review*, December 5, 2017, https://hbr.org/2017/12/clocking-in-what-its-like-to-work-a-bad-job.

2. There has been a huge growth in businesses that specialize in providing technological monitoring tools to count keystrokes, time online, mistakes, customer complaints, and so on.

3. Sadly, many companies—even service companies—now operate like the factories of the twentieth century. If you want to see what this kind of mistrustful management is like for those on the receiving end, I recommend *Rivethead* (New York: Grand Central, 1991), by Ben Hamper—a fantastic book that depicts soul-crushing assembly-line jobs and what the workers may do in desperation.

4. Maura Judkis, "'Please Don't Get It': Starbucks Baristas Are Flipping Out over the Unicorn Frappuccino," *Washington Post*, April 21, 2017, https://www.washingtonpost .com/news/food/wp/2017/04/20/please-dont-get-it-starbucks-barista-flips-out-over -unicorn-frappuccino/.

5. There were many Reddit threads highlighting the challenges, including having just two blenders, understaffing, and miscommunication about the length of the promotion. See, for example, "Day 1 of Unicorn Frappuccino and I wanna die," https://www.reddit.com/r/starbucks/comments/66ddrl/day_1_of_unicorn_frappuccino _and_i_wanna_die/. There were complaints about having just two blenders; see "Why is the unicorn frap so hard to make?" https://www.reddit.com/r/starbucks/comments /66po8d/comment/dgkckit/?utm_source=share&utm_medium=web2x&context=3; "Was the Unicorn Frappuccino that terrible?" https://www.reddit.com/r/starbucks /comments/6puz9u/comment/dksr6cg/?utm_source=share&utm_medium =web2x&context=3.

6. "QuikTrip Employee, Oklahoma Teacher Salary Comparison Sparks Debate," CBS News, January 17, 2017, https://www.5newsonline.com/article/news/local/outreach /back-to-school/quiktrip-employee-oklahoma-teacher-salary-comparison-sparks-debate /527-27e4e4e2-f3bc-4f33-98e7-f767257528fa.

7. Gregory Scruggs, "The Unmalling of America," Lincoln Institute of Land Policy, December 16, 2019, https://www.lincolninst.edu/publications/articles/2019-12 -unmalling-america-municipalities-navigating-changing-retail-landscape.

8. Jose Alvarez, Zeynep Ton, and Ryan Johnson, "Home Depot and Interconnected Retail," Case 512-036 (Boston: Harvard Business School, 2012).

Chapter 5

1. Aristotle, *Rhetoric* 1.2.

2. They also looked at firms in Denmark, where the drop in wages was 3 percent; see https://www.nber.org/papers/w29874.

3. Daron Acemoglu, Alex Xi He, and Daniel le Maire, "Eclipse of Rent-Sharing: The Effects of Managers' Business Education on Wages and the Labor Share in the US and Denmark," NBER Working paper no. 29874, March 2022, https://www.nber.org /papers/w29874.

4. "FDA Alerts the Public to Potentially Contaminated Products from Family Dollar Stores in Six States," Food and Drug Administration, February 2022, https://bit .ly/3RXvMvp.

5. Annabelle Timsit, "Family Dollar Closes 400 Stores, Recalls Products after FDA Finds Decaying Dead Rodents in Warehouse," *Washington Post*, February 2022, https:// www.washingtonpost.com/nation/2022/02/20/family-dollar-recall-fda-rodents/.

6. Ellen Gabler, "How Chaos at Chain Pharmacies Is Putting Patients at Risk," *New York Times*, January 31, 2020, https://www.nytimes.com/2020/01/31/health /pharmacists-medication-errors.html; Lucy King and Jonah M. Kessel, "We Know the Real Cause of the Crisis in Our Hospitals. It's Greed," *New York Times*, January 19, 2022, https://www.nytimes.com/2022/01/19/opinion/nurses-staffing-hospitals-covid-19 .html; Jordan Rau and Kaiser Health News, "'Like a Ghost Town': Erratic Nursing

Home Staffing Revealed through New Records," *Washington Post*, July 13, 2018, https://www.washingtonpost.com/national/health-science/like-a-ghost-town-erratic-nursing-home-staffing-revealed-through-new-records/2018/07/13/62513d62-867d-11e8-9e06-4db52ac42e05_story.html.

7. King and Kessel, "We Know the Real Cause of the Crisis in Our Hospitals. It's Greed."

8. Tanya Basu, "Timeline: A History of GM's Ignition Switch Defect," NPR, March 31, 2014, https://www.npr.org/2014/03/31/297158876/timeline-a-history-of-gms-ignition-switch-defect; Dominic Gates, "Q&A: What Led to Boeing's 737 MAX Crisis," *Seattle Times*, November 18, 2020, https://www.seattletimes.com/business/boeing-aerospace/what-led-to-boeings-737-max-crisis-a-qa/; Gabler, "How Chaos at Pharmacies Is Putting Patients at Risk"; "Chipotle Agrees to Pay $25 Million Federal Fine for Role in Some Outbreaks," *Food Safety News*, April 22, 2020, https://www.foodsafetynews.com/2020/04/chipotle-agrees-to-pay-25-million-federal-fine-for-role-in-some-outbreaks/.

9. Ruth Strachan and Sebastian Shehadi, "Who Killed US Manufacturing?" Investment Monitor, May 12, 2021, https://www.investmentmonitor.ai/manufacturing/who-killed-us-manufacturing.

10. Jodi Kantor, Karen Weise, and Grace Ashford, "The Amazon That Customers Don't See," *New York Times*, June 15, 2021, https://www.nytimes.com/interactive/2021/06/15/us/amazon-workers.html.

Chapter 6

1. Jena McGregor, "The Costco King Checks Out," *Washington Post*, September 2, 2011, https://www.washingtonpost.com/blogs/post-leadership/post/costco-ceo-jim-sinegal-checks-out/2011/04/01/gIQAh7CqwJ_blog.html.

2. The data in this paragraph comes from Costco's Annual Meeting of Shareholders on January 20, 2022, and its 4th Quarter Fiscal Year 2022 Investor presentation, https://investor.costco.com/static-files/859f72e2-5757-4507-a673-70f4268e6c0b.

3. "Why Should Taxpayers Subsidize Poverty Wages at Large Profitable Corporations," Senate Hearing 117-29, February 25, 2021, https://www.govinfo.gov/content/pkg/CHRG-117shrg44967/html/CHRG-117shrg44967.htm.

4. Costco's CEO Craig Jelinek shared these numbers during Senate Hearing 117-29, "Why Should Taxpayers Subsidize Poverty Wages at Large Profitable Companies?"

5. Here, Sinegal is talking about all the costs, except cost of merchandise, referred to as selling, general, and administrative expenses, or SG&A.

6. Chester Cadieux, *From Lucky to Smart: Leadership Lessons from QuikTrip* (Tulsa, OK: Mullerhaus, 2008), 62.

7. Joe Coulombe with Patty Civalleri, *Becoming Trader Joe: How I Did Business My Way & Still Beat the Big Guys* (New York: HarperCollins, 2021), 197. Robert Price, *Sol Price: Retail Revolutionary & Social Innovator* (San Diego, CA: San Diego History Center, 2012).

8. Isadore Sharp, *Four Seasons: The Story of a Business Philosophy* (New York: Portfolio, 2012).

9. Sharp, *Four Seasons*.

10. Even Warren Buffett admitted that Progressive has been outperforming Geico in pricing risk. Geico is the second-largest insurance company and is owned by Buffett's company, Berkshire Hathaway. Chris Westfall, "Buffett, Jain Speak the Hard Truth About Insurance," Risk Market News, May 2, 2021. https://www.riskmarketnews.com/buffett-speaks-the-hard-truth-about-insurance-at-annual-meeting/.

11. Frances Frei and Hanna Rodriguez-Farrar, "Innovation at Progressive (A): Pay-as-you-go Insurance," Case 9-602-175 (Boston: Harvard Business School, 2002).

12. Chloe Sorvino, "Exclusive: In-N-Out Billionaire Lynsi Snyder Opens Up about Her Troubled Past and the Burger Chain's Future," *Forbes*, October 10, 2018, https://www.forbes.com/sites/chloesorvino/2018/10/10/exclusive-in-n-out-billionaire -lynsi-snyder-opens-up-about-her-troubled-past-and-the-burger-chains-future/?sh =452548dd4b9c.

13. Harry Snyder's beliefs and the pay information in this paragraph are from Stacy Perman, *In-N-Out Burger: A Behind-the-Counter Look at the Fast-Food Chain That Breaks All the Rules* (New York: Harper Business, 2010).

14. As I write, Costco does carry disposable diapers because they can now sell them more cheaply than they are being sold elsewhere.

15. Zhen Lian, Sebastien Martin, and Garrett van Ryzin, "Labor Cost Free-Riding in the Gig Economy," Northwestern Kellogg working paper.

16. Anna North, "Essential Workers Are Losing Their Hazard Pay Even Though Hazard Isn't Over," *Vox*, May 18, 2020, https://www.vox.com/2020/5/16/21258834 /coronavirus-essential-workers-hazard-pay-kroger-target-covid.

17. The full Facebook post can be found here: https://www.facebook.com/tim .hennessy.965/posts/10159106775203556.

18. Clayton M. Christensen, James Allworth, and Karen Dillon, *How Will You Measure Your Life?* (New York: Harper Business, 2012).

Chapter 7

1. The name of the convenience store chain has been disguised for confidentiality.

2. Shouldice's ability to achieve the highest patient outcomes at one-third of the cost at other hospitals has made it a favorite case study among many operations management professors at business schools.

3. According to Little's Law, the average time a customer spends in the system is proportional to the average numbers of customers in the system. See John Little, "A Proof for the Queuing Formula: $L = \lambda W$," *Operations Research* 9, no. 3 (May–June 1961): 383–387. See also Wallace J. Hopp and Mark L. Spearman, *Factory Physics, 2nd Ed.* (New York: McGraw-Hill/Irwin, 2000), ch. 9.

4. As I explained in chapter 8 of *The Good Jobs Strategy* (Boston: New Harvest, 2014), the newsvendor theory in inventory management also shows operating with slack as the profit-maximizing strategy when the costs of understaffing (e.g., mistakes, lost sales, employee turnover) are higher than the costs of overstaffing (e.g., labor costs).

5. Steve Prokesch, "The Right Thing to Do," *Harvard Business Review*, The Big Idea Series / The Good Jobs Solution, December 7, 2017.

6. "How a Washington Casino Is Using the Good Jobs Strategy to Invest in Guest Experience: Q&A with Lucky Eagle Casino & Hotel CEO JaNessa Bumgarner and Hotel Director Ben Scholl," Good Jobs Institute, December 21, 2021, https://goodjob sinstitute.medium.com/how-a-washington-casino-is-using-the-good-jobs-strategy-to -invest-in-guest-experience-d7dafc478814.

7. Paul J. DiMaggio and Walter W. Powell documented institutional isomorphism in their influential 1983 article, "The Iron Cage Revisited: Institutional Isomorphism and Collective Rationality in Organizational Fields," *American Sociological Review* 48, no. 2 (April 1983): 147–160, https://www.jstor.org/stable/2095101.

8. "Costco Wholesale (COST) Q4 2020 Earnings Call Transcript," The Motley Fool, September 25, 2020, https://www.fool.com/earnings/call-transcripts/2020/09/25 /costco-wholesale-cost-q4-2020-earnings-call-transc/.

9. Aine Cain, "Sam's Club Sales Soar as Membership Swells to an All-Time High— And Walmart's CEO Says He Hasn't Seen This Kind of Growth in 19 Years," *Business Insider*, August 17, 2021, https://www.businessinsider.com/sams-club-walmart-sales -membership-numbers-spike-2021-8.

10. Lars Wulff, "Lars Wulff on the Good Jobs Strategy at Mud Bay," YouTube, https://www.youtube.com/watch?v=IV1R7wydjQw.

Chapter 8

1. I am inspired by Clay Christensen, who, in his famous book, *The Innovator's Dilemma*, wrote: "I am particularly anxious that managers read these chapters . . . *for understanding, rather than simple answers* [my emphasis]. I am very confident that the great managers about whom this book is written will be very capable on their own of finding the answers that best fit their circumstances." See Clayton M. Christensen, *The Innovator's Dilemma: When New Technologies Cause Great Firms to Fail* (Boston: Harvard Business School Press, 1997).

2. John Kotter, *Leading Change* (Boston: Harvard Business Review Press, 2012).

3. Michael Beer, Russell Eisenstat, and Bert Spector, *The Critical Path to Corporate Renewal* (Boston: Harvard Business School Press, 1990).

4. Jim Collins, *Good to Great: Why Some Companies Make the Leap and Others Don't* (New York: HarperCollins, 2001).

5. Anita L. Tucker and Amy C. Edmondson, "Cincinnati Children's Hospital Medical Center," Case 609-109 (Boston: Harvard Business School, 2009), https://www.hbs.edu/faculty/Pages/item.aspx?num=37458.

6. Kelli A. Komro, Melvin D. Livingston, Sara Markowitz, and Alexander C. Wagenaar, "The Effect of an Increased Minimum Wage on Infant Mortality and Birth Weight," *American Journal of Public Health* 106, no. 8 (August 2016): 1514–1516, https://www.ncbi.nlm.nih.gov/pmc/articles/PMC4940666/.

7. Sonya V. Troller-Renfree, Molly A. Costanzo, Greg Duncan, and Kimberly G. Noble, "The Impact of a Poverty Reduction Intervention on Infant Brain Activity," *Proceedings of the National Academy of Sciences* 119, no. 5 (February 1, 2022), https://www.pnas.org/doi/10.1073/pnas.2115649119.

8. Living wage also depends on the household size. At the Good Jobs Institute, we have been using two working parents with one child as the household size.

9. Lauren Thomas, "Here's the One Photo Walmart's CEO Keeps on His Phone to Stoke 'Healthy Paranoia' in Race against Amazon," CNBC, December 7, 2018, https://www.cnbc.com/2018/12/07/walmarts-ceo-says-this-photo-inspires-him-to-stay-ahead-of-amazon.html.

10. As we saw in chapter 7, improving data accuracy was one reason Sam's Club had to reduce employee turnover. Creating a seamless omniexperience requires highly accurate data.

11. Ryan Raffaelli, "Reinventing Retail: The Novel Resurgence of Independent Bookstores," working paper 20-068, Harvard Business School, Boston, January 2020, https://www.hbs.edu/ris/Publication%20Files/20-068_c19963e7-506c-479a-beb4-bb339cd293ee.pdf.

12. Joe Coulombe with Patty Civalleri, *Becoming Trader Joe: How I Did Business My Way & Still Beat the Big Guys* (New York: HarperCollins, 2021), 96.

13. Adam Grant and David Hofmann ran experiments to motivate health-care workers to practice better hand hygiene at work. They put up alternative signs in different bathrooms around a hospital. One sign tried to leverage self-interest: "Hand hygiene prevents you from getting diseases." The other sign emphasized the prosocial consequences: "Hand hygiene prevents patients from getting diseases." The first sign had no effect, but the second caused doctors and nurses to wash their hands 11 percent more often and to use 45 percent more soap and gel. See Adam Grant and David Hofmann, "It's Not All About Me: Motivating Hand Hygiene Among Health Care Professionals by Focusing on Patients," *Psychology Science* 12 (December 2022): 1494–1499.

14. Michael Corkery, "How a Dollar General Employee Went Viral on TikTok," *New York Times*, April 18, 2022, https://www.nytimes.com/2022/04/18/business/dollar -general-tiktok.html.

15. "Company Wage Tracker," Economic Policy Institute, https://www.epi.org /company-wage-tracker/.

16. Corkery, "How a Dollar General Employee Went Viral on TikTok."

Chapter 9

1. Gabrielle S. Adams, Benjamin A. Converse, Andrew H. Hales, and Leidy Klotz, "People Systematically Overlook Subtractive Changes," *Nature* 592 (April 2021): 258–261, https://www.nature.com/articles/s41586-021-03380-y.

2. Arthur Conan Doyle, *The Case Book of Sherlock Holmes* (New York: Doran, 1927).

3. The member perception, higher sales, and lower labor costs were mentioned in the Walmart investment community meeting on February 18, 2020. Walmart, Inc., https://corporate.walmart.com/media-library/document/2020-investment-community -meeting-transcript/_proxyDocument?id=00000170-5dc5-d590-ad71-7dcf3f370000.

4. These investments are different than what we saw in chapter 3, where companies invested in "so-so" technologies solely to replace workers. Daron Acemoglu, Andrea Manera, and Pascual Restrepo, "Taxes, Automation, and the Future of Labor," MIT Work of the Future research brief, https://mitsloan.mit.edu/shared/ods/documents ?PublicationDocumentID=7929#:~:text=Automation%2C%20which%20involves%20 the%20substitution,and%20fails%20to%20improve%20productivity.

5. Saravanan Kesavan, Susan J. Lambert, Joan C. Williams, and Pradeep K. Pendem, "Doing Well by Doing Good: Improving Retail Store Performance with Responsible Scheduling Practices at the Gap, Inc.," *Management Science*, March 2022, https://papers.ssrn.com/sol3/papers.cfm?abstract_id=3731670.

6. According to Mercadona's 2021 annual report, the monthly salary for a first-year employee was 1,425 euros and went up to 1,929 euros by the fourth year, https://info .mercadona.es/document/en/annual-report-2021.pdf?blobheader=application/pdf.

7. Frances Dodds, "Four Years Ago, This Chick-fil-A Started Paying $17 an Hour. It Transformed the Business," *Entrepreneur*, May 10, 2022, https://www.entrepreneur .com/franchise/four-years-ago-this-chick-fil-a-started-paying-17-an/425436.

8. Chad Donath told me that the implementation team wanted club managers and market managers to make the announcement because they wanted them to be the heroes.

9. Robert B. Cialdini, *Influence: The Psychology of Persuasion* (New York: Harper Business, 1984).

10. If you had been spending 1,000 hours a year to train 100 new people and now, having reduced turnover, you can spend that 1,000 hours on 70 new people, you can spend 14.3 hours training each one (instead of only 10 hours). So you've reduced turnover by 30 percent, but increased training time (investment) by 43 percent.

Chapter 10

1. Michael Beer, Magnus Finnström, and Derek Schrader, "Why Leadership Training Fails—and What to Do about It," *Harvard Business Review*, October 2016, https://hbr.org/2016/10/why-leadership-training-fails-and-what-to-do-about-it.

2. Boris Groysberg's research found that Wall Street analysts rated as "stars" did not perform as well or retain their star status after moving to another firm. Most never regained that status during the five-year study. Those who did perform well were the ones who took their teams with them; that is, they had been stars in a well-functioning system and brought that system to their new job. See Boris Groysberg, Ashish Nanda,

and Nitin Nohria, "The Risky Business of Hiring Stars," *Harvard Business Review*, May 2004.

3. Mark Bertolini, *Mission-Driven Leadership: My Journey as a Radical Capitalist* (New York: Currency, 2019), 113.

4. In a theoretical paper that models the switch from a labor cost minimization approach to a labor contribution maximization approach, my colleague Hazhir Rahmandad and I find that performance first declines before it gets better. We conclude that companies that are looking for early signals of success will wrongly conclude that the transformation is not working. See Hazhir Rahmandad and Zeynep Ton, "If Higher Pay Is Profitable, Why Is it So Rare? Modeling Competing Strategies in Mass Market Services," *Organization Science* 31, no. 5 (September–October 2020): 1053–1312, https://pubsonline.informs .org/doi/10.1287/orsc.2019.1347.

Epilogue

1. Kent Bowen and Steve Spear wrote the famous *Harvard Business Review* article, "Decoding the DNA of the Toyota Production System" (September–October 1999), https://hbr.org/1999/09/decoding-the-dna-of-the-toyota-production-system.

2. In fact, David Gelles has just published such a book, *The Man Who Broke Capitalism* (New York: Simon and Schuster, 2022).

INDEX

Note: Page numbers followed by *f* refer to figures; page numbers followed by *t* refer to tables; and page numbers followed by *n* refer to endnotes.

ACKNOWLEDGMENTS

In November 2015, Roger Martin came to our house for dinner. I had just hung up the phone with a legendary retail CEO who had read *The Good Jobs Strategy* and asked if I could help his company implement its ideas. I told this CEO the truth I had told others: I didn't know how to do it. Besides, I already had a job and four young kids. When I told Roger about this and other similar exchanges with leaders of other companies, he told me that if I ever wanted to make a real difference, I had better learn how to help these leaders. He graciously agreed to help me learn how to do it and to be the cofounder of an organization with me. A few months later, I asked Sarah Kalloch—a student of mine at MIT Sloan who stood out both in and beyond the classroom—if she would join me in spreading the good jobs strategy when she graduated in 2016. She said yes. That was the beginning of the nonprofit Good Jobs Institute (GJI). This book describes much of what we learned as a team at GJI.

Thank you, Roger, for giving me the confidence to start an organization and helping GJI all along the way—from writing our first proposal to helping us in our work with clients—and for constantly reminding us that change takes time and patience. Thank you, Sarah, for leading GJI with competence, integrity, and compassion.

We are a small organization with a big goal: to improve 10 million low-wage jobs by 2027. Sarah tirelessly works with companies, investors, and nonprofits in the good jobs ecosystem—from the Aspen Institute to JUST Capital to the National Association of Convenience Stores—to get us there. She also makes sure GJI is positioned for impact by diligently managing our financials and graciously leading our staff. I don't know how she can do so many things that well. But I do know that there would be no GJI without Sarah!

As I write these pages, our team includes Dan Ford, Riddhima Sharma, and Amanda Silver. MBA students graduate with many options. I am grateful that these talented people chose to join GJI to help companies thrive by creating good jobs. I never take them for granted. In addition to our current team, Katie Bach, my student from 2011, spent nearly two years with us before moving to Washington, DC. I am confident that she will continue working to improve job quality wherever she goes. Bridget Mehmeti and Max Kagan also worked with us.

I am grateful to our board members BJ Hess and Roger Martin and advisors: José Alvarez, Jamie Bonini, Jan Rivkin, and Mary Alice Vuicic. They brainstorm with us, guide us, and offer their expertise whenever we need them.

When Sarah first joined me, we had no clients. It was a fellowship I had received from Martin Prosperity Institute (MPI) that enabled me to offer her a position. MPI gave us another grant shortly before its closing. I want to thank Jamison Steeve for his leadership there and Darren Karn for his research assistance. In 2016, José Alvarez introduced us to the Joyce Foundation, which took a bet on us and, along with MPI, got us started financially. Thank you, José, for believing in us even before we knew what we were doing! Thanks to Roy Swan from the Ford Foundation for investing in us so that we can begin scaling our work. Rachel Kohlberg was our first program officer at Ford Foundation and made sure that we got our grant before she left for the Workers and Families Fund.

I want to thank the leaders of Toyota Production System Support Center (TSSC) and Lean Enterprise Institute (LEI), who have been generously sharing their knowledge with us. Thank you, Terry Horinouchi, for making sure that TSSC staff was available to show us how they help companies implement the Toyota Production System. Thank you, Jamie Bonini, for all that you taught me, especially during our visits to factories, hospitals, and retail stores.

When we celebrated GJI's fifth anniversary, Dewey Hasbrouck, the owner of Moe's Original BBQ, was there. Roger told him: "It takes a special person to be motivated by ideas in a book." To all those brave leaders who were motivated by the ideas in *The Good Jobs Strategy*, did the work, and made bets on their people, I thank you. I also thank countless others, only some of whom I was lucky enough to meet, who helped those leaders adopt the good jobs strategy. You read their stories in this book. I also owe thanks to Henry Armour for helping us spread the good jobs strategy in the convenience chain industry and to Ann Ruble, Raj Sisodia, and Warren Valdmanis for their advocacy for the good jobs strategy. Thanks to all our friends at JUST Capital, PayPal, and Financial Health Network who are encouraging companies to understand and improve their workers' financial wellness.

My interest in the intersection of operations and people emerged when I was at Harvard Business School. I am grateful to Kent Bowen, who accepted me into the doctoral program despite my low verbal GRE score and who taught me to work on important problems and how to set high standards and care for students' learning. Kent also introduced me to his former MIT student, Jamie Bonini, at Toyota. Jamie and I are both lucky to call Kent our mentor. Jan Hammond, Roy Shapiro, and Steve Wheelwright guided me since I was a doctoral student. Jan is my daughter Ela's godmother and holds a special place in my heart. Mike Beer showed me what it means to do research that makes a difference in companies. He also gave me the opportunity to share my research with CEOs of large companies through his Center for Higher Ambition Leadership.

Since 2011, MIT Sloan has been my professional home, where I am surrounded by wonderful colleagues. Thanks in particular to Vivek Farias, Charlie Fine, Jason Jay, Erin Kelly, Tom Kochan, Retsef Levi, Georgia Perakis, dean David Schmittlein, John Sterman, Scott Stern, and Don Sull, as well as David Autor from the economics department for supporting my work. I am grateful to my friend and coauthor, Hazhir Rahmandad; I talked about our academic papers in chapters 2 and 3.

In January 2018, we lost our dear colleague Don Rosenfield. Don and I co-taught operations strategy for seven years. Every time I pass his old office, I think about Don's care for his students and his modesty, loyalty, and generosity. One former student said, "Ten years after graduating,

I still want to make Don proud." He's a role model for all of us who have the privilege of teaching.

One of the best things about teaching at MIT Sloan is the opportunity to work with MBA students. Their various projects helped contribute to the ideas in this book. Tom De Falco, Ryan Jacobs, and Matthew Strangfels studied scheduling practices at a supermarket chain; Clemens Mewald helped create a "good jobs score" for food retailers using publicly available data; Nila Bhattacharyya interviewed store managers and analyzed Glassdoor and Yelp data; Victoria Lee studied hiring practices at retailers and even took a frontline job; Meredith Thurston worked on a project on operational complexity and customer satisfaction; Rebecca Gould, Zaafir Kherani, Kate Lazaroff-Puck, and Well Smittinet worked on quantifying the cost of mediocrity at the large retailer you read about in chapter 8; Megan Larcom, with the help of Katie Bach, built on that team's methodology to create a "good jobs calculator" (Max Kagan and Bridget Mehmeti also worked on the calculator); Matthew Kilby worked on drivers and costs of turnover at a Nissan plant; Paul Millerd helped create surveys and diagnostic tools; Cassie Zhang helped us with company data methodology and helped with our Zoom workshops during Covid-19; Riddhima Sharma did research on what companies disclose on people metrics; and Amanda Silver worked with Sarah and me on a paper on "unskilled" jobs.

In 2017, senior editor Steve Prokesch at *Harvard Business Review* asked if I would be interested in being featured in their new "Big Idea" series. I already loved working with Steve and jumped at the opportunity. Steve had terrific ideas for making the series a success and, as always, gave me the most honest feedback. That's when he planted the seed of writing a second book. That's also when I met Scott Berinato, who then moved to the book publishing side of *Harvard Business Review*—namely, Harvard Business Review Press (HBRP).

When I was finally ready to write this book, I knew HBRP would be the right home for it. My hope was to work with Scott on the book and with Steve on a magazine article. Both of those hopes came true! Scott, thank you for those conversations on how to address all the "yeah-buts," for your diligence in editing the manuscript, and for making me feel like you always had my back. Steve, thank you for being a supporter of my work since 2012 and for all the care and energy you put into improving my articles. I also want to thank several people at HBRP: Melinda Merino, for believing in this work (and Frances Frci for introducing me to Melinda); Allison Peter, for her masterful coordination of production; and Stephani Finks and her team for the book cover—with a gold star.

This book was a challenge to write—partly because I was learning as I was writing. I would present the ideas in workshops or in follow-up meetings with companies, get feedback, discuss with the GJI team, refine those ideas, present, and get feedback again. It never stopped. I couldn't have done it without my friend Barbara Feinberg. When I went in circles (I think I shared more than twenty versions of chapter 1 with Barbara!) and lost confidence, she was always the first person I called. She cheered me up and told me I could do it. I can still hear her voice: "Keep writing, keep writing." I also couldn't have done it without my brilliant editor, John Elder, who patiently read and edited various drafts. John knows this work and my voice so well and always makes me sound smarter than I am. In this book, I talk about the benefits of stability. Well, Barbara and John worked on my first book. John and I have been working together since 2005! Barbara has become my confidant and trusted adviser on a range of topics from book writing to teaching to dealing with wild turkeys in Cambridge!

There are many leaders who participated in interviews for this book or came to MIT Sloan to talk to my students. They include Mark Bertolini, Jamie Bonini, Craig Boyan, Chet Cadieux, MaryAnn Camacho, Mary Chesser, Michael Fisher, John Furner, Tricia Griffith, Scott Jeffers, Sean McKendry, Kath McLay, Todd Miner, Charlie Penner, Dan Schulman, Isadore Sharp, Tim Simmons, Jim Sinegal, Dacona Smith, Lars Wulff, and Marisa Wulff.

When the book was ready to share with others, I got helpful feedback from friends and colleagues. I am grateful to José Alvarez, Michael Fisher,

Dan Ford, Rebecca Henderson, BJ Hess, Sarah Kalloch, Tom Kochan, Roger Martin, Dani Rodrik, Amanda Silver, Lars Wulff, and Dina Zelleke. I owe special thanks to Rebecca, who gave me six pages of notes—with ideas on how to restructure the book. I ended up making a lot of changes including rewriting chapter 1 based on her feedback. Amanda, Dan, and Sarah provided examples, helped improve the argument, and saved me from making a few mistakes. Amanda, in particular, helped me with her gift for storytelling and diligence in identifying quotes and research papers.

I have dedicated my career to improving low-wage jobs in a way that benefits companies in a country that has been so generous to me. Spreading good jobs is my second-most important life mission (after raising my four kids with strong values). One of the biggest surprises and joys during the last eight years has been the support for this mission from my friends and neighbors—making connections, talking about the work and reminding me of its importance, and showing up at GJI events. You know who you are. I am so lucky to have you in my life.

I owe special gratitude to Jim Sinegal, my business hero, for showing us that it is possible to create good jobs at scale, for being so generous with his time to teach hundreds of my students and me since 2014, and for his friendship. If more leaders ran their company the way Jim did—with integrity, discipline, and humility—there would be much higher trust in our society. Shortly after the manuscript was ready, I shared it with Jim to get his blessing for chapter 6. His feedback was like his store visits, in which he stands in front of each product, looks at the display, the price, the quality—and asks questions. He read every word of the chapter, caught lots of little things, asked questions, and made great suggestions.

When Jim visits my class, I end the discussion by asking him what advice he would give his younger self. He advises paying attention to three big things: family, livelihood, and health. I've been lucky on all fronts, but especially when it comes to family. My brother Ali and I grew up in a happy and stable family. Ali, his wife Elizabeth, and their children Leyla and Kaya now live in California. Our parents, Handan and Necmi Ton, to whom this book is dedicated, and the rest of our extended family are still in Turkey. During the pandemic, what kept me sane was weekly Zoom meetings with our parents, aunt, uncles, and cousins; we even celebrated each person's birthday, with real cake and candles! When we could all get together in person for our parents' fiftieth wedding anniversary, many others joined, including basketball players my dad had coached forty years ago. Hearing all these people talk about both our mom and dad reminded my brother and me what we learned most from our parents—how to love and care for others. I hope some of what they taught me is reflected in this book.

My brother and I always knew that we came first for our parents. I hope my children—Ali, Hakan, Ela, and Kerem—feel the same way about my husband, Carlos, and me. Time is precious for working parents. Carlos and I have been able to focus on our family and on our work thanks to Nubia and Jackie, who have kept our house clean and our laundry folded for many years. When Ali and Hakan were toddlers, my mom told me, "Your children are young for a short amount of time, but your career is long." How right she was! Ali just turned seventeen and our youngest, Kerem, is already nine. Thanks to Ali for editing this section and to Hakan for sharing his insights from working at Sevan Bakery and at the Fishmonger. Thanks to Ela and Kerem for always asking me how they can help with this book. Ela, who is ten, read the entire introduction and took detailed notes. Kerem read the first two pages of chapter 1 and advised me to take out a sentence (I followed his advice). As my children enter adulthood, I hope they will each find their own way to be useful people.

For twenty-three years, I've been saying that marrying Carlos was the best thing that ever happened to me. One of the elements of the good jobs strategy is simplicity. Well, we have a very uncomplicated relationship, which makes everything else easier—including having the time to work on a book and care for our four children. I am grateful to be sharing my life with such a patient, caring, and competent person. Carlos is our family Wikipedia, our help desk, and our rock. When I married him, I didn't know how much I would also love his family, especially his parents Mary Ellen and José Ignacio Gonzalez. In September, we lost Geraldine Morales, our beloved Tia Gerrie. She was always interested in good jobs—she even attended my class remotely when Jim Sinegal was the featured guest (she loved Costco) and came to my talks in Miami. I think she would have liked this book and even made a funny (although likely inappropriate) joke about it!

So many people to be grateful for. Could I be any luckier?

ABOUT THE AUTHOR

ZEYNEP TON is a Professor of the Practice in the Operations Management group at MIT Sloan School of Management and the cofounder and president of the nonprofit Good Jobs Institute. She has received numerous awards for teaching excellence at MIT Sloan and at Harvard Business School, where she worked previously. In her research, teaching, and consulting work, Ton focuses on how organizations can design and manage their operations in a way that satisfies customers, employees, and investors simultaneously. She is the author of *The Good Jobs Strategy*. She lives in Cambridge with her husband and four children.